YZERMAN

Also by Douglas Hunter

Against the Odds
Trials (with Jeff Boyd)
Open Ice
A Breed Apart
Champions: The Illustrated History of Hockey's Greatest Dynasties
War Games
Scotty Bowman: A Life in Hockey
Yacht Design Explained (with Steve Killing)
Ultimate Sailing (with Sharon Green)
The Glory Barons
Molson: The Birth of a Business Empire
The Bubble and the Bear: How Nortel Burst the Canadian Dream

Douglas Hunter

YZERMAN

THE MAKING OF A CHAMPION

TRIUMPH
BOOKS
CHICAGO

Library of Congress Control Number: 2004110302

This book is available in quantity at special discounts for your group or
organization. For further information, contact:
Triumph Books
601 South LaSalle Street
Suite 500
Chicago, Illinois 60605
(312) 939-3330
Fax (312) 663-3557

Printed in U.S.A.
ISBN 1-57243-676-X
Jacket image: Getty Images/NHLI
Jacket design: CS Richardson
Design by Carla Kean

Published in Canada by Doubleday Canada,
a division of Random House of Canada Limited

For Jeff, a Wingnut from way back.

CONTENTS

INTRODUCTION

THE MAY 1, 2003, EDITION OF *News Night with Aaron Brown* on CNN was preoccupied with the Middle East. A presidential photo op was being orchestrated for the next day aboard the aircraft carrier *Abraham Lincoln,* from which George W. Bush would declare victory in Iraq. *News Night* opened with a Nic Robertson report from Iraq on the frustrations in the search for weapons of mass destruction. Then came an interview with a photographer traveling in country with the 62nd Medical Brigade. Next, the comedian and producer Carl Reiner dropped by the studio to lighten the mood by chatting with Brown as he plugged his autobiography.

The hour-long show then did its customary wrap-up, a review of the front pages of the next day's morning papers, which were already hitting the streets. The lead news was, of course, Iraq, from every angle. Except in one major American city.

"I want to get one more thing in quickly," Brown said as time ran out. "*Detroit News* . . . The big front-page story is a hockey story, because it's Hockeytown. 'Yzerman to Stay for Run to Cup'—or 'At Cup.' And we think that's good because we like him. He's a good hockey player."

1

Professional hockey can scarcely attract the attention of the mainstream American press at the best of times, let alone for the best of reasons (a state of affairs exemplified by Todd Bertuzzi's assault of Steve Moore, which lit up CNN in March 2004). But on a day when major media outlets were saturated with talk of Bush, Iraq and WMDs, the people at *News Night* felt it important before signing off to let everyone in the world know it was good that Stevie Y was coming back for another season in Detroit—because they, at *News Night,* liked him. And they liked him because, in Brown's succinct words, he was "a good hockey player."

Which pretty well sums up the stature of Steve Yzerman in the home stretch of his career: a *good* hockey player, in the way that "good" is used to define a good friend or a good man. There's no "great" necessarily to consider beyond it—good is plenty good enough.

It was no longer possible to say Yzerman was the best, at least by the measure of who had the most goals, assists or points in the National Hockey League—or who was the most handsomely paid: the new one-year contract wouldn't be finalized until late August, and would earn him (according to the players' association) $5,849,823, a drop from his previous $8.5 million salary (both figures are in U.S. dollars). It made him only the sixth-highest-paid player on the team he captained, and ranked him thirteenth in the league among centers, thirty-eighth among all players. Still, if you were to ask fans (and the players themselves) to name the greatest player in the game today, you certainly wouldn't find Steve Yzerman logging in around thirty-eighth. And you probably won't see Aaron Brown hold up the front page of a newspaper announcing a new contract for Alexei Yashin anytime soon.

Yzerman had not yet been awarded the Bill Masterton Memorial Trophy on the night that Brown displayed the front page of *The Detroit News*. That would come in June, when Yzerman would stride to the podium at the annual NHL awards ceremony in Toronto to accept the award, given by the Professional Hockey Writers' Association to "the National Hockey League player who best exemplifies the qualities of perseverance, sportsmanship and dedication to hockey." The Masterton traditionally goes to players who have overcome some personal hardship, often in the form of debilitating illness. Montreal Canadiens captain Saku Koivu had earned it in 2002 for his battle with non-Hodgkin's lymphoma. In 2003, Yzerman was up against Steve Rucchin of the Anaheim Mighty Ducks, who had come back from two injury-shortened seasons and the trauma of the death of his brother from cancer to play a full season in 2002–03, when his team reached the Stanley Cup finals, and Bryan Berard of the Boston Bruins, who had bounced back from an eye injury that almost ended his career.

There's something unsettling about pitting people's misfortunes against one another in an award balloting: should the death of Rucchin's brother count for more than Yzerman's battles with his bum knee? But in the end, the award went to Yzerman gracefully and unequivocally. Fundamentally, the basis for the award was his return to the game late in the 2002–03 season after undergoing major surgery on a troublesome right knee and missing 66 regular-season games. Rather than undergo full reconstructive surgery, Yzerman had opted for an osteotomy, a realignment of the knee joint—a procedure normally reserved for the elderly.

No athlete had ever used the operation as a career-lengthening measure, and in Yzerman's case, playing more hockey had been a secondary goal to ensuring quality of life in his imminent retirement years. The fact that he came back at all was incredible. Underlying the Masterton award was the knowledge of everything that had led to that surgery. After an initial injury in 1988, Yzerman's right knee had steadily deteriorated. He underwent arthroscopic surgery in mid October 2000, missed 22 games in recovery, then had another bout of surgery right before the Olympic tournament in Salt Lake City in February 2002. Yzerman had played on a knee that caused him excruciating pain all that season, helping Canada win its first Olympic gold medal in men's ice hockey in fifty years before leading his Red Wings to their third Stanley Cup title since 1996–97.

Not everyone was happy with Yzerman's decision to play the Olympic tournament on a bad knee, a move that forced him to sit out a few weeks of Red Wings games. Mario Lemieux similarly had to miss time in a Penguins uniform after the tournament when his hip gave him grief. Some Detroit fans were irate that Yzerman, in their view, put Canada's Olympic medal hopes before his obligations to his NHL team. One unhappy fan wrote *The Detroit News:* "Steve Yzerman should stay in Utah after what he pulled. Yzerman's knee flared up during the Olympics and now he's going to sit at home on his butt and miss games for the team and the fans who pay him his $8 million per year. What an outrage! Mario Lemieux is being lynched in Pittsburgh and it should be the same in Detroit for Yzerman."

By the time Yzerman returned to the lineup and won the Stanley Cup for the third time—thereby surpassing the Cup-winning heroics of his Olympic teammates Joe Sakic in Colorado and Lemieux in Pittsburgh, each of whom had won two—his problems were obvious. Each time a check sent him to the ice, he had to lean heavily on his stick just to get back on his feet; clearly, surgery beyond an arthroscopic tidying was the only answer.

One fan's example of selfish behavior is many fans' example of doing the right thing, of thinking about yourself last and the team first—or of thinking of yourself first and foremost from the perspective of what your team achieves. Yzerman had made the kind of personal sacrifice for the greater good of both teams in 2002 that is usually thought to belong to some deep past of professional sport, before athletes became pampered multimillionaires who would refuse to dress for a game if a hamstring felt a little twitchy. He had played through pain in Salt Lake City, and had probably done damage that would curtail his career. By this point, those boo birds back in Detroit should have known who they were dealing with, and how his priorities had brought them so much to celebrate after so many years of disappointment.

Even after the knee surgery, those who knew Yzerman also knew how much pain continued to be a routine component of his game. The knee hurt, all the time. But he never called a press conference to talk about how much it bugged him, nor did he blame it for holding him to one assist as his team was upset by Anaheim in an opening-round sweep in the 2003 playoffs. Yzerman had become synonymous with selflessness on the ice. He was the scoring star who had turned himself into the total player, the guy who had twice finished third in the league scoring race but had decided, in the name of winning, that he would henceforth prefer to block shots, kill penalties and back-check.

Without the background history of his professional transformation, Yzerman would appear to have been one more star player trying to extend his paydays via surgery and rest. Viewed from this perspective, the Masterton might represent a lifetime achievement award for a player who was widely admired and was not expected to last in the game much longer. There would be another season, and then—who knew, really. In March 2002, Yzerman had told the *St. Petersburg Times,* "I'm planning on playing another year, and then go from there."

People who know Yzerman say his mind has been working that way since at least the mid 1990s. Knowing that every season might be his last had helped motivate the evolution of his playing style as he reached for the championship that had eluded him and the Red Wings. When the Masterton was handed to him, it was hard to say how many more achievements might follow this salute to his career and his work ethic. The uncertainty over the collective bargaining agreement, which has made a player lockout in 2004–05 a strong possibility, may prevent Yzerman from getting back on the ice until 2005–06. He will be forty then, an age at which few athletes are still employed in their chosen fields. Yzerman has been playing professionally since he was eighteen. Entering the 2003–04 season, he had logged twenty seasons, producing 1,670 points in 1,378 regular-season games. His longest-playing teammates from his junior club, the Peterborough Petes, were long gone from the game. Bob Errey was doing color commentary in Pittsburgh, where he'd won two Stanley Cups. Dave Reid had capped a late surge in professional success with a Stanley Cup in Colorado in 2000-01, his last season. Some career ends had been more traumatic: his good friend Steve Chiasson had been killed in a car accident after his trade from Detroit. In fact, most of his peers had fallen by the wayside by the mid 1990s. His own team had tried to trade him at least twice. His one-time coach, Scotty Bowman, had put him through a professional hell that few team captains ever endure. But he had stuck it out, and in the process became the player that fans truly want to remember, and really don't want to let go of.

At the same time, Steve Yzerman has been a player these fans have found surprisingly difficult to really know as a person.

Over the course of his long career, Steve Yzerman has managed to create a life within the game without compromising his life outside it, which is to say his life of friends and family. "Steve is a really, really private guy," says Larry Kelly, an Ottawa lawyer and decent fellow who plays pickup hockey with my fellow scribe Roy MacGregor, and who has represented Yzerman for fourteen years. "I've been doing this for twenty-eight years now, and I don't know a guy who's more focused, more intense. During the season, he has two things on his mind: playing hockey to the best of his abilities, and getting whatever time he can with his family. And he's really careful not to allow anything to infringe upon them.

"It's a two-way street with him. He has never, ever, in all the years I've worked with him, phoned me at home on a weekend. Because he doesn't want to interrupt my own time with my family. There are very few players who fall into that category."

Yzerman's protection of his privacy and utter lack of show-boating don't leave much in the way of leverage if crafting a celebrity exposé is your thing as a writer. Try test-driving the memories of John Ollson, who was among Yzerman's circle of friends when he was growing up in the Ottawa suburb of Nepean. Ollson played major junior hockey with the Ottawa 67s before turning pro in the Chicago Blackhawks system and then taking his game to Europe, with a stop on Canada's national team in 1988–89. He's now an Ottawa-area golf pro, runs a Nepean sporting goods store and a hockey school that Yzerman helped him set up, and conducts hockey clinics around North America. Ottawa Senators fans well know his ads, which air on local game broadcasts.

He told me a story of the 67s sending him down to Tier II junior for a spell with the Junior Senators. Yzerman, who is about eighteen months younger than him, was starring with the Tier II Nepean Raiders, and the two teams met in Ottawa's last home game of the season. "I'd broken my nose and was wearing a face mask. I had gone from a first-place team to a last-place team, and

Steve was with a first-place team. They were kicking the shit out of us—like, 7–2."

Between the second and third periods, a draw was held for first prize in a team fundraising raffle. Ollson's own ticket was drawn. He was seventeen years old, down on his hockey luck, and he'd just won ten thousand dollars. "The place was packed, with two thousand people. We were facing off together at center ice, and Steve says, 'Well, I guess you're buying the beers for everyone tonight.'"

Little Stevie Y, sixteen years old, under age, making some crack about beer money? But there's nothing more to tell, and that's as controversial a story as you're ever likely to hear about Yzerman. For one thing, his character doesn't lend itself to controversy. ("Does he drink beer or wine?" Jacques Demers, his coach in Detroit in the late 1980s, wonders aloud.) For another, there's the intense privacy, which the people around him respect.

Yzerman's own agent is careful about dialing his client's number. "He's so focused during the season, and I'm so aware of that, that I'm careful when I call," says Kelly. "With other stars I've represented, I've never felt the need to be that way, but with Steve, I have."

His former Red Wings linemate, Gerard Gallant, who was named the coach of the Columbus Blue Jackets in 2003–04, remains a close friend—the Yzermans are godparents of his eldest daughter. But he testifies to the fear-of-phoning phenomenon that seems to surround the player. "He has so many people pulling at him. I talk to him every couple weeks, and I don't feel like calling him most of the time, even though he wants to talk."

"I'm an acquaintance of Steve," John Ollson emphasizes. "I'm not one of his 'buddies,' so to speak. But if I were to call Steve today, he'd certainly return my call. I have his numbers, but

I'd never give them to anybody. It's funny, though. He's never asked me not to. But when you get to know Steve, you just *know* what your boundaries are, and what you would and wouldn't do."

In writing this book, I began to think of what Ollson, Gallant and Kelly were describing as the "Steve Zone," a bubble of privacy that not even his own friends like to risk bursting. Wariness of that zone is contagious. Larry Kelly was unfailingly helpful in my research efforts, handing out phone numbers, suggesting people to speak with, making an advance call to Mike O'Connell, the general manager and vice president of the Boston Bruins, to pave the way for an interview that Kelly rightly thought would be helpful. But Yzerman himself turned out to be unavailable, and his number was one that Kelly wouldn't think of relinquishing. Kelly forwarded my request for an interview to Yzerman, followed up with phone calls (leaving one message, recommending that he speak with me, while I sat in Kelly's office in Ottawa). "I don't want you to take this the wrong way," Kelly advised, "but when your book is done, he probably won't even read it." And it's not because he doesn't read. It's because a book about him is background noise in his life, best left beyond the bubble of the Steve Zone.

I never did hear from my subject. Nor did he interfere in any way. Key people in the Red Wings organization, Jim Devellano and Dave Lewis, told me whatever I wanted to know. Gerard Gallant returned one of my calls from the Blue Jackets dressing room and was frank and heartfelt in his observations. There were no signals that Steve Yzerman was discouraging people from speaking with me.

And I have to admit that I, too, fell victim to the vibes of the Steve Zone. Mike Kelly had an inspiration in the fall of 2003 and gave me the cellphone number of another client, Steve Thomas, for whom he'd just completed a deal that sent the veteran to the Red Wings. Thomas was actually staying right in Steve's house. Maybe you should talk to Thomas, Kelly proposed.

And for the first time in my life as a professional writer, I found myself unable to place a call. My dialing finger went numb in the presence of the Do Not Disturb sign that others had hung for me on Yzerman's private life. Yzerman had started the season on a scoring tear, but then went into a slump. And I actually started thinking, I can't call Steve Thomas. He'll be sitting in Yzerman's living room with him, watching a movie or something. Thomas will start talking to me on his cellphone about Yzerman. Maybe he'll duck into the laundry room for privacy. Yzerman might start to worry about what Thomas is saying, and then he'll be distracted and the slump will go on forever and Yzerman won't win a fourth Stanley Cup, because I messed with his personal space with a phone call that went right into his house. So I never did call Steve Thomas.

Which worked out all right in the end, I think, because the story I was telling had particular narrative requirements that only certain people could satisfy. I was most interested in how Steve Yzerman had gone from being a prospect to an individual star to a team leader who is also a champion, and what all of that could teach us not only about Yzerman, but about the nature of winning, of becoming a winner. That requires certain people who are in the right place at the right time—sometimes people who have seen him over a long career trajectory, in order to glean the proper insights. That's why I found Jim Devellano, who drafted Yzerman in 1983 and is now the senior vice president of the Red Wings, so important. And Dick Todd, his junior coach, who deserves tremendous credit for instilling in him the fundamentals of the two-way game. And Dave Lewis, who played with Yzerman in the

1980s, served as an assistant coach during Detroit's troubled years of playoff disappointments as well as in the winning years, and is now his head coach. And Bob Errey, who was a linemate in junior, an opponent in the NHL (in particular when he led San Jose to a major upset of the Red Wings in the 1994 playoffs) and finally a teammate again on the Red Wings. And Gerard Gallant, who in addition to having been a close friend and linemate through Yzerman's most spectacular offensive years, had also played on a line in junior with Pat LaFontaine (the kid Detroit really wanted to draft in 1983) and can now speak with the added perspective of a coach about what has made Yzerman so special. And Jacques Demers, a Stanley Cup–winning coach who insisted on making Yzerman his captain in 1986 and who told me Yzerman was the greatest player he ever coached. And Mike O'Connell, another former teammate who now, as a senior executive with the Bruins, has some idea of the qualities of great players and where Yzerman fits into their pantheon.

I also enjoyed meeting and speaking with John Ollson, the childhood friend who insisted to me that he should not be considered a buddy of Steve's. Nevertheless, let the record show that, near the end of the 2000–01 season, Ollson took his son Matty to Detroit for his twelfth birthday. They did the full tour of sporting sights, capped by a Red Wings game, courtesy of two tickets from Yzerman.

"After the game," says Ollson, "Anna Kournikova's with us, and we go down to the locker room. I'd known Kris Draper from the national team, and when I walk in, it's, 'What the hell are you doing here?' Matty's in the room, he's talking to Chelios, Scotty Bowman, the whole thing." They went to leave Joe Louis Arena with Yzerman, and the captain said, "Let's go out across the ice." As they shuffled across the rink, Yzerman turned to Ollson's son.

"He says, 'Hey, Matty. You should have seen it when we got the Stanley Cup. There was confetti coming down . . . ' We walk out past everybody, past two security guards. Two people still snagged him for an autograph, and then we're out the back door and in his Land Rover and gone."

The Red Wings had beaten Washington 2–1 on an Yzerman goal just seconds into overtime. "Dad called your goal before you even got it," Matty told the captain. After the game, it was learned that Yzerman had been playing, as he'd suspected, with a broken bone in his foot. Ollson spoke with him about it a little later. "I had some family coming down, and I knew you were coming down, and I didn't know if it was broken or not, so I decided to play," Yzerman explained.

"He played for *those* reasons," Ollson emphasizes. Because friends and family had come all the way to Detroit to see him. Considering how exercised some Red Wings fans would become over Yzerman representing Canada in the Olympic tournament despite knee problems, it's hard to imagine what they would have thought of him having played on a broken foot, right before the playoffs, because he didn't want to disappoint people who had driven down from the capital of Soviet Canuckistan. And as it turned out, he only managed to appear in one playoff game for Detroit, against Los Angeles in the opening round, before the foot forced him onto the injured list. But he has always played for the fans, and fans are the last people who should complain about his priorities. If he had played only for himself, his game would never have gone through the transformation that it did in the 1990s. And there would have been no confetti falling on them in June 1997.

Just getting to June 1997 was a veritable odyssey for Yzerman and his many admirers. Which brings us to how he came to skate his first NHL shift.

ONE

"How many lines did the Red Wings use when they finally started winning Stanley Cups?" Dick Todd asks.

Four, is the answer.

"And how many lines are the winning teams now using?" he continues.

Four. The same number that the Peterborough Petes used when Todd coached them in the 1980s, when Steve Yzerman was his most spectacular—but far from the only—graduate to the NHL.

"During the time I coached in Peterborough," Todd states with unabashed pride, "we put more underage players in the NHL than any junior franchise has ever put in. I've had the highest winning percentage of any coach in junior hockey. I think that my system worked well and developed a broad base of players."

Todd's coaching record is indisputably impressive. In addition to his achievements in Peterborough, Todd was assistant coach in 1990, and head coach in 1991, of Canada's entries in the World Junior Championships, which won back-to-back gold medals. He had worked with Roger Neilson in the Petes organization in the 1970s before "Captain Video" moved up to the NHL in 1977, and he later joined Neilson as his assistant coach with the New York Rangers. The Petes organization had a long-standing reputation for training prospects to play in both directions; many forwards who did graduate to the NHL, such as Craig Ramsay and Bob Gainey, were renowned for their defensive abilities and went on to excel in off-ice roles as well. Peterborough was not, however, an organization that turned out high-scoring forwards. Considering the way that Yzerman's professional career initially unfolded, as an offensive star, his Pete pedigree stands out as the most surprising aspect of his amateur career. But from the perspective of Yzerman's maturation as a total player, having been a Pete was absolutely fundamental.

When people talk of Stevie Y's junior career, they repeat this mantra: You've got to remember that four-line system in Peterborough. It taught him things about two-way play. It didn't let him hog ice time, or run up huge personal scoring stats.

"I don't know whether Steve would admit to this," says Todd, "but we really stressed to him to learn the game at both ends of the rink. He was an excellent defensive player for us as well as contributing offensively."

"We were never the top line in juniors," says Yzerman's linemate on the Petes, Bob Errey. "We played four lines under Dick Todd," he explains, as everyone who knows of those days feels obliged to point out. "We might play the second power play, and kill penalties. We had no more ice time than anyone else."

"I didn't know that much about Steve when I was in junior," says Gerard "Turk" Gallant, his future linemate in Detroit, who was playing in the Quebec Major Junior league for Verdun, waging shootouts with Mario Lemieux's Laval Voisins. "But you heard they played a four-line system, that everybody did the same things— killed penalties, were on power plays. Steve didn't get twenty-five minutes of ice time a game, but that was probably better for him in his career. It might have been hard to say when he was playing there, but he learned both ends of the rink, and about team chemistry, and about winning. And sure enough, in the last ten years of his career, when he was winning those Stanley Cups and he played his best hockey, it was about 'team' winning and not just carrying the team offensively. It was about playing defensively, and killing penalties."

Yzerman never made the OHL's top-ten scoring list, or its All-Star team. He didn't even lead his own team in total points. In his first season, 1981–82, he produced 21 goals and 43 assists, tied with Dave Morrison at 64 points and trailing Larry Floyd (69), Doug Evans (66) and Vinci Sebek (65). In 1982–83, Yzerman was bested by his left winger, Errey, in goals (53 to 42) and points (100 to 91); both finished behind their line's right winger, Scott McLellan, who led the team with 101 points.

So much for statistics. For, as is often the case, they hardly tell the whole story—or even the real story. "His numbers weren't out of this world," says Todd, "but for a seventeen-year-old, they were very, very good. And," he proposes, laughing, "they would have been better had Bob Errey been able to convert the number of opportunities he was given by Steve. He could set Bob up once a period for a breakaway.

"Steve was the catalyst for Bob putting up the statistics he did," adds Todd. "Bob was an exceptionally strong skater. He was *so* quick. This made them a real threat all the time, because Steve could put the puck on Bob's stick at the right moment and have him break loose. And Bob, you could tell, was intelligent. He was quiet, and thankful to be playing with Steve. I don't think he wanted to do or say anything to rock his position."

There is, persistently, the issue of age with Yzerman. A young man in a pragmatic, impressive hurry. He was only sixteen when he began his first season as a Pete, only eighteen when he made the Red Wings lineup, only twenty-one when the Red Wings made him their captain. Many other players have reached significant career thresholds at a tender age, but few have done so and left such a consistent impression of their character and ability. There would be a flip side to this rush of accomplishments for Yzerman: disappointments in not making Canada Cup squads, or the fourteen-season wait to be a league champion. But rather than becoming a young talent who blossomed early and then faded through frustration or adversity, or who tasted success so soon that he lacked the motivation to keep on achieving, Yzerman became a persistent, versatile talent for whom people can point back to his Peterborough days and recall him not only playing there, but *being* Steve Yzerman there, while still a youth.

The qualities that would make him a star in the NHL were already to be seen when Yzerman was playing for his hometown Tier II junior club, the Nepean Raiders. The Petes had the fourth pick overall in the draft, and Todd, who was then the team's trainer and business manager, was involved in the picking. "I remember we were trying to decide between Brian Bradley and Steve Yzerman." After Peterborough chose Yzerman (in part on the recommendation of Jacques Martin, the future Ottawa Senators coach who was then bird-dogging talent for the Petes), Bradley went to the London Knights. He stayed with them for the better part of four seasons and produced two 100-point efforts before turning pro with the Calgary Flames organization. When his NHL career ended in 1997–98, he had appeared in 651 games with Calgary, Vancouver, Toronto and Tampa Bay, where he served as captain.

"From a junior point of view, Bradley played four seasons and Steve played only two," says Todd. "As a team, we might have been better with Bradley. But we always went with the guy who we felt was the best NHL prospect."

"Brian Bradley was a great NHLer," says John Ollson, who grew up with Yzerman and played against both him and Bradley in junior. "Those guys are really similar: right-hand shots, the same size, skated the same way, handled the puck well. Steve is probably a more complete player, but he didn't become a more complete player until about the last ten years, because for the first ten years he just scored. Steve had a great brain. Him, Mario Lemieux, Joe Sakic, Wayne Gretzky . . . there are only five or six guys that play with their eyes more than they play with their body. They really are true thinkers out there, and they don't look like they're working very hard. They let their minds do so much of it. It's just a big chess game to them."

Ollson slips into an almost poetic recitation of Yzerman's abilities. "Slippery, sleek, agile, mobile, fast. Fedorov is like him. They create their own time and space."

"He had tremendous insight into the game," says Todd of Yzerman in Peterborough. "He was outstanding. We had another player who was nineteen and would play a few NHL games. He was extremely jealous of Steve and the amount of attention he started getting in Peterborough." Todd inherited the unhappy fact of this streak of jealousy when he took over the Peterborough bench, his first coaching job, after the former NHL and WHA goaltender Dave Dryden was canned in midseason. "When I took over, it was unfortunate that that was there, but Steve made the best of the situation."

Yzerman was hardwired for stardom, but not celebrity. He didn't make a fuss about himself. Once he turned pro, he would have no time for players who turned on the charm for the endorsement biz, who became someone that they weren't in the dressing room. He has shown himself to be proud, but not vain; ambitious, but not deluded by notions of entitlement. What he has asked in return for his own effort on the ice is results, not accolades.

Jealousy dogged both Yzerman and Errey within their own team. Todd faced the challenge of placating older team members who no longer enjoyed the privileges that had only recently accrued to nineteen- and twenty-year-old juniors. Players who had begun their junior careers before the NHL draft age started dropping in 1980 (first to nineteen, then to eighteen in 1981) had been part of a system in which certain perks, such as a prime spot on the power play, extra ice time, or a pairing with a star forward, were often reserved for the most senior players. The lowering of the draft age meant that the pecking order on junior rosters had been turned upside down: the best players were now generally the youngest ones; who stuck around to the end of their junior eligibility tended to have been passed over by the NHL. Part of Todd's motivation for a four-line system, for using two power-play units, neither one getting more ice time than the other, was to promote team chemistry, to prevent his oldest charges from being marginalized, even if not all of them saw it that way.

And while neither Yzerman nor Errey served as captain, they were unquestioned team leaders. "They led by their example," says Todd, "more than they did vocally. They were both never a problem. There was never an ego situation with them, no agendas. They were elite players, playing with older people. They were quiet and unassuming, and intent on doing what was right for the team."

For a prospect with such obvious talent, Yzerman was noticeably down-to-earth. He boarded in Peterborough with the Garvey family, who lived near the Memorial Centre, where the Petes played. "They were very middle class, barely middle-class people," says Todd. "I think Vince [Garvey] was a truck driver at one point. Steve took to them, and they took to him. Steve's parents would come down and spend the week at their camp at a trailer park in the summer. I can remember being invited out for a barbecue one night at the camp, which was unusual to have happen with a junior player. Later, Vince would wear a 'Steve Yzerman' Detroit Red Wings jacket around town. Vince adopted the boy. He would make sure that they had a euchre game on Monday nights. Two tables of guys would come to Steve's boarding house. It was a really close-knit atmosphere. The support was terrific."

Bob Errey made his own contributions to team cohesion. As a local boy, it became his duty to squire other players around town. "I showed them the good things and the bad things of Peterborough," he says, laughing, and leaves it at that.

It is to the credit of Yzerman's parents that they were able to support their son's ambitions without warping his ego or annoying the hell out of everyone with whom they came into contact on his way up. Todd pays special tribute to them. "Many times, you'd have a kid with the talent that Steve had, and you'd have difficulties with parents because they'd be looking for more recognition for him, or were behaving like they were a step above everybody else. But Steve's people were so down to earth and so supportive of our team, our city and his career here. Steve was very conscientious and hardworking. Just an honest kid that gave you what he had."

Yzerman's father, Ron, was an Ottawa civil servant, and Ron and Jean Yzerman had tried to raise their five children (four boys and girl) to pursue postsecondary academics, which they all did— except for Steve, who had become totally focused on a career in professional hockey before he even reached high school. Though born in Cranbrook, British Columbia, Steve had been raised in

Nepean, which in the 1970s was a small Ottawa suburb just emerging from its dairy farming past. A telecommunications revolution was helping change the capital's landscape; the 'burbs began to boom as greater Ottawa turned into a center of high technology thanks to the burgeoning success of outfits like Mitel, Bell Northern Research (where Yzerman's sister became a computer programmer) and Northern Telecom (later Nortel Networks). Amid this next-big-thing economic growth, Yzerman was pursuing the old-economy dream of playing pro hockey.

"We played ball hockey together, hockey with and against each other," John Ollson recalls of growing up in Nepean with Yzerman and others in their circle of friends, which included Darren Pang, a goaltender who had a cup of coffee with the Chicago Blackhawks and went on to work for ESPN. Ollson was about eighteen months older than Yzerman, but Yzerman's skills have always, it seems, let him excel beyond his age bracket. "We were all pretty good athletes in terms of playing other sports." There was baseball in the summer, and Ollson would become a golf pro in addition to running his hockey school. "Hit a ball, catch a ball, shoot a puck, anything like that, we could all do it reasonably well with little effort. You started with hand-eye coordination and talent, and then you had to be mentored in the right way."

Hockey was their unquestioned priority, and they were all good at it. One of the biggest headaches plaguing amateur hockey today is the effect of the multimillion-dollar salaries earned by players like Yzerman on parents who think their tykes are destined to make that kind of coin, too. Studies have been pressed, with limited success, upon these glassy-eyed dreamers, showing that a boy playing in the Canadian minor hockey system has only a slightly better chance of having an NHL career than he does of discovering intelligent life elsewhere in the universe. When

Yzerman was young, it was still the kids, and not the parents, who entertained pro ambitions most ardently. And while the rise of the World Hockey Association as a rival to the NHL helped force up professional salaries overall, the effect hadn't been great enough to convince many that it was necessarily wise to become totally focused on a hockey career.

But the WHA also radically changed the path to a professional career for players like Yzerman who would come of age in the early 1980s. The instigator of that change was Ken Linseman, an impatient teen with the Kingston Canadians.

Linseman—later nicknamed "The Rat" for his bent-over skating style—was a top prospect in Ontario major junior hockey, a forward who had racked up more than 100 points in both his second and third seasons with his hometown Canadians, when the Birmingham Bulls chose him eighty-third overall in the 1977 WHA draft. He was a smart young man (today he is a commercial real estate broker in Connecticut) from a big Kingston family, was gifted on the ice, and had lost his mother at a young age. He would turn nineteen in August, before the start of the new season, and after three years of major junior competition, he felt ready to make his own way in the world and was eager to turn pro. And why not? The WHA, although struggling—having by this time shrunken from a high of fourteen teams to just nine— was still paying the kinds of salaries that cause NHL executives to go into conniptions. Every year that the start of a young man's playing career was delayed carried a six-figure penalty.

It wasn't the first time the Bulls had had designs on an under-age talent. In 1975, in their previous guise as the Toronto Toros, the team had signed and iced an eighteen-year-old named Mark Napier after he had played just two seasons of junior hockey with the Toronto Marlboros. The WHA as a league had agreed, as the

NHL had, not to sign players in the Canadian amateur system to contracts before their twentieth year, so as not to rob junior hockey of its star attractions. The NHL had allowed for a limited number of underage players to be drafted in 1974, but that was a one-year experiment. By signing Napier as a free agent and putting him on the ice two full seasons before the Montreal Canadiens chose him in the first round of the NHL draft, Toros owner John Bassett broke ranks with both leagues. There were other underage signings in the WHA, but the practice ceased shortly thereafter in the wake of vehement objections from the Canadian Amateur Hockey Association. The CAHA was determined to keep the rosters of its major junior teams intact, and to that end used its clout as the primary venue for the development of new talent, to wrest agreements out of the NHL and WHA that prevented players from turning pro before turning twenty. The drafting of Linseman was another rogue maneuver on Bassett's part, and the WHA ruled that the young centerman was ineligible to play.

Back in the days of the Original Six, players routinely began their professional careers at the age of eighteen, and in some cases even younger. Before the amateur draft came along, players' NHL rights were formally secured at sixteen, usually with what was called a "C" form, a promise of professional services that gave the NHL club the right to call upon the player to sign a pro contract within one year's time. Linseman had no intention of being forced to play a fourth season of junior hockey. Through his agent, Max Kaminsky, he arranged to have a young lawyer named John Hughes file an antitrust suit against the WHA in the state of Connecticut.

Hughes had a good feel for the issues, having once been a Toronto Marlie and property of the Toronto Maple Leafs. A

Scarborough lad, he had gone to Cornell University on a hockey scholarship, where he played alongside the imminently famous goaltender, Ken Dryden, and served as captain. While Hughes' destiny was to practice tax and real estate law from his New York City law office, it was in sports that he became truly famous: first, for his hockey exploits at Cornell; second, for filing the Linseman suit; and third, for fathering a figure skater named Sarah who, at age sixteen, scored a major upset at the 2002 Olympics by winning the women's singles gold medal.

The Linseman case was not a long, drawn-out affair. "John got an injunction within two weeks," Linesman recalls. The WHA mounted a "coercion" defense, asserting that it had been forced not to employ young men like Linseman because of pressure exerted by the CAHA. That defense failed; Linseman had every right to make a living. The Linesman injunction compelled the NHL to begin rolling back the draft age to eighteen, thus accelerating the professional debuts of new prospects like Yzerman.

Although resolved quickly, the dispute made a lasting impact on case law. "I have friends who are lawyers, and the first case they studied in sports was me," Linesman says. It also got Linseman into a WHA uniform and a handsome pay schedule that fall. As he recalls, he was paid a signing bonus of $100,000 on a $1 million contract, payable over six years. "The next year, I think my signing bonus was $150,000." The money Linseman made in the dying days of the WHA would put to shame the salary Steve Yzerman would draw just a few years later, when he turned pro as a Red Wing at eighteen.

People who excel at something, whether it is sports, software design or playing the violin, tend to be a wee bit fixated in their youth. Obsession as a developmental process produces a lot of waste—most obsessed youths aren't going to make it big in whatever has them in its seductive grip—but those who do succeed do so because of that obsession, which might be described more benignly as dedication. Unlike software code and classical instruments, the professional hockey development stream—especially since the draft age was rolled back beginning in 1980—hasn't required a postsecondary education. Yzerman did pay attention to his schooling while in Peterborough, enough to be singled out among players for his academic effort. But there was no longer any time for university for a top prospect. With the draft age reduced to eighteen, players were now entering the profession straight out of high school. That required a young man to get serious about the job while still in high school, so that he could be properly prepped in junior. A parent confronted with a child's determination to play pro hockey, and inclined to agree that the boy might be onto something, had to buy into the dream pretty quickly.

By all accounts, once the Yzermans accepted their son's fixation—and it was hard not to notice how good he was—they supported him unequivocally. In the mid 1970s, there were roughly 2,400 kids in the Nepean minor hockey system, where Yzerman began playing at the Atom A level, and the emphasis was more on house league than tournament-caliber play. Yzerman's parents sent him to hockey camp in the summer to help him refine his skills, and at fifteen he was able to join the Nepean Raiders, a Tier II Junior A team that had played in the Central Junior league since 1972. The Raiders at least had a terrific facility to call home: the NHL-sized rink at the Nepean Sportsplex which was built in 1973. (After Yzerman led the Red Wings to their 1998 Stanley Cup win and earned the Conn Smythe Trophy as the most valuable player in the playoffs, this rink was renamed Steve Yzerman Arena.) At 200 feet by 85, there was a lot of ice for a teenager to cover. Most small-town rinks are ten to fifteen feet shorter than regulation, and at the time there were even some NHL rinks that were less than full size: Boston Garden measured 191 by 83; Buffalo's "Aud," 193 by 84; Chicago Stadium, 185 by 85. Yzerman was exposed to the full sheet, and the consequences of not patrolling all of it, at a very young age.

Like many future NHL stars in a hurry to make their way up through the development ranks, Yzerman didn't stick with the Raiders long enough to rewrite the team record book. He played only one season, but did register his first junior hat trick with the Raiders by scoring shorthanded, at even strength, and on the power play in one game. Pursuing his hockey dream meant lighting out for Peterborough at age sixteen to play for the major junior Petes. Oddly enough, the move up from the Raiders to the Petes put him on home ice that was ten feet shorter than in Nepean.

"He was more mature than most people his age," Errey says of the young Yzerman. "He was a real professional. He knew the game was about more than scoring goals. Steve was as happy to win 2–1 as he was 7–5. That's not typical of a junior player, who usually likes to score a lot of goals. He was ahead of his time. And he always had a work ethic, constantly training, working on his deficiencies instead of his strengths. I remember how, after his first season, he went home and did a lot of skating. He came back, and was way faster at training camp. He went from being an above-average skater to being a great skater.

"You couldn't tell him he couldn't do something. It would make him strive that much more. I don't think I was much different. Some of it was because you were told you were too small."

In Yzerman and Errey's second season together in Peterborough, the NHL's Central Scouting Bureau came calling. The bureau had been created by the league in the 1970s to provide a pool of wisdom about prospects that would be available to all teams. It was a measure to help the expansion clubs, which tended not to have the extensive scouting programs that the established teams did, to make more intelligent drafting decisions. Bad teams drafted high, and if they didn't do their homework properly they would draft as badly as they played—or they wouldn't bother drafting at all, choosing instead to deal away future draft picks to talent-laden teams in exchange for proven, if aging, players. League parity depended in part, then, on better intelligence about amateur players for all. And so the bureau called on the Petes, to have a look at what they had coming down the pipeline in preparation for the next entry draft in June 1983.

Errey and Yzerman were both up for the 1983 draft. Errey had turned eighteen in September, at the start of the 1982–83 season, while Yzerman wouldn't reach that milestone until May 9, just a month before the draft. Central Scouting didn't only assess each prospect's skill on the ice; there was also the matter of sizing them up physically. Errey and Yzerman took no chances, stuffing foam into their socks to increase their height; Errey also remembers wrapping some foam around his torso, under his shirt, to seem more imposing, and thinks his linemate may have done the same.

The NHL record books say Bob Errey stands five feet, ten inches tall. "I've never been five-ten in my life," he says. The best he could hope for in a legitimate measurement was five-nine and a half. "But you wanted to get that 'five-and-double digit.'"

"There definitely was a concern about size," says Dick Todd, agreeing that the five-and-double-digit threshold got everyone in knots. He remembers a scam Keith Acton tried to pull while he was with the Petes in the mid seventies. "Keith had wooden heel inserts in his socks. He got to five-ten or something with a guy from Central Scouting." Problem was, a teammate, Mark Kirton, came along to the measuring ceremony after him. "Mark was taller than Keith and hadn't done anything like Keith had, and he measured five nine and a half. He started to scream right in front of the scout: 'I'm taller than him and I always have been! What's going on here? How come I'm not measuring up?'" In the NHL record books, Keith Acton has been busted down to five-eight, while Kirton is listed at five-ten.

"Scouts were under a great deal of pressure to do their job and get the right numbers," says Todd. "Because once the NHL club had the player under contract and did their own measurements, they'd go crazy if the numbers were different. Sometimes, Central Scouting would say to a scout, 'That guy is *not* five-ten. You go back and measure him.' They might also send in an independent scout, a western scout or somebody else to measure the guy. That happened several times—not necessarily on my team, but it was happening."

Yzerman was hardly diminutive, but his size was enough to set off alarm bells. Conventional wisdom had it that five-ten was the threshold at which scouts began to express a host of concerns. Below that height, scouts—and general managers—began to view a player as an exceptional prospect, which meant he would have to demonstrate exceptional abilities. After all, five feet, ten inches is barely above the fiftieth percentile of the U.S. National Center for Health Statistics' growth chart for boys between two and twenty years of age. At age twenty, the typical midsize male is five foot nine (about five-eight-and-a-half at eighteen) and 155 pounds. And as a rule, professional contact sports are not populated by adult males of average size.

The kids Yzerman had grown up with were really going to have a hard time proving they belonged in the major league.

John Ollson reached five-nine, and while he finished eighth in the Ontario Hockey League in scoring with the Ottawa 67s in 1982–83—well ahead of Yzerman with 122 points—no NHL team even drafted him. Their buddy Darren Pang, the 67s goaltender who had also played on the Nepean Raiders, was only five-five, and would be signed by the Blackhawks as a free agent.

Every rise through the game's hierarchy thinned the herd. Players once deemed exceptional often became merely average in their later teens, and those who were merely average became unemployable. A player who measured below or even around the five-and-double-digit level would prompt scouts to ask, What makes this kid so special that he can be so small and still compete?

Desire was hardly ever at issue. Smaller men, including players like Yzerman on the size bubble, were accustomed to training and playing hard simply to hold their own, to prove that they belonged. The urge to have a greater presence in the game than their physical stats would allude to sometimes made them excel beyond reasonable expectations. Desire and intensity led to a hard work ethic that in turn usually paid off in better-than-average skating, passing and shooting skills, which ultimately were the keys to their survival. And which were what the scouts started looking for when a player touched that trip wire. At five-eleven, average skating speed might be okay. But at five-ten or less, the scouts began looking for speed that could give the smaller player an edge. In fact, they were looking for every element of a small player's game, short of bodychecking and fighting, to be a cut above the rest. And the shyer a player fell of five and double digit, the less he could do, short of levitation, to convince a scout that he belonged in the NHL.

There was no great science behind this fixation on height, only the experience of seasons past, of training camps and so many young prospects who had sparkled on the way up only to hit a physical wall when they reached the big league. And that wall was a fairly recent development. Prior to the 1970s, size never seemed to be a major issue in the National Hockey League. There were large, powerful men, like Gordie Howe, Frank Mahovlich and Jean Beliveau, but no one ever said that a player had to be large in order to excel. There were many players—great players—who would scarcely draw a second glace in street clothes. Ted Lindsay, the ferocious captain of the Red Wings in the 1950s and Howe's linemate on the famous Production Line, was only five-eight. Tim Horton, the stalwart blueliner of the Leafs of the 1950s and '60s, also stood five-eight, although he was incredibly muscular. Meet a group of Original Six players today, and even allowing for a bit of natural height loss that comes with aging, it's striking how perfectly ordinary they seem in stature. Indeed, many have thickened up around the middle, and you have to remind yourself that they tended to play at weights at least twenty or thirty pounds lighter than what you see standing in front of you.

The giants started showing up in force in the 1970s, ushered in by the accelerated pace of league exapansion and the brawling made famous by Philadelphia's Broad Street Bullies. At the same time, physical conditioning was instilled in the NHL game after the example set by the great Soviet and other European teams. Players overall became faster, better skaters, with greater endurance. They also hit harder, and the ice surface wasn't getting any bigger. Big centers came into fashion because they could outmuscle their opponents during face-offs. A big man parked in the slot in front of the goaltender required another big man to move him out of the way. Soon it was an exception to the rule for an NHL defenseman to be less than six feet tall and two hundred pounds.

The lowering of the NHL draft age to eighteen, which was completed just two years before Steve Yzerman became eligible, put scouts in the unfamiliar position of having to assess players not only before they had fully mastered their hockey skills, but before they had finished growing, both emotionally and physically. The emotional component is impossible to quantify, but on the physical side there's plenty of pediatric data to draw on. By the age of sixteen, boys have pretty well finished growing, height-wise; they'll typically gain, at most, another inch by age twenty as their torso catches up with the initial growth spurt of arms and legs. Scouts talk of a draft prospect "filling out" as he grows older because, even at eighteen, a typical young man hasn't finished with skeletal growth. The final stage involves the broadening of the chest and shoulders, and this doesn't usually finish until age twenty. Upper-body strength, then, is one of the last things a prospect adds to his physical repertoire, and it's often not completely in evidence at draft age. The average young man naturally will pack on another ten pounds after turning eighteen as the upper body finishes growing; an athlete who has finished growing will bulk up even more when he hits the weight room. As a result, scouts have had to grow accustomed to sizing up the sometimes gangly proportions of a young prospect and struggling to predict how big he might ultimately become.

The job of rating prospects during their growing years presents another considerable hazard: players are also growing at different rates at the same time that they're developing their skills. Kids who go through their growth spurt early can skate all over their opponents while they're still in midget competition. A prospect can look brilliant in junior because he's physically more mature than his opponents, but once everyone is done growing at age twenty, those gaps have closed; a player who looked positively electric at age seventeen or eighteen may turn out to be utterly ordinary in his early twenties.

"It's all just a big guess," Dale Derkatch, a scout with the Washington Capitals, says of his job. "You do your best." He speaks with heartfelt experience about how difficult it is to judge the professional potential of a junior player. "I'm in lots of meetings where a guy will say, 'Look at that player and all the points he has.' And I'll say, 'I'll show you guys with tons of points in Juniors who didn't make it in the NHL.'"

As was the case during Yzerman's—and his own—junior years in the early 1980s, Derkatch and his fellow scouts today "are watching guys seventeen, eighteen years old. This season he'll be great and have a ton of points, but we ask: is he still growing, not just physically, but in his skills, and emotionally? You're looking years down the road with them. I'm hoping for the best for every kid. I really am. But sooner or later, you have to make your decisions."

He agrees that size continues to be a prime concern in the prospect hunt. And the days of five-and-double-digit are gone. "Six feet and 200 are now the magic numbers." Derkatch notes how many of the gifted forwards today, including Paul Kariya, Peter Forsberg, and yes, Steve Yzerman, don't measure up to those magic numbers. There are a lot of great forwards around five-eleven, maybe six feet, and 180 pounds. "It's true in some ways that you want a player to be bigger because he has to be able to handle the rigor of the NHL season, and handle the Derian Hatchers. But usually, the smaller guys have determination and heart. They play hard."

Derkatch should know. He was one of the brightest talents ever to come out of junior hockey in western Canada, and became draft-eligible in the same year as Yzerman. He presented the NHL's scouts with a profound dilemma. On the one hand, he was a dazzling playmaker and exceptionally gifted scorer who produced goals not by shoveling in rebounds, but by virtuoso rushing and passing displays. On March 26, 1982, he set a WHL postseason assist record by setting up seven goals in a 13–6 shootout with the Brandon Wheat Kings. He scored 84 goals that season, along with 95 assists, and was on another tear in 1982–83. But he was shy of that five-and-double-digit tripwire by four full inches, and weighed only 140 pounds. He was such an enigmatic talent that there were people who believed he would either be chosen in the first round, or not at all. Of all the players eligible for the draft in 1983, Derkatch was the wild card, the one who made predicting where Yzerman, Errey, and everyone else might end up so unusually difficult as the season unfolded.

Ken Linseman's experience in making the jump from junior hockey to the professional ranks was significant for more than lowering the draft age: he was also part of a trend among hockey people to place a premium on aggression. By 1983, quite a few general managers wanted to see a mean streak in a prospect, especially one on that five-and-double-digit bubble. Players were routinely encouraged to start fighting, to double their penalty minutes in order to get themselves noticed.

Linseman's epiphany came from playing in his rookie season in Kingston with a defenseman named Mike O'Connell, about whom he cannot say enough good things. "He was a like a Bobby Orr," says Linseman. "Very talented. But then he got hurt"—a knee injury forced him to miss twenty games—"and he didn't get drafted until the third round." Despite notching 73 points from the blue line in 50 games, O'Connell was chosen forty-third overall by Chicago in the 1975 amateur draft.

A year later, while O'Connell broke into the pro ranks with the Dallas Blackhawks of the Central league, Linseman managed a very respectable 112 points with the Canadians. And now Linseman got to watch a bruiser of a Kingston defenseman, Mark Suzor—much bigger than O'Connell, but without his many skills—get chosen seventeenth overall by the Philadelphia Flyers in the first round of the 1976 draft. The Broad Street Bullies had just lost the Stanley Cup finals to Montreal.

"Right then, I started thinking that I had to make sure people didn't think size was an issue with me. I had to play aggressively, more than was my nature." He was committed to making sure he went no lower in the NHL draft than the second round, because he figured that "the higher you're drafted, the more they're committed to you."

A talented scorer, Linseman would also gain a reputation as one of the nastiest opponents in the professional game. In 1976–77, his final junior season, his penalty total leapt from 92 minutes to 210. Along the way, he garnered a criminal conviction for assault after he kicked another player in the head with his skate. In 1978, the Flyers made him their second choice, seventh overall, in the NHL draft, and he would win a Stanley Cup with Edmonton, in 1984. Many fans who watched the "classic" outdoor game at Edmonton's Commonwealth Stadium between the Oilers and Montreal Canadiens oldtimers in 2003 were probably surprised by the nifty goal Linseman scored to open the game for Edmonton. It was a reminder of just how good he had been at putting pucks in the net, not just at tormenting opponents.

Linseman's career also illustrates how absurdly small the world of professional hockey can be. Six degrees of separation are seldom required to link one person with another. In Linseman's case, there were direct lines to Yzerman, not only through the impact of the lawsuit on the draft process.

Mike O'Connell, the skilled defenseman whom Linseman had so admired, wound up a teammate of Yzerman's in Detroit. (Linseman and O'Connell would eventually play together again, in Boston.) And when Linseman was charged with assault as a junior, there was a young lawyer working on the case in the Crown Attorney's office by the name of Larry Kelly, who offered some advice on how he should handle his plea. A dozen years later, Kelly would become Yzerman's agent. Small world indeed.

Growing up in Kingston, Linseman had watched his younger brother Johnny play against Yzerman in junior, and he eventually tangled with Yzerman in the NHL. "He's a class act," Linseman says of Yzerman. "It's neat to see a guy with his personality persevere. He always played with his skills, and was never intimidated. He was totally comfortable with his surroundings on the ice. Skillful guys can sometimes show some softness, but he didn't have any."

It's a sincere tribute from a player who feels he had to become someone he says he wasn't in order to make it as a pro. Change in general was a condition of employment for many prospects seeking a niche in the NHL. Scorers became checkers. Checkers became fighters. These were transformations not everyone knew how to make, or could tolerate making. Particularly if brawling was their only option.

Other prospects in 1983 had the mean streak that made them more appealing than Yzerman to scouts and general managers, but they never parlayed that nastiness into the stardom that Yzerman achieved. While intensely competitive and occasionally prone to emotional blowouts, Yzerman never had to demonstrate or cultivate a mean streak the way Linseman and many others did. But once in the NHL, Yzerman would undergo perhaps the most remarkable transformations of any player of his time—first becoming the scoring star his junior career didn't necessarily predict, then becoming a defensive marvel for which the Petes system ably prepared him. Yzerman would fulfill every ounce of the potential he demonstrated in Peterborough, changing the nature of his game to suit the needs of his team, as its success became his priority as a professional.

TWO

IF CERTAIN PHYSICISTS ARE TO BE BELIEVED, OUR UNIVERSE is but one of an infinite number of parallel universes. And infinity being what it is, that means everything you could ever imagining happening on earth, has happened or will happen in another universe. Somewhere out there, the Toronto Maple Leafs have won every Stanley Cup final ever. Somewhere out there, Paul Henderson's famous series-winning stab at his own rebound sent the puck bouncing harmlessly off the goalpost. Somewhere out there, Pat LaFontaine has led the Detroit Red Wings, under general manager Bryan Murray, to the Stanley Cup while Steve Yzerman toiled in comparative obscurity as a Minnesota North Star, albeit with such celestial skill as to prevent the team from moving to Dallas. There's another universe in which Yzerman has led the Ottawa Senators to a Cup victory after a blockbuster trade that saw the Red Wings swap him for Alexei Yashin. Somewhere out there, Stevie Y ended up playing in Düsseldorf, simply because cosmology suggests that, given infinite universes, anything can and will happen.

Somewhere, there's a universe in which Steve Yzerman played harmonica in the Yardbirds.

We don't have time to imagine, let alone visit, all those universes. But that doesn't stop people, especially those in the business of professional sports, from wondering aloud about might-have-beens and could-have-beens. The star-crossed fortunes of so many talents in the Original Six era of the NHL, who never cracked the ranks of the big league, is a bottomless source of musing on the cruel nature of Fate. On the other hand, Dick Duff, who in this universe won a slew of Stanley Cups with the Toronto Maple Leafs and the Montreal Canadiens in the 1960s, once cut short a "Whatever happened to . . . ?" conversation with this writer by succinctly declaring: "Everybody who should have made it, *made it.*" But like the beat of a butterfly's wings in the Amazon rainforest that ultimately spawns a Category Five hurricane over the Atlantic Ocean, the smallest permutations in a player's unfolding career are routinely weighed and measured, the alternate realities imagined. Professional sport is especially prone to such ponderings because the twists and turns of fortune and misfortune have such easily defined crossroads: the dropped ball, the missed field goal, the freak injury, the too-many-men-on-the-ice penalty. (Somewhere, there is a universe in which Don Cherry's Boston Bruins are the 1979 Stanley Cup champions.) Not to mention the trades, the trades and the trades.

And the amateur draft. There is no greater display of fate than this annual cattle call of fresh talent, because the whole process is predicated on the expectation of what will come. God, as Einstein once said, does not play dice with the universe, but in professional hockey, scouts and general managers gather every summer for a crap shoot of talent selection. In hockey, the stakes are especially high for the players, because free agency is beyond their reach until they are thirty-one; few players will have the good fortune (in addition to the pure talent) to last in the league long enough to have some say over where they play. The kids come out for the annual talent auction—which isn't really an auction at all, because there's no bidding, just taking, in a set pecking order—and when the last crumbs of potential have been spoken for, those selected are locked into a career path that is in so many ways about as much within their control as a car with a gas pedal but no steering wheel. When each selected hopeful hears his name called and is handed a team jersey to pull on at the draft, there's no fooling around. As soon as the team comes to an agreement with the player's agent, the prospect is a franchise's contractual property, to be played, traded, promoted, demoted, or discarded at will.

It's not just where they're going to play. It's who they're going to play with, who's going to coach them, whether or not their skills will fit the talent mix of the team and the system of play currently in favor there. Whether or not management is even serious about winning anything, or is happy just to put fans in seats. "He should have played with or under so-and-so," you will hear people say.

Or he should have played somewhere entirely different. John Ollson, Yzerman's childhood friend, reminisces about a prospect they both knew who went high in the amateur draft, made it to the NHL, but never really had the career people thought he should have. "He was ten times the athlete Steve was. The best physical specimen of a man I've ever seen. Could throw a ball a mile, could play volleyball, could shoot the puck like nobody else. He was running a five-minute mile in high school with no training. All he'd say is, 'What's the best time? Well, I'll just beat it.' And that's all he'd need, to be able to do it." In the NHL draft, he went to a team with especially bright city lights. "Eighteen years old, lots of money. Too many off-ice problems. Not necessarily with drugs, just staying out late and having a good time. I said to him, 'You needed to be drafted by *Winnipeg.*' He could have focused on hockey, and he would have been great. He just went to the wrong damned team."

On the other hand, getting drafted by Winnipeg could mean being a star on a team that never achieves anything. Think of Dale Hawerchuk. Your talent would be obvious to everyone, and you would win your share of accolades, but true greatness would elude you. The Calder Trophy, All-Star team appointments, 100-point seasons, Canada Cup victories, more than 1,100 regular-season games, even an induction in the Hockey Hall of Fame—all yours. But there would be no championship at the end of the long grind, despite trades that took you all the way to Philadelphia and a playoff run in your final season that landed you, at last, in the Stanley Cup finals in the spring of 1997 . . . only to encounter Steve Yzerman's Red Wings, tired of coming up short themselves, ready to sweep you in four games. Hawerchuk could not have done more than was ever asked of him, but the lack of the championship ring, combined with the more obscure years in Winnipeg, would leave him an underappreciated talent in the modern game.

Or you could be the player who was kicked off the train just as the championship club hit full steam. You could be Dave Lewis, a New York Islanders draft pick in 1973 who soldiered his way through every playoff disappointment on the Islanders blue line. And just as the Islanders were about to get it all together and launch their dynastic streak of Cup wins in 1980, that trade deadline came along and the Islanders decided they needed another experienced, points-producing center, while Los Angeles needed another experienced defenseman. Had there been any justice in the world, Marcel Dionne would have been sprung loose from L.A. and at last given the chance to win something. But Dionne would have cost far, far more than a Lewis. He was too good to get a chance to win. So Lewis was parcelled off to the Kings and Butch Goring, rather than Dionne, became an Islander and celebrated four successive Cup victories. Meanwhile, Lewis watched from the west coast, where Dionne continued to be living, breathing proof of what it's like to be a great talent in the wrong town.

The problem with these what-if scenarios is that what actually happened may never have happened without those heartbreaking trades. Could the Islanders have won with Lewis, and without Goring (and his 19 points in 21 playoff games)? Maybe—but it doesn't matter. Everything that happened, happened the way it did, with the personnel it did. The universe has unfolded in precisely the way that it can't be refolded. We can only look back and consider the consequences of the when and where.

Because a player's career is subject to so many capricious whims beyond his own control, to the unforeseen consequences of so many hairpin turns in the destinies of people he's never met in places he's never been, that he either can go insane thinking about it all or try to make the most of the hand he is dealt. Strange things are going to happen, both to him and, sometimes, because of him. Fans wonder at the apparent randomness of it all, and are glad when something approaching a deserved outcome comes along in any player's life.

The one place where the player is free from the machinations of the business of the game is within the game itself. Nobody knows what's going to happen next once the puck is dropped. The great players have always found their sanctuary in the chaos of the game. It's where *they* can make things happen. They prepare, they show up, they play. Weird things do happen within the game, and these will inevitably generate their own cascade of should-have's and could-have's—those errant passes, those shots that hit the post, the foot that was or wasn't in the crease, the hit that blew someone's knee apart. The best players don't lament the fact that they can't change what happened; they try to make sure that those things don't happen to them again, but are adamant that the negatives remain locked up in the there and then. They learn and improve. The good things, they try to make them happen over and over again.

But they still have to start somewhere, and draft picks are like the sea turtles hatching on the beach and making a desperate run for the water before the frigate birds eat them. The number of hopefuls who actually make it, to the extent that they hold a starting job in the NHL for enough seasons to have something like a career, and also accomplish things that truly matter in the eyes of the fans, teammates, friends and family—not to mention themselves—is microscopically small. In the thirty-team NHL, the number of players who have had careers numbering in the hundreds of games, without leaving much of an impression of any kind in the sport's collective memory, are legion. Many are called, and many are chosen, but precious few are remembered.

Nobody should hold a tag day for anyone who manages to crack the lineup of an NHL team, no matter how their career turns out, and especially not for those who had a great career, but no championship to show for it. But the bottom line is that the number of players who have the dream career, with the near-perfect narrative arc, are few and far between. There is a thimbleful of room in this universe for a Jean Beliveau: hailed as the next great thing, proven to be the next great thing, an individual star and a team leader who racks up the championships and actually retires with the Stanley Cup in his hands. Conversely, there is an ocean of room for promising prospects who fail to deliver on their promise, or never find a team that properly exploits their talent, or who find the right team but at the wrong time, or get hurt, or get traded, and, sometimes, never really get over it.

And everything starts with the draft.

Halfway through the 1982–83 season, the new crop of talent that would come up for grabs at the June 8 draft in the Montreal Forum wasn't inspiring much enthusiasm among the professional onlookers.

"The consensus among National Hockey League scouts is that 1983 is going to be a poor draft year," wrote Peter Swan in a draft preview published in *The Hockey News* on March 11. There was no obvious talent to cause frantic maneuvering for a high pick, the way there had been a year earlier, when a "Brian Bellows derby" had broken out. Bellows, a left winger from the Kitchener Rangers, was the sought-after prize who went second overall to Minnesota, using a pick Detroit had traded away. And people were already looking ahead to 1984, when the Laval Voisins' Mario Lemieux would go on the block. Yzerman and Lemieux both played at center, but their games were entirely different. Five months younger than Yzerman, Lemieux was a good six inches taller and a highly touted scoring machine. He produced 184 points for Laval in 1982–83, and would set Quebec Major Junior Hockey League records for goals (133), assists (149) and points (282) in 1983–84.

Yzerman was coming onto the market just as the Edmonton Oilers, led by Wayne Gretzky, were hitting their stride. They would lose to the New York Islanders in their first Stanley Cup finals appearance, right before the 1983 draft, but in 1984 they would win their first of five Cups in eight seasons. The Oilers epitomized a leaguewide trend toward a high-scoring game. Back in the Original Six era, teams had typically averaged between two and a half and three goals per game. Between 1978–79 and 1981–82, the offense was ramped up dramatically, from 3.3 goals per game to 4.0, and the level would hover above 3.8 through 1985–86. The Oilers, particularly early on, would far prefer to win a hockey game 7–5 than they would 3–1. They were a very young team, and in their attitude toward offensive production they were very much like a bunch of junior players, thinking about goals, goals, and more goals. A determined coach might try to stress defense, and might even get his charges to play his way, but in their heart of hearts, as Bob Errey has noted, teenage hockey stars liked scoring goals. It was what made them happy and what made them popular, and if the drift toward shoot-'em-up offense in the NHL was any indication, it was also what would make them rich. The kids who tended to generate a lot of excitement as draft day approached, at least in the media, were invariably also the ones with big offensive numbers, the ones who looked like they were cut from the same template as the up-tempo Oilers. Within the scouting ranks, however, a keen eye was still kept peeled for all-round skills such as Yzerman demonstrated.

After polling his various contacts in the NHL scouting ranks, Swan saw a "dead heat" for the first-overall selection among Pat LaFontaine, Pierre Turgeon, Yvan Lambert, Cam Neely, Steve Yzerman, Adam Creighton, Andrew McBain and Brian Lawton. All but Lawton, a teenager playing high school hockey in Rhode Island, were in the Canadian junior system. In a photo finish, Swan ranked Yzerman first. He warned, however, that scouts looking at the Ontario prospects "are divided in their evaluations of Yzerman, Creighton and McBain." On the one hand, Yzerman was "relatively small," but he had more refined skills and was closer to his full potential. Creighton and McBain, meanwhile, were "imposing physical specimens but are only just beginning to show their potential."

In ranking Yzerman ahead of the other two, Swan made this capsule comment:

> A complete player with sound instincts. Yzerman was selected for the Canadian national junior team because of his versatility. He is regarded as having all the skating and passing skills necessary to be a fine center in the NHL, but some scouts have questioned his physical strength. According to one scout, however, 'Yzerman is deceptive. He often has scored goals with a defenseman draped all over him.'

Few today would disagree with Swan's conviction as to where Yzerman belonged in the 1983 class of prospects, regardless of where he actually ended up being drafted. But the field was crowded, and as Swan had noted, there was no clear first choice. Complicating matters was the challenge that confronted any team taking a risk on a smaller player like Yzerman, LaFontaine, Turgeon—or Derkatch, who continued to be a total enigma. In the first half of the WHL season, the Regina Pats center was on a furious scoring streak, and Central Scouting had him ranked as high as twelfth.

By the time Swan's article appeared in *The Hockey News,* the small-man debate was fully engaged. Chicago had done well with Denis Savard, taken third overall in 1980 from the Montreal Junior Canadiens and already producing 100-point seasons. But there was "Savard" small, which was also LaFontaine small and Yzerman small, at around five-ten, and then there was Derkatch small. Some media reports had him as short as five foot three, when he was really five-six.

Derkatch was good enough to beat out Bob Errey for a spot on the national team that represented Canada at the 1983 World Junior Championships in Leningrad over the Christmas–New Year's holiday. (Errey remembers him as a "water bug" on the ice at the tryouts, but also as a player who practiced so hard that he made himself physically sick.) It was the second year of the Canadian Hockey Association's new Program of Excellence, which was meant to reverse several years of indifferent perform-ances, during which Canada was consistently far from the medal podium at the Junior Worlds. Rather than continue to send a Memorial Cup–winning team, or a pickup All-Star squad (as was done when Gretzky participated in 1978), there was a proper scouting, tryout and selection process. The new approach had paid off immediately with a gold medal in 1982. Initial evalua-tions for the '83 squad were held in Manitoba in the summer of 1982, and final selections were made at a December camp, right before the departure for Leningrad. That summer evaluation camp doubtlessly contributed to Yzerman's determination to improve his skating before the start of his second junior season. Yzerman made the World Junior team at seventeen.

Also on the team was Mike Eagles, a left winger with the Kitchener Rangers who just barely reached the five-and-double-digit mark. He would turn twenty in March 1983, and his NHL rights had already been claimed by the Quebec Nordiques, 116th overall, in the 1981 draft. Eagles would defy the minimal prom-ise posed by his draft position by carving out an 853-game NHL career. While he had produced sixty-point seasons in Kitchener, in the NHL he found his meal ticket as a checker, only twice reg-istering more than five goals in a single season.

Eagles is a good example of the kind of "game smarts" the sport tends to produce. If you want to understand the nuances of NHL hockey, you're generally best served by a conversation with a goaltender or a utility forward, not a scoring star. The role players often have a much more coherent view of the game as a team sport, because they're accustomed to being the mortar that holds a group effort together. A native of New Brunswick, Eagles' savvy saw him hired as the coach of St. Thomas Tommies in the Atlantic Universities Hockey Conference after retiring from the NHL in 2000, and he was named CIAU Coach of the Year in 2003.

Yzerman was so reserved, so self-contained, that he scarcely registers in Derkatch's memories of the 1983 Junior Worlds. Eagles remembers Yzerman more clearly from the tournament. "He was just not—" he struggles to come up with a capsule description "—somebody you would see being a class clown. He just quietly went about his business of being a good hockey player."

But Eagles does remember Yzerman arriving hurt in Leningrad. "If my memory serves me correctly, he had a bad knee going into the tournament. He was nursing it. I don't think he was really able to play up to his abilities. He certainly didn't play a lot of minutes, and was probably used more on the right side than in the middle."

The bum knee at the World Juniors apparently flew under the scouts' radar. While it might have hinted at serious problems to come in his professional career, the knee problem, however troublesome it truly was, had shown up on the other side of the world, away from the eyes of NHL decision makers. It may also have been overlooked mainly because the team was loaded down with top prospects who weren't necessarily seeing a lot of ice time. It was easy to put Yzerman's reduced role down to a coaching decision rather than a physical problem. The injury also foreshadowed the reputation he would gather in the NHL for playing through pain, especially during playoffs, which he equated with tournaments—if you showed up, you participated, come what may.

(Jim Devellano, who drafted Yzerman for Detroit, says an injury to Yzerman's knee at that time "is news to me . . . I have no knowledge, and did not have any knowledge, of a knee problem then. I don't think it was ever an issue.")

The 1983 Canadian World Juniors team was stacked with future NHL talent: Mario Lemieux, Dave Andreychuk, Mike Vernon and Sylvain Turgeon, to name just a few. But as can happen in the junior game, the workhorses of the Canadian effort, which amassed a 4–2–1 record and won the bronze medal, were players who would never register with future NHL fans. Dave King of the University of Saskatchewan Huskies hockey program was back as coach, having brought home Canada's first World Junior gold in 1982, and he expected a disciplined two-way effort. (His expectations didn't prevent a 7–7 tie with Czechoslovakia and a 7–3 loss to the Soviets.) Lemieux and Andreychuk didn't see much ice, and neither did the injured Yzerman. Canada's top centers were Dale Derkatch and Mark Morrison, another WHL player, who only measured five-eight and had been selected fifty-first overall in the 1981 draft by the New York Rangers.

In the last game of the tournament, against Norway, Lemieux and Andreychuk were turned loose together on a line. "They put on a clinic," Eagles recalls of the 13–0 rout, in which Andreychuk registered a hat trick, while Lemieux popped in four goals—which is still a record for a Canadian player in the tournament. As a result of the outburst, the pair led the team in scoring—eleven points for Andreychuk and ten for Lemieux. But game in and game out, it was Derkatch who had been the top player, gathering seven points, third-best on the team, ahead of Turgeon and Eagles, with six each, and Yzerman, with five.

"I think Dale was a tremendous player," says Eagles. "At that time, he was unbelievable. He and Morrison were playing ahead of Hall of Fame guys." Morrison would spend much of the 1983–84 season on Canada's national team. Derkatch would star on Canada's 1984 Olympic team. Yzerman didn't even get an Olympic tryout invitation.

Today, as an NHL scout, Derkatch understands the distorted view of a prospect's NHL potential that tournament performances can give. Events like the World Juniors and the Memorial Cup (Canada's national junior championship) may well showcase talents, but often "it's just what a player does at that time, in that tournament." It is the nature of junior hockey that many players have great junior careers but never make the transition to the professional game. The circumstances that made them great among their peers as a teenager aren't there to allow them to shine when they have to play against adults who have been the cream of many crops harvested over the years.

Back home, Swan in his *Hockey News* draft preview quoted one anonymous coach as saying that Derkatch could go midway through the first round, and Swan placed him twelfth, but no one really knew what would become of Derkatch in June. There were so many other players now considered to be first-round material, including Dave Gagner, John Tucker, Normand Lacombe, and Bobby Dollas. A bunch of others also had the potential to go high: Bob Errey, Cam Neely, Alfie Turcotte, Russ Courtnall, Wayne Presley, John MacLean, Bruce Cassidy, and Brian Bradley, the player the Petes had passed over in order to choose Yzerman.

As the draft approached, the Memorial Cup playdowns injected a new dimension into the debate. The Petes had won the

Memorial Cup in 1979, but in 1981 and '82 they were eliminated in the opening round of the OHL playoffs by the Oshawa Generals, a much more physical club. The Petes and Generals, their arenas and fans separated by a fifty-mile bus ride (85 km), had a real hate on for one another. The last time they met during the 1982–83 season, there was a bench-clearing brawl. While the Petes had the third-best record and the Generals the fourth-best in the OHL that season, the Generals had amassed the league's second-highest number of penalty minutes, while the Petes had the second lowest. Yzerman tried to soldier through the Generals in the third straight opening-round series between the two clubs, contributing a goal and four assists, but to no avail.

"We did not have a tough guy," says Todd. "We got run over by Oshawa. Steve, I think, to this day has a scar on his lip from that playoff series." Indeed, in the final game, Yzerman was clipped by a high stick that made such a mess of his upper lip that he required emergency plastic surgery. "After Steve left Peterborough, I never let that happen again, and I brought in guys like Tie Domi."

With Yzerman's postseason experience having been limited to four games and a torn lip, it was left to other juniors to garner more headlines. The Generals advanced to the Memorial Cup tournament in May in Portland, Oregon, after sweeping the first-place Sault Ste. Marie Greyhounds in the OHL finals. The event yielded scouts a chance, with the NHL entry draft only weeks away, to give further consideration to such prospects as John MacLean of the Generals, Pat LaFontaine of Verdun, and Cam Neely of the Portland Winter Hawks, who contributed a hat-trick to the tournament-clinching 8–3 defeat of Oshawa. Mike Vernon, the goaltender on the World Junior team whom Portland had picked up from the Calgary Wranglers for the tournament, was also getting another look. And the spotlight shone a little more brightly on the Hawk's Alfie Turcotte, the tournament's MVP. Like Yzerman, he was a modest-sized center, but he had outscored him, producing 127 points in the WHL regular season and 32 more in 14 playoff games. With the draft only days away, the heightened profiles of the Memorial Cup standouts, gained while Yzerman was out of action, gave the NHL's scouts and general managers a last-minute reason to reconsider their priorities.

Over the course of the twelve rounds of the June 8 draft, held at the Forum in Montreal, a total of 252 players would be spoken for: 146 Canadians, 62 Americans, and the rest from various European nations and the Soviet Union. The fortunes of an NHL franchise can hinge on the outcome of a single draft, and can also come unhinged at one. A precious first-round pick can be squandered as the business plan of a multimillion-dollar sports franchise is derailed by a teenager's inability to live up to the demands of the professional game. On the other hand, a longshot hunch, taken in a later round, can perform beyond the wildest expectations. Draft lore is full of dramatic contrasts and fateful decisions. For every Ray Martiniuk, the Flin Flon Bombers goalie chosen fifth overall by Montreal in the 1970 draft, and who never played a single NHL game, there is an Andy Moog, the Billings Chiefs goaltender chosen 132nd overall by Edmonton in 1980, who went on to become one of the league's winningest netminders with the Oilers and the Boston Bruins.

The draft is supposed to be where teams secure their futures, where leagues ensure some hope of parity among teams by allowing the teams with the worst regular-season record to choose first from the latest crop of talent. But it's a deeply flawed, or at least deeply unscientific, process.

"There's a lot of luck," says Jim Devellano, echoing the opinion of Derkatch. Now a senior vice president and alternate governor with the Detroit Red Wings, he was the team's newly minted general manager in 1983. He is a small, stocky man, with a passing resemblance to the late comic Buddy Hackett. A self-described "trenches guy," the man better known as Jimmy D, has as much pride in his drafting record as Dick Todd does in his coaching resumé. As far as luck in the draft is concerned, his choice of Yzerman, the first player he ever selected for Detroit, may have been of the four-leaf shamrock variety. Yzerman was a peak achievement for Devellano in an area of the game in which he had already enjoyed many successes.

Devellano had been around the NHL since 1967, when Lynn Patrick hired him to scout amateur talent in Ontario for the new St. Louis Blues franchise. A former minor hockey coach, he came aboard at the same time that Scotty Bowman did as coach of the Blues. Bowman had been one of several talents in the Canadiens' pool of potential successors to Toe Blake, running the bench of the Montreal Junior Canadiens, when he was offered the job of coach of the Blues by Lynn Patrick. Bowman had coached Lynn's son Craig in junior hockey, and in the inch-deep, mile-wide world of professional hockey characters, these connections—Bowman to Craig Patrick, Bowman to Devellano—were going to count for something, someday.

After the Blues were eliminated from the 1971 playoffs—the first time in their short history that they didn't make the Stanley Cup finals—the owner's son, Sid Salomon III, inadvisably ousted Bowman, who was by then the general manager and who had reluctantly resumed the bench duties he had tried to hand over to defenseman Al Arbour. Bowman immediately landed on his feet as the new coach of the Montreal Canadiens. Jimmy D lasted another year with the Blues before being canned as well. Devellano put it down to a final housecleaning of Bowman's people: whatever the cause, he was not out of work for very long. A new franchise, the New York Islanders, was about to start playing on Long Island, and general manager Bill Torrey hired Devellano as his chief scout.

The Islanders were run in a much different way than the Blues had been. There had been no universal amateur draft until 1969, so Bowman had been most successful in assembling a contending team from scratch by gathering up veteran Original Six players, many of them from the Canadiens system, where Bowman himself had long been employed as a scout and a coach of junior and minor pro teams. With the Islanders, however, the focus was going to be on building through draft picks—first making sure, as Bowman and Patrick had done in St. Louis, that there was strength in defense and goal. Trading a draft pick was okay, but only after the player had been actually drafted. The picks themselves, particularly those vital first-rounders, were not to be placed on the auction block.

It was a risky strategy. The castoffs that existing teams made available in the expansion draft wouldn't give the Islanders much hope of winning, and in the short term it would be far easier to deal away future entry draft picks to bring in some more talented players. But in 1972, the trade value of draft picks was seriously depressed; the World Hockey Association was about to begin its first season, and players drafted by NHL teams were perfectly free to sign with a WHA team instead. The Islanders had already watched eight of their twenty-three selections in the expansion draft choose to play in the rival league rather than report to Nassau Coliseum.

The Islanders' twelve wins in seventy-eight games in 1972–73 set a new league record for futility. But that lack of success earned them the first pick overall in the 1973 amateur draft, and Devellano and Torrey used it to snare the highly touted defenseman Denis Potvin. The Islanders went on to make one smart choice after another, coming up with solid talents even after the team's improving regular-season record began to deny them the highest draft positions. Among those they snagged later in the draft were Ken Morrow (sixty-eighth, 1976) and John Tonelli (thirty-third, 1977), not to mention Bryan Trottier—claimed in the second round in 1974.

The Islanders did such an effective job of drafting that, of the twenty-two players who shared in the first Stanley Cup win in 1979–80, all but six had played their entire NHL careers exclusively on the Island. And of those six exceptions, one, goaltender Billy Smith, was the sole holdover from the inaugural 1972–73 roster, having been acquired from Los Angeles in the expansion draft. Another was one Jean Potvin, the older brother of Denis, whom the Islanders acquired from Philadelphia during their first season to help ensure that the as-yet undrafted Denis would show up to play in Long Island rather than answer the siren call of the WHA. Five more players would participate in the subsequent Cup wins of 1981 through 1983, and only one arrived via a trade. The Islanders' success at building a championship club from within has never been surpassed.

Devellano began to move up through the Islanders management ranks in 1979 with his appointment as general manager of the team's Central league affiliate, the Indianapolis Checkers. After *The Hockey News* named him its minor-league executive of the year, Jimmy D returned to Long Island to become assistant general manager of the Islanders under Torrey in 1981. (Devellano had also begun accumulating Maple Leaf Gardens stock in 1976. This financial interest in one NHL club while serving as a senior executive with another would become a minor source of concern to league president John Ziegler in the 1980s. Devellano finally disposed of his shares, which represented one percent of the corporation's equity, in the 1995 takeover of Maple Leaf Gardens by Steve Stavro—after he held out for a better offer, of course.) Despite the fact that he seemed well positioned for promotion within an organization that was just beginning its string of Cup victories, Bill Torrey was ahead of him, holding down the big job, and wasn't going anywhere soon.

Being offered the job in Detroit "was the culmination of a dream for me as a young person," says Devellano. "I had started in the NHL as an area scout and worked my way up to assistant general manager of the Islanders, and we were in the midst of winning four consecutive Stanley Cups. When I had the chance to be the general manager of an Original Six team, I had to grab it. I knew how horseshit the team was. But I more than doubled my salary and got a four-year contract." Twenty-two years later, Jimmy D is still in Motown.

Devellano was hired on July 12, 1982, a month after he worked the entry draft for the Islanders for the last time. The timing of the new job gave him plenty of time to prepare for the 1983 draft, to attend about seventy junior hockey games, and to think about what he wanted and what he was capable of getting.

When Devellano was chief scout with the Islanders, he was lucky enough to find Bryan Trottier still available in the second round in 1974 and Mike Bossy loitering, as yet unspoken for, when the Islanders got to make their first pick at fifteenth overall in 1977. Trottier and Bossy each produced more points in their careers than every player selected before them in their draft years. Those kind of breaks with nascent superstars are what give general managers perpetual hope that the talents that might not seem so obvious are often diamonds in the rough, that scouting works, that informed hunches and instinct make more of a difference than dry statistics or the pack psychology that is sometimes behind the consensus as to who the top prospects are.

Scoring stats are often the first thing seasoned scouts throw out the window, particularly since so-called "underage" players became draft-eligible in 1980. Once that happened, it was possible for exceptional players to jump to the NHL before they had completed their junior careers, leaving other, perhaps less talented, players to carry on in the junior ranks, get bigger and stronger, and put up numbers at age twenty that were inflated in part because they were playing against much less experienced seventeen-year-olds. Different junior leagues also had different playing styles; in leagues where backchecking and punishing hits were rarer, for instance, goals were easier to come by. Different teams also gave their top players different amounts of ice time, and asked them to fill different roles when they were on the ice. All of which would help explain why Steve Yzerman, an eighteen-year-old of unexceptional size, who wasn't even the top scorer on his team, who didn't make the Ontario Major Junior Hockey League's top-ten scoring list or its postseason All-Star teams, nevertheless was capable of going high in the opening round of the 1983 draft. The question, of course, was how high, and to whom. And there was a larger question: How would those answers affect the way he developed as a player and the kind of career he would end up having?

THREE

Speramus meliora. Resurget cineribus.

"We hope for better things. It will rise from the ashes."

The city of Detroit came up with this motto after a catastrophic fire in 1805. The state seal of Michigan, created in 1827, wrapped Detroit's Latin motto around an image of two women who represent the city's history. One, weeping, is the Detroit of the infernal tragedy, which appears in flames behind her. On the right is the Detroit of the future, personified by a woman giving comfort to her alter ego, before a newer, better city. This seal should have been stitched into a special shoulder patch to be worn by the Red Wings in the 1980s, as it applied all too well to both the city and the club that the Ilitch family and Jim Devellano strove to rebuild. Soon after acquiring the Wings, the Ilitches would also find themselves pouring dollars into the redevelopment of the downtown core, gutted not only by the more recent fires of urban riots, but by a socioeconomic implosion.

It may not be possible to overstate how much was riding on Jim Devellano's debut performance as general manager of the Detroit Red Wings at the entry draft in 1983. He had one first-round pick, one shot at one kid who could lead the franchise out of its devastation. And Devellano would have to find a player not only who could lead the team's recovery, but who would want to actually stick around long enough to do the job.

The Red Wings were a sporting ruin within the ruin of Detroit itself. No metropolis better exemplified the decay of urban America than Detroit, which reached its nadir in the 1970s, after the double whammy of the OPEC oil embargo and the rise in consumer appeal of fuel-efficient imports devastated the auto industry that was the heart of the local economy. Michigan's automakers went from building half of the cars sold in the world in 1950 to one in every thousand in 1990. But the roots of decay went much deeper, into the boom years of the auto industry, when the racial divide between black and white was deep, bitter and violent; when blacks were employed as strike-breakers and antiunion goons even as black workers were treated badly by unions themselves. Beginning in the 1950s, the white managerial classes began to flee the urban center for the suburbs above the northern city limit of 8 Mile Road, or to the east along the Lake St. Clair shoreline.

The outflight of the middle class of all races accelerated after the horrific riots of 1967. A police raid on a speakeasy deteriorated into an explosion of violence that claimed the deaths of forty-four people and led to the arrests of seven thousand, while more than $30 million in property damage was recorded. And when the economy turned against Detroit in the 1970s, the downward spiral was viciously steep. A study by a Michigan State University geographer has shown that Detroit went from having 42.3 percent of the region's population and 49.6 percent of its wealth in 1960, to only 27.6 percent of its population and 16.5 percent of its wealth in 1980. Between 1972 and 1991, the number of manufacturing, wholesale and retail establishments in the city dropped by more than 45 percent. In 1980, the Big Three automakers—General Motors, Ford and Chrysler—laid off a quarter million people, and their suppliers axed another 450,000, with most of the jobs being lost in the Detroit area. Major employers like Uniroyal, Vernor's Ginger Ale and Revere Copper simply closed their Detroit operations and left them to decay. When the Red Wings finally became a Stanley Cup contender again in the early 1990s, Detroit was still blighted by empty lots and abandoned buildings. In 1995, the urban policy publication *City Journal* reported: "Parts of Detroit have reverted to prairie, so lush that Michigan's Department of Natural Resources exports Detroit pheasants to the countryside to improve the rural gene pool."

Detroit did bounce back economically, creating 241,850 new jobs in the 1990s, resurging as the Red Wings did. The Ilitches would help the city recover some of its former glory by renovating the five-thousand-seat Fox Theater in 1987. Once restored, the ornate facility, built in 1928, anchored the rebirth of the old theater district. In 1993, the Ilitches acquired the Second City Theater next door, and in 1996 they created Olympia Development to further the cause of downtown resurrection.

But in June 1982, when Mike Ilitch bought the team from the Norris family for just $8 million, the prospects for both city and franchise were extraordinarily bleak. This was not Hockeytown. The Wings' miserable performance, which earned it the unofficial nickname the Dead Things, was one more kick in the teeth for a city that appeared to embody every futuristic cliché of the post-apocalyptic urban nightmare. Detroit was in the grip of a full-blown crisis—which is saying something, given that crises had been a consistent background rumbling in city life for more than a decade. While the opening of the waterfront Renaissance Center in 1977 and renewed interest by the auto industry in investing in the downtown had provided some hope, the Iran hostage drama set off another oil debacle that pushed American consumers even more forcefully in the direction of imported cars. And that move away from Detroit metal came in lockstep with the particularly tough recession of the early 1980s that created the Rust Belt of the northeastern and midwestern U.S. and blighted Detroit, Cleveland, Pittsburgh and other big-iron industrial cities. Detroit was also hit by a serious fiscal shock in 1981, causing it to teeter on the verge of bankruptcy. The controversial mayor, Coleman Young, was compelled to freeze wages of city workers, raise income taxes, sell off municipal assets such as hospitals, and scrap such public services as meat and milk inspection.

Just a few years earlier, the city of Detroit had even come close to losing the Red Wings, when real estate interests in the satellite city of Pontiac, about twenty-five miles north of downtown, made the Norris family an offer it seemingly couldn't refuse: abandon the aging Olympia Stadium for a new arena that would be built next to the Silverdome, home of the National Football League's Detroit Lions. The club would pay nothing to build the new rink, and would also pick up about $3 million a year in profits from the facility. The Norrises barely managed not to take the bait. (Among the recent accomplishments of the Ilitches' Olympia Development was its role in the creation of new side-by-side stadia in downtown Detroit: Comerica Park for baseball's Tigers—which the family bought in 1992—and Ford Field for the Lions, thereby reversing the Lions' previous flight to the suburbs.)

When we consider the storied Olympia, we can begin to understand why so much was hanging on Devellano's performance in the 1983 draft. The arena had been built in 1926 under the aegis of the Detroit Athletic Club, with funding from such local high rollers as the Ford family, to ward off a rival arena construction initiative. Artificial ice was a newfangled attraction in the east, even though such arenas had been created in Vancouver and Victoria before the First World War.

The new arena model had allowed the National Hockey League to expand south of the border—and institute a longer playing season—in the good times of the Roaring Twenties. In 1923, there were just four clubs in the NHL, all of them in Canada: the Ottawa Senators, Toronto St. Patricks, Montreal Canadiens and Hamilton Tigers. Two new clubs, the Boston Bruins and the Montreal Maroons, were brought aboard in 1924. The Tigers shifted to New York City to become the Americans in 1925, and the Pittsburgh Pirates were added at the same time. The league agreed to have a total of ten clubs operating in 1926. Joining the fray would be the Chicago Blackhawks, New York Rangers, and a new outfit in Detroit.

The three new teams were stocked largely by buying up player contracts from the NHL's erstwhile professional rival, the Western Hockey League, which folded after the 1925–26 season. The league's Victoria Cougars, who had won the Stanley Cup in 1925 and lost the 1926 finals to the Montreal Maroons, would be the basis for Detroit's new NHL entry—which went as far as to retain the Cougars nickname.

Like a lot of other enterprises dependent on discretionary spending, the NHL was hit hard by the Depression, and it would contract to seven teams by 1938. The downturn affected the Olympia and the Detroit franchise, whose name had changed to the Falcons, and they were placed on the selling block in 1932. Team and arena were both acquired by the Chicago grain magnate and boxing impresario Jim Norris. Norris had been a member of the Montreal Amateur Athletic Association, whose hockey team had won the Stanley Cup three times beginning in 1893, when Lord Stanley simply directed that his new Cup be presented to the MAAA after it won an amateur tournament on New Year's Day. The late-nineteenth-century cycling craze had seen to it that the emblem of the club was a bicycle wheel powered by wings and that the club's sports teams were known as the Winged Wheelers.

Why Jim Norris decided to filch the Winged Wheelers symbol for his newly acquired NHL team is a matter of speculation. It was probably a combination of sentimental attachment to his old club and their historic association with the Stanley Cup. Having a wheel as the focal point of a team logo in a city whose economy was powered by the automobile didn't hurt. And so, at the beginning of the 1932–33 season, the Red Wings were born.

The team would remain in the Norris family for almost fifty years. At the height of his league powers, "Big Jim" Norris essentially controlled the NHL thanks to a series of Depression-era bailouts and cheap-dollar investments. In addition to his acknowledged ownership of the Red Wings, he had silent control of the Chicago Blackhawks (achieved through his acquisition of Chicago Stadium in 1935) and a hefty sway over the New York Rangers (through a large block of shares in Madison Square Garden) and the Boston Bruins (through mortgages he held on Boston Garden).

When the patriarch Norris died in 1952, the Blackhawks were given to his son Jimmy to run, while daughter Marguerite assumed control of the Red Wings. Another son, Bruce, subsequently won a power struggle with Marguerite to gain control of the Red Wings, and ran the team thereafter with an incompetent if jolly brand of meddling.

"The problem in Bruce's ownership of the Red Wings was that he never could decide whether the team was a hobby or a business," wrote Alison Cruise and David Griffiths in *Net Worth*.

"Sometimes he'd tinker with it like a toy; other times he'd throw himself into it as if it were the only thing that counted. And worst of all, Bruce would never admit to what he didn't know, confusing good intentions with sound action." Toronto Maple Leaf fans who loved to complain long and loud about the horrors of having Harold Ballard as team owner were well advised to sit down and shut up in the presence of long-suffering Red Wing fans. It was on Bruce's watch that the club rolled downhill, along with the Motor City itself.

In the 1970s, Detroit scored the hat trick of foibles for floundering sports franchises: playing badly, selling tickets badly and drafting badly. The Red Wings were alone among the Original Six franchises in not enjoying consistent success against the first wave of expansion teams in 1967, nor against those that followed in the 1970s as the NHL tried to ward off the territorial challenges of the World Hockey Association.

The club was already in deep trouble when Mr. Hockey, Gordie Howe, retired at the end of the 1970–71 season, having missed the playoffs in four of the past five seasons. He was the last vestige of the great teams of the 1950s and '60s, when the club was known more for its stellar goaltending and defensive work than it was for its goal scoring. Even at Detroit's height of greatness in the early 1950s, when it won four Stanley Cups in six seasons, the Wings were, offensively, a one-line phenomenon: the Production Line of Howe, Sid Abel and Ted Lindsay.

Things went so badly in Howe's last season that the Wings finished behind two brand new expansion franchises, the Buffalo Sabres and Vancouver Canucks, in the standings. Only the persistently awful California Golden Seals fared worse. Fans might have taken some consolation in the fact that Detroit at least held the second-best draft position in 1971.

There was enough talent in the 1971 draft pool that Larry Robinson would still be available in the second round. Far and away the top prospects were two gentlemanly, high-scoring, playmaking sensations: Guy Lafleur of the Quebec Remparts and Marcel Dionne of the St. Catharines Blackhawks. Because California had chosen to build with veterans rather than new talent, it had dealt away its pick to the league's strongest team, Montreal. Either young francophone star would have been a perfect choice to succeed Jean Beliveau (who, like Howe, had just retired) as the core of a new Canadiens dynasty. Montreal opted for Lafleur. And Detroit immediately moved in to claim Dionne.

At first it appeared that Detroit had made the wiser choice, as Lafleur struggled to fulfill such enormous expectations while Dionne broke Gilbert Perreault's rookie point record, only to be edged out by Ken Dryden in Calder Trophy (rookie of the year) voting.

In Dionne, Detroit had the foundation for a new era of on-ice success, but the team didn't keep up with its star. "They made bad trades, the people didn't come up through the system, and they made more bad trades trying to fill the holes," Gordie Howe would later say. For his part, when he decided to come out of retirement in 1973, it was to play not for Detroit again, but for Houston of the WHA.

In the first few seasons of Dionne's NHL career, Detroit trades led nowhere while drafting failed to build any semblance of a winning team. In 1974–75, Dionne had his first 100-point season, with 47 goals and 74 assists, which meant he was involved in nearly half the entire team's offensive production of 259 goals. The Wings missed the playoffs (for the fourth straight time) and Dionne wanted more money than Detroit was willing to pay. His rights were traded to the Los Angeles Kings. A playmaking and scoring star and team leader had gone begging. And once in L.A., Dionne's career shifted into overdrive. He played in eight of the next ten NHL All-Star Games (never having appeared as a Red Wing), earned two Lady Byng Trophies, was voted the league's top player by his playing peers in 1979 and 1980 (earning him the Lester B. Pearson award), and won the league scoring title in 1980. When his career wound up in 1988–89 in New York, only two players, Wayne Gretzky and Gordie Howe, were ahead of him in all-time points production.

Dionne was the might-have-been of Detroit's rejuvenation, had management been able to see past the short-term pain of his contract demands. Sweating under the salary pressures created by the rival WHA, some NHL owners and managers had sworn themselves to not getting sucked into a salary war. It was a line that a club with a superfluity of talent, like the Canadiens (who, as the game's greatest dynasty, were also an emotional draw for players), could afford to take. Detroit, however, with so little going for it, courted franchise disaster by not keeping Dionne happy.

And the efforts to replace Dionne, either through trades or draft picks, continued to fall flat. In 1977 the Wings thought they had another franchise cornerstone in Dale McCourt, an Ontario Hockey League scoring phenomenon who had been named tournament MVP in the 1976 Memorial Cup. McCourt produced a respectable 72 points in his first Red Wings season, 1977–78, as the team doubled its wins to 32 and made its first playoff appearance in eight seasons, sweeping Atlanta in an opening-round best-of-three before losing in five to the defending (and eventual) Stanley Cup champions, the Montreal Canadiens. But then the protracted search for Gordie Howe's successor went awry in August 1978, when Detroit made a rare move by signing L.A.'s star goaltender, Rogie Vachon, as a free agent. As compensation, the Wings were ordered to hand McCourt over to the Kings, but the forward refused to go, and he remained in limbo, his fate tied up in litigation. Detroit finally made the expensive decision to regain its rights to McCourt by assigning the Kings its first-round picks in 1980 and 1981. More rebuilding opportunities went down the drain, and to add insult to injury, McCourt was traded to Buffalo in December 1981. But McCourt didn't fit Buffalo's plans, either, and Sabres general manager Scotty Bowman made the expensive decision to buy out his contract in 1983. McCourt would later say that the legal squabbling over where he should play sapped his enthusiasm for the game.

For much of this time, Detroit was being managed by that Original Six warhorse, Ted Lindsay, who had taken over as GM in 1976. In the late seventies, Lindsay began reshaping the Wings along more pugnacious lines. When his term ended in 1980, another throwback to Detroit's glory years of the 1950s, former coach and chief scout Jimmy Skinner, assumed the manager's job for two seasons.

How bad were these lost years? Seven different people served as captain in 1973–74 alone, as Detroit experimented with a rotational captaincy. Between 1974–75 and 1980–81, a span of seven seasons, the Wings went through eleven captains and six coaches. After reaching the Stanley Cup finals in 1966 and losing to Montreal in six games (after winning the first two), the Wings saw playoff action just twice—in 1970 and 1978—over the next seventeen seasons, winning three of nine games. When the Red Wings franchise changed hands in the summer of 1982, fans had not seen their team in a playoff series against the New York Rangers since 1950, against Boston since 1957, against Toronto since 1964. The team's position in the honor roll of Original Six clubs was an artifact of history, not a living legacy of any deep-seated rivalries.

The final indignity for many diehard Red Wings fans was the team's decision to abandon the beloved Olympia. On the verge of losing the team to the proposed new rink in suburban Pontiac, the city of Detroit came to something of a rescue, at least for the downtown if not for the actual Olympia, by offering the Red Wings control of a new waterfront facility, Joe Louis Arena, along with the 12,000-seat Cobo Arena and two parking complexes. For one-third the rent cost of the Pontiac overture, the Wings would also pocket whatever revenues these facilities generated. And so, prior to the 1980–81 season, the Red Wings relocated to a new home, "The Joe," on the city waterfront.

Although the Olympia, also known as the Red Barn, was more than fifty years old, not all fans were happy to part with it. The arena wasn't in a part of town that frightened them away from attending games, and the building was beloved for its sight lines, acoustics, and not least of all the rich history that had transpired within its poured concrete walls: the seven Stanley Cups the Red Wings had won; the concerts by Elvis; the boxing matches featuring Joe Louis, Thomas "The Hitman" Hearns and so many others, including back-to-back matches between Jake LaMotta and Sugar Ray Robinson in 1943. All of it was being cast aside for something new and soulless, and largely cut off from the urban streetscape (which many doubtless felt was a good thing). The city's deal with the Norrises also specified that they could not hold events at the Olympia that competed with those put on in the city-owned Joe Louis Arena, or sell it to anyone who would try to do the same thing. That stipulation signed the grand old building's death warrant; it would be torn down in 1986.

Opponents of the move from the Olympia to Joe Louis Arena claimed that there was no problem being solved in the process, pointing out that the Red Wings had been setting new attendance records in the old building, although the house was probably being heavily papered: by the early 1980s, there almost wasn't such a thing as a Red Wings fan left on the planet surface. More people believed that extraterrestrials controlled the White House than were convinced the Red Wings could ever win another Stanley Cup. Season-ticket sales were down to about 2,100. The team had won just twenty-one games in 1981–82 and finished last in the Norris Division for the fourth year in a row. They were an embarrassment to their division's name.

We can therefore sum up the transfer of ownership of the Red Wings in the summer of 1982 as the sale of a professional hockey team on death's door playing in a city on death's door. The white knight, Mike Ilitch[1], had made a private fortune in the pizza restaurant business, with the Little Caesars chain. A self-made man, he had opened his first pizza parlor in 1959 with his wife Marian, and these first-generation Americans of Macedonian descent built the restaurant business outward from the Detroit suburbs, making it the cornerstone of a multifaceted family enterprise with a large degree of involvement from their seven offspring. A former minor-league prospect in the Detroit Tigers farm system whose baseball career is said to have been finished by a broken ankle, Ilitch was bitten by the hockey bug. He created the suburban Little Caesars Amateur Hockey League in 1979, and just three years later, he was playing with the big boys in the NHL.

Considering the degree to which franchise values were to appreciate over the next two decades, the Ilitches' purchase of the

---

[1] While the Red Wings are owned by both Mike and Marian Ilitch, he serves as the team governor on the NHL board. For simplicity's sake, Mike Ilitch henceforth in this book will be referred to as the team's owner.

Red Wings was a steal (they paid only $3 million more than Big Jim Norris had invested in 1932). But the Red Wings weren't exactly unloaded into a seller's market; in fact, the league had lately been allowing other (albeit newer) franchises, to hopscotch all over the continent in search of a friendly audience and a profitable location. The Atlanta Flames, created alongside the New York Islanders in 1972, had moved to Calgary in June 1980. The Kansas City Scouts, born in 1974, had shuffled off to Colorado in 1976 and again, at the very moment Ilitch was buying the Wings, to the New Jersey Meadowlands.

But there was no conceivable way anyone would be allowed to pull out of an NHL location as storied as Detroit. And with Ilitch as the owner, the Red Wings weren't going anywhere—geographically speaking, at least. If they were going to make a move upward in the standings, Ilitch would need to recruit some new management blood from out of town.

At the time, the two clubs with the greatest track records were the Montreal Canadiens and the New York Islanders, the Canadiens having won six of nine Stanley Cup finals between 1971 and '79, while the Islanders had since won all three Cups. Both operations had strong management, in the front office and behind the bench, and had built their winning lineups overwhelmingly through the draft, even in years in which their top finishes didn't grant them the best positions in the pecking order.

Ilitch had bought the Red Wings just a tad late to take advantage of the diaspora of management talent that struck Montreal after the Bronfman family decided to sell the Canadiens to Molson Breweries in 1978. Sam Pollock, the mastermind of the Canadiens operation, who had been in the team's management structure since he was hired to coach the Montreal Junior Canadiens in 1947 and had been GM of the Habs since 1956, left hockey entirely in 1978 when he went to work for the Bronfmans after the team's sale. Scotty Bowman, the gifted coach and former Canadiens scout who had aspirations toward managing, didn't get the signals he was looking for from upper management after Pollock's departure, so he responded to the overtures of the Knox family and became coach and general manager of the Buffalo Sabres in 1979. Al MacNeil, another key member of the Canadiens front office, went to Atlanta that year to serve as coach of the Flames, and after they relocated to Calgary, he moved up to assistant general manager under Cliff Fletcher.

It would be more than a decade before Ilitch got the chance to tap into the Canadiens legacy, by hiring Bowman. And it was Jim Devellano, the man he plucked from the NHL's current dynasty on Long Island, who would recommend Bowman. In the meantime, Devellano's job was to build a team that a man like Bowman would even want to coach.

"The cupboard was bare," Devellano would recall of the roster that he took over in 1982. The Wings "had eighty-one players under contract and seventy-five couldn't play." The 1983 draft was his first real opportunity to do something about replenishing that cupboard.

Until 1980, the NHL entry draft (known prior to 1979 as the amateur draft) was a closed-door affair. Team representatives gathered in the ballroom of the Queen Elizabeth Hotel in Montreal, where they'd divvy up the available players in private, then let the players, their agents and the media know who had ended up where. For the 1980 draft, the first to follow the death of the rival World Hockey Association, Jim Devellano pressed the league to open up the event to generate publicity for the game, and the selection process moved into the Montreal Forum. It would take until 1984 before the proceedings were televised, but at least in 1980 the draft became a forerunner of reality TV's *American Idol.* Fresh-scrubbed young hopefuls—still in the throes of acne, their hair slicked back or spiked up with gel, sporting ties picked out by their moms—turned out with their parents, siblings, friends, girlfriends and agents, along with thousands of other spectators, to see who would win the top prize and go first overall. But there were so many other prizes on which to hang one's hopes, beginning with just being selected, and moving up to being picked respectively high and by a team you'd like to play for. Teams started adding to the spectacle by bringing a supply of jerseys to be donned by their top picks (sometimes with their names already sewn on the back) for photo ops.

For all the bright and shiny PR the draft came to generate for the league, its teams, the newly minted players and their agents, there was a cruel Darwinian component to the increasingly public event. Too many kids showed up only to be humiliated in front of friends, family and teammates (and in due course, television audiences) as they were claimed disappointingly deep in the draft, or not at all. Those professionals associated with this cattle call who had an ounce of compassion would try to discourage kids from attending if there wasn't a solid chance that they were going to be selected in one of the early rounds, but many kept coming anyway, either because they were firmly in the grip of the major-league dream, or they had been brought by parents who hadn't got the message that their son was not destined for the big time.

They came in part because all those inspired "sleeper" picks of yore were a constant reminder that being picked late didn't necessarily mean being a career longshot. Even as the league's executives and scouting staffs gathered in Montreal for the 1983 draft, another rink-rat-to-riches story was unfolding. The top scorer in the Ontario Hockey League that season was a slight dynamo named Doug Gilmour, who played for the Kingston Canadians. The St. Louis Blues (whose owners, the animal chow folks at Ralston Purina, had just been denied permission by the league to sell the limping operation to a Saskatoon syndicate, so they abandoned it, leaving the franchise in such a state of suspended animation that it wouldn't even participate in the June 1983 draft) had been seemingly prescient enough to claim Gilmour way down at 134th overall in 1982. But the Blues were so suspicious of Gilmour's ability to survive, never mind thrive, in the NHL that Gilmour's agent, Larry Kelly (who would eventually represent Steve Yzerman), was preparing to have Gilmour play in Germany before the Blues at last came through with a satisfactory offer.

Teams often took risks in the draft counting on other teams not to be interested in a marginal prospect like Gilmour, enabling them to leave his selection for a later round and use an early pick to secure a player who was going to attract plenty of attention. But if there was one lesson that had sunk in from the 1970s, delivered in large part by Montreal general manager Sam Pollock, it was that weak teams should not deal away draft choices in the early rounds.

Still, the urge for some teams to deal away the future to fill present needs hadn't abated, despite the example set by the New York Islanders, who had iced their fourth consecutive Cup title just days before the draft. If anything, the let's-make-a-deal mentality was alive and well in part *because* of the Islanders, who, as their lineup matured, were willing to turn loose spare talent in exchange for the high draft picks their strong regular-season finishes now denied them. And over in Buffalo, general manager Scotty Bowman was busy casting off a host of veteran players on a strong team in plain pursuit of higher picks in the draft. As a result, four of the top six draft positions in 1983 were held by teams that had traded for them, rather than earned them through crummy regular seasons. Looked at another way, four of the top six drafting teams had chosen to deal away those prime positions in favor of immediate returns in on-ice personnel. While the exact pecking order of the draft was not settled until the end of the 1982–83 season, the identities of the teams that would actually wield those high picks had been coming together through trades for more than two years.

The first pick, which had been deservedly earned after they won just eighteen of eighty games in 1982–83, belonged to the Pittsburgh Penguins. But the previous October, the Penguins had dealt away that choice to the Minnesota North Stars in one of the stranger trades involving a draft selection. Minnesota had used its first pick in the 1981 draft (thirteenth overall) to take the eighteen-year-old defenseman Ron Meighan of the Niagara Falls Flyers. He was given a seven-game look in 1981–82 before being sent back to the OHL, where he was a first-team All-Star and was voted the league's top blueliner. But the North Stars obviously thought they could do better, so they sent Meighan and left winger Anders Hakansson to Pittsburgh in exchange for the Penguins' opening-round pick in 1983 and second-string center George Ferguson. As it turned out, Meighan never did secure an NHL starting job. Pittsburgh would fare brilliantly with Hakansson, not on the ice but by using him in one of the NHL's most lopsided swaps: a one-for-one trade with Los Angeles for the rights to Boston College left-winger Kevin Stevens, who would be a key figure in Pittsburgh's (and later New Jersey's) Stanley Cup successes.

Hartford would follow Minnesota, by virtue of the fact that it had the second-worst record in 1982–83, which was one slim win better than that of Pittsburgh (both teams had 45 points). The rights to the third pick rested with the New Jersey Devils, who had just completed their first season after being transplanted from Colorado. In their third home in nine seasons, they were considering wandering yet more, threatening to leave New Jersey altogether in hopes of landing a better lease arrangement than they had at the Meadowlands Coliseum. A top draft pick would have come in handy in the summer of 1983, but back in their woeful Rockies days the team had tried to dig itself out of a hole in the Smythe Division standings by loading up on spare Islanders. Into the mountains at the start of the 1981–82 season went Bob Lorimer and Dave Cameron, and out to Long Island went the Scouts/Rockies/Devils' first-round pick in 1983. Which meant that the winner of the last four Stanley Cup titles was picking third overall.

That deal also meant that Jim Devellano's former employers were going to have a tremendous effect on his first draft with his new club, the Red Wings, who were set to choose behind the Islanders, in the fourth spot. Unlike New York, they had got into this position in the honest, old-fashioned way: by playing terribly, as they had largely been doing since the last Original Six season in 1966–67.

In fifth was Buffalo, with a spot Scotty Bowman had secured from Los Angeles in a 1981 trade for Richard (Rick) Martin, the celebrated left winger of the Sabres' French Connection line. Unless he could pull off some eleventh-hour miracle, there was no way for Scotty Bowman to get in the way of Jim Devellano's drafting plans. It wasn't for a lack of trying: at 4 a.m. on the morning of the draft, Bowman did seal a deal with the Quebec Nordiques for the rights to the eleventh pick overall, giving him three first rounders in all. But the Red Wings were still free and clear of him. Devellano had only to worry about which young men the three teams ahead of him—Minnesota, Hartford, and the Islanders—might call down from the Forum seats to don a jersey.

Strange things happen at drafts. Not often, but often enough to discourage notions of foregone conclusions. In 1981, Bowman had surprised his own scouting staff by making a Czechoslovakian teen, Jiri Dudacek, the Sabres' first pick, seventeenth overall. While Central Scouting had named him the world's top junior player that June, the fact that he was on the wrong side of the Iron Curtain made him too risky for most general managers to consider claiming him in the first round. Dudacek never made it to the NHL. Bowman may have gambled on him because the draft pick hadn't cost him anything—he hadn't given up any player in a trade to secure it. The next season, he made amends with another surprise, taking an American teenager, a smallish defenseman playing for South St. Paul High School in Minnesota, sixth overall. Phil Housley immediately proved to be an inspired choice, producing 86 points from the blue line in 1982–83 and finishing second in Calder Trophy voting.

Ever since the U.S. Miracle on Ice at the 1980 Lake Placid Olympics, when a bunch of college kids coached by Herb Brooks upset the mighty Soviet Union and then downed the Finns to win hockey gold, American NHL teams had been desperate to capitalize on fan enthusiasm by offering homegrown talents. There had been a stampede to sign up the 1980 gold-medal squad, with most being offered pro contracts. But the American invasion of the NHL, if it was going to happen in a sustained way, would have to be mounted by a new generation. Trouble was, while hockey did have a following as a recreational sport, mainly in a few corners of the northeast, the talent pool was extremely shallow. While there were some top-notch college programs, the best players tended to be Canadians on scholarships. Nevertheless, Bowman had been a pioneer when he chose an American, Mike Ramsey of the University of Minnesota, with his first pick, eleventh overall, in 1979; that same year, the North Stars chose Ramsey's teammate Neal Broten in the second round. Both had been part of the 1980 Olympic victory and both secured starting jobs in the big league. The NHL's managers scarcely had time to digest the lessons of their success before another complication cropped up: the draft age was lowered to nineteen in 1980, and then eighteen in 1981.

The lowering of the entry draft age meant that the league was back to hiring teenagers, the way it had been in the Original Six days. But there was an important difference, in that the NHL clubs no longer owned the amateur development system, the way it once had. Junior clubs were no longer sponsored by NHL teams, and prospects were no longer scouted and their playing rights spoken for when players were fourteen or even younger. The NHL scout was now an outsider. Instead of bird-dogging the hinterlands and trying to get the signatures of sixteen-year-olds on C-forms, they were forced to do their best to assess teenage talents that hadn't been brought along within their own club's hierarchy of sponsored amateur teams. That difference made the young players less familiar, and the commitment made at a draft became much riskier.

The sheer difficulty of assessing talent at the age of eighteen rather than twenty was one factor that encouraged teams to trade away high draft picks. Clubs could point to past drafting foibles and conclude that they would be better off dealing away an unknown quantity, a future draft pick, in favor of a known, "proven" player who could provide leadership, the experience of winning, and marquee value for season-ticket sales.

The lower draft age had the greatest impact on scouts covering the American development system, such as it was. In Canada, it meant only that scouts were paying closer attention, at an earlier age, to the same juniors they were already tracking. But in the States, where there was no equivalent of the Canadian junior system, the need and the opportunity to choose teenagers meant suddenly trying to rate prospects, for the most part, purely on the basis of their play in high school. Before 1980, no American high school prospect had ever figured in an NHL draft. That summer, when the drop in draft age was cross-pollinated with the desire for red-white-and-blue talent after the Lake Placid Olympics, seven were chosen. When the draft age dropped to eighteen the next year, seventeen high schoolers were drafted. And in 1982, the year of the Housley selection, the number jumped to forty-seven.

While scouts could be comfortable about assessing the skills of Americans who had come to play in the Canadian junior leagues, many hockey people still discounted the idea that somebody playing high school hockey in the States was sufficiently trained to be considered as a topflight NHL prospect. Housley erased many lingering doubts that a team could pluck a kid straight out of an American high school team's lineup and make him an NHLer. Not only could it be done, but teams could be sufficiently confident of the talent to use a first-round pick. The Housley selection said that American teenagers deserved to be in the front ranks of the draft.

But there was also the danger of an overreaction from general managers of struggling American franchises: that the recent success of Bowman with Housley could provoke them into gambling the franchise on successfully selecting a homegrown star in the opening round of the draft. Because in some cases, gambling with the franchise is exactly what it seemed like. Some teams were in such dire shape that they desperately needed a fresh young talent to build a lineup around that would excite the fans.

There were a number of American prospects worth watching for the 1983 draft, and one of the most promising was Pat LaFontaine. Born in St. Louis, LaFontaine had been raised in the Detroit suburbs—his dad was a Chrysler executive—where he played in the Compuware-sponsored minor system. (There was already a rivalry between Compuware owner Peter Karmanos and Mike Ilitch, both of whom sponsored Detroit-area minor hockey programs. Ilitch had moved into hockey's big leagues by acquiring the Red Wings in 1982, and Karmanos was nursing similar ambitions. He would buy the Windsor Spitfires, a major junior franchise across the Detroit River, in 1984, and eventually realized his dream of owning an NHL team when he acquired the Hartford Whalers in 1994, turning them into the Carolina Hurricanes in 1997.)

LaFontaine outgrew the U.S. system, churning out 324 points in 79 games at the midget level with Compuware in 1981–82. Drafted by teams in three different Canadian junior leagues, at seventeen he chose to move to suburban Montreal to play with the Verdun Junior Canadiens. In 1982–83, he led the Quebec Major Junior Hockey League in goals (104), assists (130) and points (234), and also produced the most assists (24) and points (34) in his fifteen playoff games. In the process he broke Mike Bossy's rookie scoring record and beat Mario Lemieux to the scoring title. Named to the QMJHL's First All-Star team, LaFontaine was also voted Canadian major junior hockey's player of the year—the first time the honor had gone to a non-native son.

In another example of how small the hockey world can be, Pat LaFontaine's left winger in the last half of his only season of Canadian junior hockey was Gerard Gallant, who would become

Steve Yzerman's linemate in Detroit. A Prince Edward Island native, Gallant had outgrown the island at seventeen, leaving the Summerside Islanders to join the Sherbrooke Beavers of the Quebec Major Junior league in 1980. The Red Wings chose him 107th overall in the 1981 draft after he turned in a 100-point season in Sherbrooke. A trade at Christmas 1982 sent him to Verdun, where he was paired with LaFontaine.

"Both are great players," Gallant says of the two centers. "Pat was a quick guy who could turn on a dime. He had a Denis Savard type of quickness, while Stevie was a powerful type of skater, not explosively fast. When Pat came to the Quebec league, after only forty games, they were talking about him breaking the record for points. At the time, he didn't play defense, and when he was on the ice he had the puck most of the time. Stevie was smooth, but he wasn't about quickness. He was about making plays and seeing the game more."

To an NHL franchise based in the U.S., LaFontaine represented the total package: not only homegrown and hugely talented, but smart, well spoken and matinee-idol handsome. "He had talent, good looks, and marketability," Detroit's Devellano sums up. The importance of presentation tends to get lost in the stat-freak dissections of draft prospects, but it isn't overlooked in the discussions among managers and owners. The NHL, after all, is in the entertainment business. Teams need stars who can sell season tickets. If they can't score, people are not going to show up in droves to watch them, the way they do to watch Anna Kournikova fail to win tennis tournaments. But if all else is equal, a team is going to put a premium on the player who is most articulate and presents himself best. Perhaps it's some lurking fear about appearing homoerotic, but the professional game generally doesn't 'fess up to the fact that a sports star who looks like a movie star (and acts like a movie star who doesn't punch out paparazzi) is literally an attractive asset.

LaFontaine wasn't the only hot American prospect available in the 1983 draft. Brian Lawton was an eighteen-year-old left winger with Mount St. Charles High School in Providence, Rhode Island, who had contributed four points in the U.S. team's fifth-place showing at the recent World Juniors. There was also the Memorial Cup MVP, Alfie Turcotte: born in Indiana, groomed in the Detroit Compuware machine, where he produced 283 points in 93 games in 1981–82 as a teammate of LaFontaine's, before choosing, as LaFontaine did, a team in the Canadian major junior system (in his case, an American-based team, the Portland Winter Hawks) as his finishing school. Also getting some serious attention was Tom Barrasso, an eighteen-year-old goaltender with Acton-Boxboro High School in suburban Boston.

For the Detroit Red Wings, choosing LaFontaine was a slam dunk, and Jim Devellano knew it. But he couldn't be certain that LaFontaine would last in the draft long enough to be chosen fourth overall. To improve its chances, a team in Detroit's position could try to make a deal to move up, and Lou Nanne, the general manager of the North Stars, who held the first pick overall, was willing to listen to proposals. He had, after all, made a last-minute deal himself, with the Bruins' Harry Sinden, to get the second pick in 1982, netting him Brian Bellows. "I'll trade it if I get what I want," Nanne told the *Toronto Sun*'s John Iaboni in late May. "The price is high and it's going to hurt if someone wants it."

The problem was, the Red Wings had nothing to offer Nanne. They couldn't trade an established star, the way winning teams could, precisely because they weren't a winning team with any established stars. All they could offer for a higher draft position was a future first-round pick. And there was no guarantee that Detroit's first round pick in, say, 1984 would be better than, or even as good as, the fourth overall it managed in 1983. In fact, if LaFontaine worked out the way he was supposed to, Detroit would move up in the standings, and would be assigned a much later slot in the draft order, devaluing their first-round pick for whoever got it.

All Devellano could hope for was at least one left-field surprise from a general manager picking ahead of him, a repeat performance of Bowman's pick of Dudacek, only in the top three selections. That, and another two general managers who decided they wanted any one of several compelling prospects other than LaFontaine. As draft day dawned, it didn't seem likely that LaFontaine still would be hanging around in the Montreal Forum seats when it was Devellano's turn to speak. Devellano would have to be satisfied with holding the fourth pick and evaluating his options should LaFontaine not be available.

Devellano would need to be ready with a Plan B, and perhaps even Plans C and D. He would also need, it would turn out, a junior hockey coach who didn't deploy his stars in a predictable way—who made use of four forward lines, who stressed play in both ends of the ice and not just firepower, who didn't give them the individual ice time required to pile up the scoring stats.

"Jimmy Devellano has a little saying," says Dick Todd. "It's, 'Thank God for Dick Todd, or we'd never have gotten Steve Yzerman.'"

Besides LaFontaine, the Red Wings also liked Sylvain Turgeon— "a very strong, well-developed junior," says Devellano. He had acquitted himself well at the World Juniors, and was bigger than LaFontaine and Yzerman, showing up in Central Scouting's logs as six feet and 190 pounds. Turgeon produced 163 points with the Hull Olympiques in 1982–83, but he also had Yzerman's defensive skills to complement his offensive firepower.

Finally, there was Yzerman, esteemed by Devellano for all the reasons one would expect: "an excellent player with a mature, professional approach, even at that age." And Detroit knew all about Dick Todd's four-line system and what effect it had had on Yzerman's scoring stats. Even though he had been rated highly by Central Scouting, there was a good chance that Yzerman could be overlooked in the early going of the first round; his was a talent that had to be scouted properly and understood. He didn't boil down to a no-brainer choice, based on stats alone.

Mike Eagles, for one, had never let the minimal ice time that Yzerman received when they played together at the World Juniors cloud his impression of the Petes center's ability or potential. "I knew how good he was because I'd played against him for two years, when I was with Kitchener. I had a better idea of what Steve Yzerman brought to the table than most people. But even from juniors, you didn't know how good he was, because Peterborough tended to roll four lines. How many points would he have gotten on a team that played two, or two and a half lines? You could tell he was really good, but he just didn't put the numbers up."

With three teams drafting ahead of the Red Wings, there remained a possibility that none of their top three choices—LaFontaine, Turgeon or Yzerman—would still be available. Devellano had already pretty well resigned himself to not getting LaFontaine. He was too good not to go first or second.

According to Frank Orr of the *Toronto Star*, the word all spring was that the draft would be a one-two American punch. Pat LaFontaine would go first, followed by Brian Lawton. If Lawton did go high in the draft, Devellano would be able to choose at least one of his three priorities, and it would probably come down to a choice between Turgeon or Yzerman.

Lou Nanne had told the *Toronto Sun's* John Iaboni in late May that he would choose either Lawton or LaFontaine. "It'll be one of those two," he said coyly. "I've made up my mind, but I don't want to say who it is right now." And while he publicly toyed with the idea of trading away the pick, and Philadelphia was thought to have expressed interest, no deal transpired. With days to go until the draft, Nanne revealed that he would in fact take Lawton.

"We need a bigger and stronger player, especially since the playoffs are so grueling and competitive now," Nanne said. As tempting as LaFontaine was, Lawton was a good three inches taller. And there was more than height standing behind the North Stars' decision. "He's nasty, and that's what we need," said Glen Sonmor, Minnesota's director of player development.

Detroit had also factored nastiness into its 1983 draft plans. Devellano had a shopping list of tough characters that he coveted: Joey Kocur, Bob Probert, Lane Lambert. But they could wait until the later rounds. The first pick was to be spent on talent, pure and simple.

At nine in the morning on June 8, Lou Nanne made it clear that one of Devellano's three "priority" players would still be available to the Wings when he announced to the Montreal Forum that the first pick of the 1983 entry draft was Brian Lawton.

Devellano has never quite gotten over Nanne's choice. "He took a *high school* kid," Devellano says. An American kid who'd played only forty-nine games over two seasons at Mount St. Charles. "We didn't have Lawton rated highly."

"We knew Steve could go anywhere in the first five," says Todd. "From our perspective, we thought he should be number one. We'd heard of Brian Lawton, but we'd never seen him play."

The North Stars, predictably, had bet the farm on an American, just as Detroit hoped to do—on someone who could put fans in the seats in an American hockey hotbed. But in so doing, in the name of size and nastiness, they hadn't bet the farm on LaFontaine. The Detroit product was still available.

LaFontaine had been led to believe he would go second, to the Hartford Whalers, but he was also well aware of how much Detroit wanted him. Then the Whalers (whom Al Strachan of the *Globe and Mail* would assert were actually expected to choose Andrew McBain of the North Bay Centennials) popped for Sylvain Turgeon.

This was an unexpected development. The Red Wings organization had built its draft strategy on the presumption that LaFontaine wouldn't last more than two picks. Suddenly, he was still in the talent pool, and only one team stood between Devellano and his dream selection: his old employer, the New York Islanders.

Once he had been passed over by Hartford, LaFontaine thought he was headed for Detroit. The New York Islanders, he heard, would take McBain, paving the way for him to fulfill a natural destiny by playing for his hometown team. McBain was being touted as a big guy who could handle the physical side of the game as well as contribute both offensively and defensively, and it was understood that the Islanders were concerned about LaFontaine's size.

For that matter, Yzerman, sitting in the Forum seats with his parents and his agent, Gus Badali, also thought LaFontaine was headed for Detroit once Hartford surprised everyone with its selection of Turgeon. He, too, assumed, that the Islanders would pass on LaFontaine, and if that happened, he couldn't imagine Detroit not choosing the local boy. "I don't think Mr. Devellano could pass on a guy of his ability," Yzerman said later, with unaffected modesty.

Yzerman understood that LaFontaine was the greater prize, and he wouldn't have blamed Devellano for taking him. But Yzerman dearly wanted to go to Detroit. Devellano had known he might have a selling job to do with the players on his draft wish list. He'd also wanted to be sure that whomever he chose would arrive at training camp eager to make the team, and would then want to stick with it through the rebuilding years. So before the draft he had brought four prospects—Yzerman included—to Detroit, to show them around and reassure them that he and Ilitch were serious about resurrecting a tarnished Original Six franchise. Devellano had taken Stevie Y to dinner, and swung by the old Olympia with him to show him where Gordie Howe had brought glory to Motor City. It was a move calculated to say: It's been done here before by a great player, and it can be done again. You can be that player.

Yzerman had his heart set on being a Red Wing. And two picks into the 1983 draft, Pat LaFontaine unexpectedly stood in the way.

But for all the talk that the Islanders would spring for McBain, LaFontaine had a natural predecessor on the Islanders: Mike Bossy, another former scoring machine from the Quebec Major Junior league. In the opening round of the 1977 draft, the Islanders had been debating whether to choose Bossy, a scorer who wasn't much of a checker, or another player, a checker who wasn't much of a scorer. Get me the scorer, Bill Torrey had instructed Devellano. I can always teach a scorer to check. I can't teach a checker to score.

And Devellano saw more complicated machinations with the current draft. Torrey, still running the Islanders, was his old boss.

And when Jimmy D came to Detroit, he had brought with him Neil Smith, an Islanders scout, to serve as his director of player personnel. Besides knowing Torrey's affection for natural goal scorers, Devellano knew that Torrey knew how much Devellano and Smith wanted LaFontaine. It was a bit of wisdom around which great deals could be manufactured in the future. The marketing potential in Detroit of LaFontaine would give him a bonus value in a trade that Detroit, and only Detroit, could be prodded into paying in order to get him. Rather than a one-for-one trade of players of equal worth, LaFontaine could net the Islanders a bonus prize of a future draft pick or an additional player as a deal sweetener. LaFontaine's talents alone would have made him an excellent choice for Long Island. Detroit's longing made him an inevitable one.

Bill Torrey chose Pat LaFontaine.

Mike Ilitch, sitting beside Devellano at the Red Wings' table, visibly slumped. Yzerman, hearing Torrey speak LaFontaine's name, was overcome with relief.

"Who else?" Torrey replied when he was asked why he chose LaFontaine. "He's a good entertainer. He blows people out of their seats. When you watch a game, he's the player your eye automatically goes to. Right now he does some great things that are instinctive. In the areas where he has to do some maturing, he can develop."

Two out of Devellano's three priorities were out of action. Yzerman was still standing. At 9:14, Devellano rose to announce, "The Detroit Red Wings are proud to take Steve Yzerman from the Peterborough Petes."

Right after him, Scotty Bowman uncorked a double-whammy surprise selection: Tom Barrasso, who was not only an American teenager from a Boston-area high school team, but was a goaltender to boot, a position that teams rarely pursued early in the draft. Even though Barrasso had said before the draft that he expected Buffalo to choose him, his high draft position was still exceptional. While Grant Fuhr had been taken eighth in 1981 by Edmonton, no team in 1982 had picked a goaltender before Toronto chose Ken Wregget, forty-fifth overall, in the third round. Mike Vernon waited until the the fifty-sixth pick to be claimed in the same draft as Barrasso, despite his solid, high-profile play in the Memorial Cup and for Canada at the World Juniors. One scout before the draft told the *Sun*'s Iaboni that Allan Bester of the OHL's Brantford Alexanders was more highly rated than Barrasso. But Bester, at five-seven, lacked Barrasso's height, and tall goaltenders were all the rage. Bester was picked forty-ninth, by Toronto. And Yzerman's good friend Darren Pang, still playing goal for the Ottawa 67s at nineteen, was passed over in the draft yet again.

With that, the story of the 1983 draft was written. An American, Brian Lawton, was the top pick for the first time in the entry draft's history. Two more Americans, LaFontaine and Barrasso, were in the top five. Amid the media hoopla surrounding this unprecedented domination by Yankee prospects, Steve Yzerman was essentially forgotten. The biggest story after the unprecedented rankings of American talent was the wily job Scotty Bowman had done in accumulating three first-round picks for Buffalo. Al Strachan's *Globe and Mail* article praised Bowman for "wheeling and dealing head and shoulders above everybody else." Frank Orr of the *Toronto Star* agreed that Bowman was the big story, followed by LaFontaine ending up in Long Island. He viewed the ascent of American high school players in the draft as "more of an inevitability than a surprise." Neither had anything to say about Yzerman.

Bob McKenzie wrote a two-page feature on the draft for *The Hockey News* that also overlooked Yzerman. The story's focus, as the issue's cover line read, was "The Young Americans." Lawton, LaFontaine and Barrasso posed together on the cover, wearing their new team jerseys over their shirts and ties and with Old Glory in the background. McKenzie's article also pointed out how two other Americans, Alfie Turcotte (who went seventeenth, to Montreal) and David Jensen (a center from Lawrence Academy in Massachusetts, who went twentieth, to Hartford), had been claimed in the first round. The 1983 draft, wrote McKenzie, was "forever to be remembered as the year of the Yankee." Even Yzerman's hometown paper, the *Ottawa Citizen,* chose as its sole picture from the draft a shot of Lawton and LaFontaine in their new team jerseys.

Perhaps the greatest snub, from Yzerman's perspective, appeared in the Montreal *Gazette.* Columnist Michael Farber portrayed Devellano's failure to secure LaFontaine as nothing less than a franchise disaster. After the Islanders chose LaFontaine, he wrote, "The Red Wings chose hara kiri. At one moment, Devellano looked as if he had a stab at the one player who could rouse a moribund franchise. At the next moment, the only stab was the blade in his chest."

Farber wrote that, earlier in the week, Devellano had said that if LaFontaine proved to be still available at the fourth pick, it would reconfirm his faith in God. "We rated our top players one through four," Devellano explained in Farber's column. "Pat was our number one. We drafted fourth, and we took the fourth player on our list." Devellano was being kind, because the Wings actually had no interest in Lawton, but he was not about to dis a teenager on his big day.

Farber allowed that Yzerman was a "useful center," adding:

"He has only one weakness as far as the Red Wings are concerned. But then, everyone cannot be named Pat LaFontaine."

The story line shaping around Detroit's draft experience—that failing to get LaFontaine was a horrible disaster, without considering Yzerman's merits—obviously made Devellano uncomfortable. "In no way will I denigrate the player we chose, so I'm having trouble saying much now with everyone asking me about Pat," he told Farber. "I like both boys. LaFontaine is a good player. But so is the player we chose. After all, they're both still kids. I mean, who the hell knows?"

LaFontaine was disappointed not to be going to Detroit, but ecstatic that he was going to a storied club like the Islanders. "I would have loved to go to Detroit. My heart was there. Jimmy D is a super guy and he's going to build a winner there. But when the Islanders called my name, it was a shock. I'm very happy."

"I was happy and surprised to go high," Yzerman told the *Peterborough Examiner* on draft day. "I knew I was rated high, but you never know how things are going to turn out. . . . I really hoped [Detroit] would pick me. They're rebuilding and I figured I would have a good chance of making it this year. They expect me to make it and told me to just give it my best shot."

"Detroit is a super club with a lot of class," Yzerman told the *Detroit Free Press* after his selection, starting off on the right foot with the local scribes. "They still haven't forgotten the days when they were the greatest."

The Detroit media were less apoplectic about the missed opportunity with LaFontaine. They had been primed for the Verdun star to go elsewhere; any other result would have been a genuine surprise. Rather than paint Yzerman as a consolation prize, the *Free Press*'s Bill McGraw was careful to stress his assets: "He was considered one of the most skillful players in the OHL, although he was not among the top 25 league scorers. He is known as a superb puck-handler, a good passer, and a fine skater. Off the ice, he won an award last year for his scholastic achievements."

In his own predictably quiet way, Steve Yzerman went to work ensuring that the draft would be eventually remembered not as the one in which Bowman was proved a deal-making genius or in which the league went wild on American talent, but as the one in which Stevie Y was still available after the first three picks—and in which nobody even seemed to notice when the Red Wings did speak for him.

The class of '83 was divvied up without any spectacular surprises once selections moved past the top five. The players flagged to go in the first round generally did so. Sixth, to New Jersey, was John MacLean from the Oshawa Generals, his stock having risen sharply after the Memorial Cup. Seventh, to Toronto, was Russ Courtnall of the Victoria Cougars. Choosing eighth, Winnipeg took Andrew McBain, the player the Islanders might have taken third. Cam Neely went ninth to Vancouver, and Adam Creighton eleventh to Buffalo.

Steve Yzerman's linemate, Bob Errey, went exactly where he had been told he'd go: fifteenth, to Pittsburgh. When Errey was drafted into major junior hockey, he'd been deeply disappointed to have had to wait until the fourth round to be picked by his hometown club, the Petes. There was no such mystery this time around. The night before the draft, Eddie Johnston, the new general manager of the Pittsburgh Penguins, came to his hotel room. He was close to Errey's agent, Bill Watters, and Johnston already had a Penguins jersey to present to Errey. And so he went, right on schedule, to Pittsburgh.

Only Dale Derkatch failed to make good on the high expectations established earlier in the season. His central scouting ranking had slid into the forties as the season drew to a close, as his goal scoring didn't maintain quite the breathtaking pace set earlier in the schedule. Winnipeg, which held two first-round picks, steered well clear of their favorite son, taking McBain eighth and Bob Dollas fourteenth. Derkatch didn't even bother to attend the draft. When it was over, Barry Fraser, the chief scout of the Edmonton Oilers, phoned the Derkatch home and told Dale's dad that his son, one of the most exciting and talented forwards ever seen in the Western Hockey League, had been spoken for in the seventh round, 145th overall. The two agreed that it wasn't even worth Derkatch's time to report to the Oilers training camp in the fall. He returned to the Regina Pats lineup and played on the 1984 Canadian Olympic team, winning gold at the World Juniors that year as well. With the Pats in 1983–84, he set a WHL scoring record that still stands. Then he took his game to Europe, where he played professionally for eleven seasons before becoming a scout.

As far as both Errey and Yzerman were concerned, the draft had worked out well for them. They were going to weak teams that would give them a chance to crack the starting lineup. But the opportunity wasn't all that it seemed cracked up to be for both of them.

Players don't choose their position in the draft; if they did, they'd be wise to decline the opportunity to go first overall. It's far better to go respectably high, and have the endorsement of a team's scouting staff and the attention of the general manager when it comes time to sign the first contract, than to be the top choice overall and have to bear the burden of being the most anticipated new star in the entire NHL. Before the 1983 draft, there was concern expressed about how much pressure LaFontaine would have faced to resurrect the Red Wings, had he lasted until the fourth pick, although there can be little doubt that he would have risen to it. Many players, on the other hand, would have been far better off being ignored entirely in the first or even the second round, so that they could have the pleasure of showing up for training camp with only moderate (or no) expectations and prove to be a pleasant surprise. Barry Fraser, the chief scout of the Oilers, had blessed numerous future stars with no-pressure draft selections: Mark Messier went forty-eighth and Glenn Anderson sixty-ninth in 1979; Jari Kurri was sixty-ninth and Andy Moog 132nd in 1980; Steve Smith went 111th in '81; and at the 1983 draft, Edmonton made one of its last inspired picks, taking Esa Tikkanen eighty-second.

By comparison, going first and second overall in the 1983 draft did no great favors for Brian Lawton and Sylvain Turgeon. Both played in the NHL, but neither had the careers expected of them. Lawton was probably just overhyped, although he did produce five goals for Team USA in the 1984 Canada Cup tournament. Turgeon never converted his size and skill into the star-quality career the way most everyone anticipated. After the draft, Barry Fraser said that Andrew McBain should have gone first or second overall. He went eighth, and never excelled as predicted.

Lawton would end up being vilified by North Stars fans, who lamented Nanne's choice when, just below him in the draft, LaFontaine, Yzerman and Barrasso, who all proved to be stars, were there for the asking. Unhappily, Lawton (who is now a player agent in Minneapolis) has become a fan favorite in barstool debates when the question of the all-time NHL draft-pick blunder is on the floor. (A skate-off on the Web site www.fan.ca contested the relative ignominies of Lawton's choice by Minnesota in

1983 and Greg Joly's by Washington in 1974. "He racked up impressive offensive numbers playing in front of mothers and girlfriends," one fan sneered in his assessment of Lawton's performance at Mount St. Charles High School.)

Jimmy Devellano can't resist playing the what-if game with the 1983 draft. "If Yzerman in hindsight had gone first, like everyone now says he should have, to the Minnesota North Stars, would the North Stars still be alive and not in Dallas?"

If, if, if. And if it's tempting to imagine Yzerman as a North Star, helping keep his team in Minnesota, consider LaFontaine as a Hartford Whaler instead of Turgeon. Perhaps that franchise doesn't move to Carolina. Perhaps Hartford fans pack the arena to watch their winning team. Peter Karmanos, whose Compuware amateur empire in Detroit gave LaFontaine his start, never gets the chance to buy the team as a result. Or—who knows—maybe if, after Minnesota does the right thing and takes Yzerman, Hartford can't resist a talent from nearby Rhode Island and goes for Lawton. That leaves the Islanders still in the driver's seat when it comes to the Detroit franchise's destiny. Does Bill Torrey still take Pat LaFontaine? Or does he go for McBain, as LaFontaine thought they would, or opt instead for Turgeon, who is still available—the bigger kid with the skills that earned him Memorial Cup MVP honors just a few weeks earlier?

And when Jimmy Devellano makes the fourth pick and gets his hands on LaFontaine, the dream selection for the Red Wings, then what? Does history still unfold the way the Red Wings hope, with a Stanley Cup celebration for the first time since the mid 1950s and LaFontaine hoisting the trophy in the air? Or is that a prospect best left to someone else's universe?

As it happened, Devellano did not look back. He didn't get LaFontaine. It didn't matter. Yzerman hadn't been an entirely helpless pick of whatever team felt like taking him. He had demonstrated a genuine desire to become a Red Wing. The Devellano tour had sold him on his destiny. Commitment like that, in a teenager with as much skill and poise as Yzerman, is a hard thing for a team to ignore.

"When we drafted Yzerman," Devellano recalls, "I said, 'We will build our team around our young player.' He was the first piece of the foundation of a competitive team."

FOUR

BOB ERREY HAD SCORED 53 GOALS IN HIS LAST SEASON AS A Peterborough Pete, and scoring goals is what Pittsburgh expected him to do when they drafted him fifteenth overall in 1983. The Penguins had tied Hartford in 1982–83 in the league cellar, with 45 points, having plunged thirty points in one precipitous season. The club had the second-worst offense and the second-worst defense. It allowed 137 more goals than it scored.

Back in his bantam days, Bob Errey had a game in which he wore out the scorekeeper's pencil with seven goals and five assists. It was the first time he thought that he might actually be able to do this for a living. He'd skipped midget altogether, going straight to Junior B, then overcame his disappointment with his late draft by the Petes to star on his hometown team alongside Steve Yzerman. Then came the first-round pick in the NHL entry draft. Turning nineteen just before the start of the 1983–84 season, Errey was handed a starting job with the Penguins, and nobody would have blamed him if he had handed it right back.

It wasn't simply that he had reached a plateau of offensive skill in Peterborough—the carpet had been yanked out from beneath him. Stevie Y was no longer his centerman, setting him up for breakaways every period, converting his passes into assists. His speed, which had been exceptional in junior, made him just one more capable winger among many in the NHL. And worse, Errey's professional rookie season with Pittsburgh informed him with brutal frankness that he was not a natural goal scorer. "I didn't have a great shot," Errey says he learned. "I had to score from five feet in."

Pittsburgh had not drafted and signed him to stand in the slot and whack home the odd rebound, on those occasions when one of the league's hulking defensemen forgot to drive his five-and-maybe-double-digit body into the ice. But did Pittsburgh send the struggling teenager back to Peterborough or down to the minors for more seasoning? No. The Penguins left him in the lineup, striving against all probability to live up to his billing as a big gun. He dressed for 65 games and scored a total of nine goals, with thirteen assists. In this way, Errey helped the Penguins lower their wins from 18 to 16, their total points from 45 to 38, their total goals from 257 to 254. While Bob Errey expresses no complaint of his own today, it can be said, without any cruelty, that by struggling painfully night after night with his obvious shortcomings as a scoring star, he did a good job for Pittsburgh of making sure they finished emphatically last in the overall league standings, thereby winning the Mario Lemieux Derby at the 1984 entry draft. With Super Mario secured, the Penguins then demoted Bob Errey to the Baltimore Skipjacks of the American Hockey League, with whom he scored only seventeen goals in fifty-nine games in 1984–85.

Things went a little differently for Steve Yzerman in Detroit.

The stats for Steve Yzerman at the 1983 draft reported that he was five-eleven and 178 pounds. When Yzerman showed up for Red Wings training camp that September in Port Huron,

Michigan—across the Bluewater Bridge from Sarnia, Ontario—Jim Devellano says that the kid couldn't have weighed more than 155 pounds. Maybe his summer training regimen had melted away undetected excess fat, but Devellano wasn't confident that his top pick was capable of playing in the NHL. Devellano had already taken some heat publicly for selecting Yzerman, the non All Star, non top-ten scorer, non (need it be said?) LaFontaine, about whom many of the top hockey sages had scribbled nary a word in their coverage of the draft. Now he was wondering if the young man about whom he had publicly declared, "We will build our team around him," could even secure a starting job.

There were bad signs before Yzerman set foot on the ice. Weight was one issue. Strength was another. Nick Polano, who was beginning his second season as Detroit's coach at training camp in 1983, would recall to the *Calgary Sun*'s George Johnson how his trainer phoned him him to complain about the kid called "Why-zerman." He told Polano that Why-zerman couldn't bench-press a hundred pounds, and that he should be sent home. A blustering Polano told the trainer that this was a boy they'd spent the fourth-pick overall to get, and that he was supposed to lead them into the playoffs.

Before the scrimmaging began, Devellano says he approached both Yzerman and his agent, Gus Badali (famous for negotiating the twenty-one-year contract that bound Wayne Gretzky to Peter Pocklington), to forewarn them of what might transpire. "I said to them that, because of Steve's weight, there was a possibility that we'd return him to Peterborough for another year of juniors if he couldn't hack it. I didn't want Steve to be disappointed. I wanted him to understand where we stood." There was no great shame in this. The Islanders had left Bryan Trottier, another center not far into the five and double digits, with his junior club, the Lethbridge

Broncos, for another season after taking him in the underage draft of 1974. And after he piled up 144 points in the Western Canada Junior Hockey League, an older, more polished Trottier joined the Islanders at nineteen and produced a ninety-five-point rookie season, winning the Calder Trophy.

Devellano joined Polano in the arena stands to watch Yzerman in his first practice scrimmage. "We were anxious to see how he'd handle things," he recalls in a triumph of understatement.

They watched Yzerman pull the puck through the legs of defenseman John Barrett, deke goaltender Greg Stefan, and stuff a shot into the roof of the net.

"After Steve skated two shifts," says Devellano, "we looked at each other and said, 'Holy cow—he's the best player we have.'"

His language might have been a little stronger than "holy cow."

Polano (who actually recalled being on the ice with the team, not in the stands) said he skated over to his trainer and asked him if he still thought he should send Why-zerman home.

The good news, says Devellano, was that, as far as they could tell, the Red Wings had chosen superbly in the draft. The bad news was that "our youngest player, at 155 pounds, was our best player." And that meant the *rest* of the team was pretty damned bad.

The Red Wings signed Steve Yzerman to a five-year contract. In addition to a $90,000 signing bonus, he would be paid $70,000 in year one, $85,000 in year two, $95,000 in year three, and $100,000 in each of years four and five. If he won the Calder, he'd get another $25,000.

It was hard to imagine anyone asking more of Yzerman in his first NHL game, which was in Winnipeg against the Jets. (His debut took place just as the Buffalo Sabres were placing Detroit's one-time draft hope, Dale McCourt, on waivers.) He got a goal and an assist, both points coming off quality efforts, and he also looked strong on the power play. But Yzerman was the one asking more. Congratulated on his effort after the 6–6 tie, he turned the remarks aside with self-criticism.

"I was kind of disappointed with my defensive play," he told the *Detroit Free Press*'s Bill McGraw. "And I was disappointed with my face-offs. I had little lapses. I'm always learning, and I want to cut down on my mistakes each game."

Okay, but Steve, you had that great goal to give the Red Wings a 3–1 lead in the first period. You shook off two checkers to get a shot on Doug Soetart, and then stuffed in your own rebound. And with the score tied 5–5, you backchecked your way into owning the puck, turned on the Jets' goal, blew past your fellow rookie, defenseman Bob Dollas, and sent the puck to Eddie Johnstone, who stuck it behind Soetart and then praised your passing ability. A shame that Doug Smail then burned Brad Park and tied the game with a hat-trick effort, but couldn't you be a little happy with yourself?

"It was one of my better games," he finally conceded to McGraw.

"He always looked dangerous," Nick Polano told McGraw. "That tells you something, especially on the road. This was a good test for Steve. He showed us he's ready to play."

A month later, Yzerman was centering a line with left winger John Ogrodnick and right winger Ron Duguay as the Red Wings hosted the Chicago Blackhawks at "The Joe." Yzerman picked up two goals, including a twenty-five-foot slapshot that he whistled past Murray Bannerman as Detroit romped to a 7–4 win before a boisterous crowd, who were rapidly warming to the idea of an exciting new era for the Wings with Yzerman's arrival. But early in the third period, Chicago's

Behn Wilson smacked Yzerman in the face with his stick and sent him, bleeding, to the bench.

Wilson was a remarkable piece of work, a defenseman who was playing on left wing that night, filling in for several injured Blackhawks. As a Kingston Canadian teammate of Ken Linseman, he was drafted sixth to Linseman's seventh overall by the Flyers in 1978. He set a team points-production record for blueliners with Philadelphia before being traded to Chicago. He was also a feared fighter, an accomplished actor who appeared in Shakespearean plays, and a guy who, like Linseman, tended to be a bit careless with his stick.

It was debatable whether or not he intended to give Yzerman the chop in the face. The referee didn't see the incident; no penalty was called. Yzerman was led away, had his broken nose tended to, and was back so quickly he didn't miss a shift.

"I've been hit by bigger and better guys than him," Yzerman told the *Free Press's* McGraw.

The Red Wings submitted a tape of the incident to the league, and Wilson was given a four-game suspension. "He deserved something," Yzerman allowed, and that was the end of it. The NHL's welcome-wagon of brutality had officially paid its visit to the rookie center. And he had established he would not be shaken off his game.

He kept on scoring, until he had 39 goals and 48 assists, enough to lead the Red Wings in total points. The entire team scored 298 goals in 1983–84, meaning that Yzerman was personally involved in just under 30 percent of them. His first NHL hat trick came against Toronto on December 23, as he victimized Mike Palmateer. His steady contribution was underlined by his ability to pick up at least one point in sixty-one of eighty games. The Wings went from 21 wins to 31, from last in the Norris

Division to third. The team returned to the playoffs after a five-season absence, and although Detroit was eliminated in the opening round by St. Louis—by a margin of three games to one—the Blues required back-to-back overtime wins to get rid of the Wings. Yzerman contributed three goals and three assists, leading the team in goals and total points, in his first, all-too-brief taste of postseason NHL hockey.

Yzerman's regular-season points total was, at the time, the ninth-best performance by a rookie in NHL history. Of the eight players ahead of him, six had set their marks in just the previous three seasons. Peter Stastny led the recent freshman efforts with 109 points in 1980–81; Dale Hawerchuk was second with 103, Neil Broten third with 98 and Barry Pederson fifth with 92 points, all in 1981–82; and Steve Larmer was seventh with 90 points in 1982–83.

Yzerman had arrived in Detroit just as the league was experiencing its historic plateau of wide-open offense (or, looked at the other way, porous defense). During the dozen seasons beginning with the NHL's expansion from six teams to twelve and ending with the WHA's last competitive gasps, scoring rose by 20 percent, from 5.5 goals per game to roughly 6.6. As soon as the WHA was gone, and four surviving teams (Hartford, Winnipeg, Quebec and Edmonton) joined the NHL, league scoring began a steep climb, reaching eight goals per game in 1981–82 and remaining above 7.5 through 1985–86.

Yzerman came along when the NHL, at twenty-one teams, had never been bigger. The focus of the game he joined was on firepower. The top clubs also knew how to prevent goals and not just score them, but the overall emphasis was on putting pucks in the net. Even struggling teams looked for offense while hoping their defensive competence would catch up. Fourteen of the league's twenty-one teams scored more than 300 goals in Yzerman's rookie season, and Detroit, at 298, just missed that plateau. Beginning in 1980–81, a player couldn't make the list of top-ten scorers without a 100-point season. Back in 1973–74, only the top three players broke 100 points, and Dennis Hextall squeezed into the top ten with a twenty-goal season.

Of the six early-eighties rookies who ranked ahead of Yzerman, all but one, the right winger Steve Larmer, was, like him, a centerman. Power-play goals figured significantly in their output: Yzerman got a third of his goals in man-advantage situations in his rookie season, with the gamut running between 18 percent (for Neal Broten) to 37 percent (for Marion Stastny).

Yzerman stood out from this crowd by being an offensive success on a team that was weak defensively. The Red Wings of 1983–84 had the worst team plus-minus record (minus-25) of any of the clubs that produced early-eighties rookie offensive stars. Yzerman's plus-minus (in even-strength situations) was minus-17, which made him better than the team, but didn't put him in the same camp as players like Larmer (plus-44), Pederson (plus-27) or Broten (plus-14), who were on teams with good scoring surpluses. And Peter Stastny had produced a plus-11 rating on a team that overall was minus-4 on the season. It would take Yzerman until his fifth NHL season to move his even-strength performance into the positive range, but the Red Wings as a team weren't doing any better, and in fact were generally a lot worse.

Yzerman was also breaking into the NHL in a strikingly weak conference. The ten teams in the Norris and Smythe divisions of the Clarence Campbell Conference were the worst offenders when it came to taking care of their own end. The North Stars, Detroit's divisional rivals, managed to finish first in the Norris in 1983–84 by scoring 345 goals—and allowing 344.

Every other team in the Norris allowed more goals than it scored. Only two other teams in the Campbell Conference, Edmonton and Calgary over in the Smythe Division, managed a scoring surplus, and all ten allowed well over 300 goals, surrendering an average of 4.23 goals per game. In the Prince of Wales Conference, seven of eleven teams had a scoring surplus, and only four allowed more than 300 goals. Wales teams allowed an average of 3.68 goals per game, and that figure was inflated by two particularly poor performances, by Pittsburgh and New Jersey. Drop those miscreants, and the Wales' defensive game improved to 2.84 goals against.

Boiled down to plain language, the Red Wings were better once Yzerman joined them, but still not very good, and their division and conference weren't any great shakes overall, either. It made him shine all the more brightly.

In so many ways, Yzerman had gone to the right team. They needed him desperately, and gave him the chance to play a leading role. Had he been selected by a top club in the Wales Conference, such as Boston, Buffalo, the Islanders, Washington or Philadelphia, he might not have had the opportunity to be such an immediate standout, although there's no doubt he would have found his way forward. Other good prospects had to spend additional time in junior or go to the American league to wait for a starting job on a strong NHL roster to open up. Detroit was also ideal for him because it wasn't an impossible distance from his home in Nepean. Family and friends could make the drive to Detroit for a game and a visit, rather than have to board a plane to Los Angeles, Vancouver, St. Louis or any number of other NHL locales.

And while Yzerman brought the self-disciplined professionalism he'd already displayed in Peterborough to his NHL career, Detroit helped minimize off-ice distractions—the bane of so many teenage rookies with more money than they'd ever seen in their life—by being such a dreadful urban center. Downtown Detroit was not a place you hung around after a game or a practice, the way you might in Manhattan or in the trendier environs of L.A. Forget Studio 54, supermodels and movie stars. Detroit was in such horrible shape that players and fans alike drove into the enclosed garage in the civic center attached to The Joe, attended the game, then fled immediately to the suburbs.

"After the game, we'd get out to the suburbs where we lived to get something to eat," says Gerard Gallant, who became a close friend as well as a linemate of Yzerman's in Detroit. The players' homes were a thirty-five-minute drive north, above 12 Mile Road. "Very seldom did we stay downtown. We'd go to Greektown every once in a while, but that was about it. We'd go to a Tigers game if we had time, but otherwise I was never downtown."

As a place to play, Detroit, says Gallant, "was perfect for Steve. A bunch of us arrived around the same time. We were all young guys and we had fun, and we wanted to win. We all knew the team was going to get better in a year or two. It was just a matter of taking the time. And in a couple years we went from being a laughingstock of the league to being a pretty good team."

As Mike Eagles has noted, Peterborough's four-line system had left people unable to predict what Yzerman was really capable of as an offensive threat. He also showed with the Behn Wilson incident that he could not be intimidated out of the rink.

Sometimes the concern about a teen's ability to play at the NHL level gets stood on its ear. Rather than give them more than they're ready for, the big league provides exactly what they need:

better competition, bigger challenges, better linemates. The game makes the player better, and the player makes those around him better at the same time. The young star progresses in the NHL in a way that more seasons in junior hockey can never bring about.

That said, Yzerman was going to have to get bigger. Gallant, who was about the same height, had been only 160 pounds when he made his training camp debut alongside Yzerman in 1983, having already been drafted in 1981. He spent 1983–84 in the AHL with the Adirondack Red Wings, and his playing weight eventually was muscled up to 190 pounds. In 1986–87, he started playing on a line with Yzerman, a combination that lasted four seasons. For almost ten years with the Red Wings, Gallant watched his friend change, every season for the better.

"This guy came to work. It wasn't just what he did on the ice. When he joined Detroit, he was a scrawny kid without much strength. He worked in the weight room as much as any player I saw there. His discipline was second to none. We can say that about a lot of guys, but I've seen it with Steve. He'd come to training camp every year in the top two or three in conditioning on the team. He got stronger, and it made him a better player. He wasn't getting pushed off the puck. He was confident in his game. He improved every year because he made himself improve."

Dick Todd saw how Yzerman's quick start to an NHL career had paid off when the player came to practice with the Petes to get back in form after a broken collarbone cost him part of the 1985–86 season. He only turned twenty-one in May 1986, but the better part of three seasons in the NHL had done wonders. "When he came back to Peterborough to work out with us, it was great of him to do that, because it helped out our team. I remember doing skating exercises and conditioning drills. He really showed the kids what an NHL player could do.

He was so far ahead of everybody else, it was incredible. He just demolished them."

Todd has lately been watching another Peterborough product, Eric Staal—a six-foot three-inch forward chosen second overall in the 2003 entry draft by the Carolina Hurricanes, who could turn out to be an early success in the NHL the way Yzerman was. Staal was still eligible to play junior hockey, with his nineteenth birthday approaching at the start of the 2003–04 season, but Staal appeared to have "big time" stamped on his professional passport. "I think he's almost a Jean Beliveau," says Todd of Staal. "Peterborough was hoping to get him back, but there's no way. I think that, once he plays with good players, he'll be better, and he'll make the people around him better because he has such great vision and an understanding of the game. That's an aspect of Steve's career, as well. When he plays with good guys, he makes them better."

But there didn't seem to be much for Yzerman to work with, teamwise. "When he went to Detroit, they had a horrible team," says Todd. "There were a lot of selfish guys in Detroit at the time. The whole inference was, you get rewarded for points."

Job one for Devellano was to put more bums in arena seats and have fewer bums in the lineup. He freely admits to having signed veteran players for their marquee value, taking a chance on getting a few more miles out of names that might bring more paying customers into The Joe. In the middle of the 1982–83 season he sent Mark Kirton (the former Peterborough Pete who'd been whipped into a lather by Keith Acton's wooden sock inserts) to Vancouver to get Ivan Boldirev, who had played his first NHL game, with Boston, way back in 1970–71. Then he made a six-player deal in June 1983 with the New York Rangers to bring in Ron Duguay, Ed Mio and Eddie Johnstone.

Duguay was a glamour-boy forward who had lit up the Manhattan nightclub scene and modeled professionally while in New York, and he is probably the only NHL player ever to have served as a judge at a Miss World beauty pageant (in Japan, no less). Duguay had been at the peak of his career just two years earlier, playing for Canada in the 1981 Canada Cup and then scoring forty goals for the Rangers in 1981–82. He'd been plagued by injuries for several consecutive seasons—a severed leg tendon, a dinged shoulder, stomach muscle problems—when Devellano brought him to Detroit for Yzerman's rookie season. He did produce seasons of 80 and 89 points before being sent to Pittsburgh at the trade deadline late in his third Detroit campaign.

Later in the summer of 1983, Devellano had also signed veteran Rangers defenseman Brad Park as a free agent, and midway through the season he picked up Rick MacLeish, who'd had a fifty-goal season with the Flyers in 1972–73. MacLeish played the last twenty-five games of his NHL career that season in Detroit. In 1984–85, Devellano brought in two former Leaf attractions, Darryl Sittler and Dave "Tiger" Williams, hoping they might lure some southern Ontario hockey fans across the Ambassador Bridge. It was Sittler's last season and his least distinguished; Williams was shipped to L.A. for "future considerations" before the season was even over. And Devellano still had as his captain Danny Gare, a star attraction of the Sabres of the 1970s whom the Red Wings had acquired in the deal that sent Dale McCourt to Buffalo. Along the way, three future NHL coaches—Ted Nolan, Colin Campbell and Barry Melrose—were also on hand.

It was an odds-and-sods team: players on their way down; a lot of players on their way nowhere; a few players who could get the job done, but were often focused on fulfilling contracts that paid them to score; and a stream of new, young players coming in through the draft. There was friction between the high-priced free agents with their bonus clauses and the lower-paid newcomers and grinders. Reed Larson, who had been with the team since 1976, was a constant on defense, but goaltending was undistinguished.

Detroit could provide Yzerman initially with at least one good linemate: left winger John Ogrodnick, who had been a longshot draft selection, at sixty-sixth overall, for the Wings in 1979. He reached two Memorial Cup finals with the New Westminster Bruins in 1977 and 1978, winning on the second try. Ogrodnick had been a right winger in junior, but as a pro he switched to the left side. Once he broke into the Red Wings lineup full time in 1980–81, he proved to be a highly capable forward, lasting more than 900 games with solid offensive numbers and an appearance on the First All-Star Team in 1984–85. He set a Red Wings record for points by a left winger that season, with 105, which was seventh-best in the league, and his 55 goals were topped only by Wayne Gretzky, Mike Bossy and Jari Kurri. But there was also some animosity between Ogrodnick and Yzerman; the winger was heard complaining that Yzerman wasn't getting him the puck enough in those years when the Red Wings weren't winning and paydays depended on points production.

Devellano also made sure he didn't repeat the mistake the Petes had made by leaving Yzerman without protective muscle. Later in the 1983 draft, he selected two enforcers, Bob Probert (forty-sixth overall) and Joe Kocur (ninety-first). Both earned spots on the Wings roster in 1985–86; Kocur led the league that season with 377 penalty minutes, while Probert did the same, with 398 minutes, in 1987–88. Having "Probie" in particular ride shotgun made Yzerman's life far less dangerous, but it was hardly free of cheap shots, painful hits and debilitating injuries.

Among the top picks in the 1983 draft, Yzerman was an offensive standout. His 87 points topped all rookies; only Sylvain Turgeon outdid him in goals, with 40. Brian Lawton had fizzled, producing just 31 points (with 10 goals) in 58 games, and would spend half of the next season down with Springfield in the American league. Andrew McBain, whom so many had argued should have been chosen higher, even first overall, came up with only 30 points in 78 games in Winnipeg.

If amateur rankings are not as good an indicator of professional promise as draft pick order, and if draft pick order is not as good an indicator of NHL ability as first-season performance, then first-season performance is not a perfect indicator of long-term ability. By design, a number of the top picks didn't even come into the NHL straight away in 1983–84. Pat LaFontaine skipped most of the NHL season, playing on the U.S. Olympic team. John MacLean, selected sixth by New Jersey, was still with the Oshawa Generals for most of 1983–84, and won gold for Canada at the World Juniors. His twenty-three games with New Jersey that season saw him put one puck in the net and contribute no assists. Russ Courtnall, taken seventh by Toronto, also hung back in junior for most of the season, won gold at the World Juniors and played for Canada in the Olympics. Cam Neely, chosen ninth by Vancouver, got a start on his NHL career, but spent nineteen games of his rookie season in junior, and wouldn't begin producing significant scoring numbers until he was traded to Boston in 1986, where he became a franchise player. Normand Lacombe, the tenth pick, by Buffalo, spent the season in the American league. While he never developed into a franchise player, he would win a Stanley Cup with Edmonton in 1988. Adam Creighton, another Buffalo first-round pick, at eleventh, spent the bulk of 1983–84 with his junior club, the Ottawa 67s.

For all the complaining about 1983 having been a weak draft year, history proved it to be full of quality players. In addition to the first-round picks who managed long and in many cases highly productive careers, once they were ready to have them, there were the usual surprises from deeper draft rounds. Claude Lemieux, a future nemesis of Yzerman and the Red Wings, had gone twenty-sixth overall. Edmonton pulled out a plum at number eighty-two with Esa Tikkanen. Detroit's choice at eighty-eight netted Czech forward Petr Klima. The Red Wings scouting had been keen on Czech players in general, but was reluctant to commit high draft picks on them as long as the Iron Curtain was intact. Gary Galley, a defenseman chosen 103rd overall out of Bowling Green, would play more than 900 NHL games. Kevin Stevens, who would have two seasons of more than 100 points in Pittsburgh, went ridiculously deep, at 112th. Rick Tocchet was still available at 125th. Buffalo found Christian Ruuttu at 139th. Slava Fetisov, a Soviet defensive stalwart who had been chosen originally as a draft after-thought by Montreal in 1978, re-entered the draft and was selected 150th by New Jersey. A 1995 trade would make him a key component of Detroit's Cup victories. Brian Noonan, an American high school player, went 186th to Chicago, and in addition to assembling a lengthy NHL career, he won the Stanley Cup with New York in 1994. And way down at 241st, another Soviet veteran, Sergei Makarov, was filed under "you never know" by Calgary. His performance in San Jose in 1993–94 would bring much grief to Yzerman and the Red Wings.

Among the draftees who logged full seasons, there were two exceptional performances, from Yzerman and Tom Barrasso, the

Acton-Boxboro High School netminder selected fifth overall by Bowman's Sabres. Both were nominated for the Calder Trophy, the league's rookie-of-the-year award, voted on (like most of the NHL's trophies) by members of the Professional Hockey Writers' Association in all NHL cities. Lately, the writers had been favoring with the Calder the new stars who were helping the league achieve such inflated scoring stats: Peter Stastny won it in 1981, Dale Hawerchuk in '82, Steve Larmer in '83. Defensemen rarely won the Calder unless they showed offensive flair, the way Ray Bourque had in 1980, or Denis Potvin in 1974—or Bobby Orr, the prototypic Calder-winning blueliner, in 1967. No goaltender had won it since Ken Dryden, in 1972. The odds seemed to favor Yzerman to continue the trend of awarding the Calder to scoring stars, and *The Sporting News* did name him its NHL Rookie of the Year.

But Yzerman's rookie season, as strong as it was, didn't quite reach the superlative heights of his predecessors. He'd come up short of a forty-goal season by one goal. We can play "what if" around the consequences of Yzerman having dinged one less goalpost or crossbar, because if scouts liked to see five-and-double-digit in the measurement stats, Calder voters had become enamored of youngsters who turned in a ninety-point effort, with or without forty goals. Neal Broten had managed 98 points, but Dale Hawerchuk cranked out 103, and that had sealed the Calder for him in 1982. In 1983, Steve Larmer had no scoring competition when he squeaked through with 90 points; Mats Naslund was the next best rookie with 71. Despite the fact that the 1982 draft was considered to be rich in defensemen (they went first, third, fifth and sixth, with nine in all being claimed in the opening round), none of them—not even Calder runner-up Phil Housley—was considered sufficiently stellar to divert enough votes from a goal-scoring forward.

Like Larmer, Steve Yzerman had little real scoring competition in 1983–84, with Sylvain Turgeon trailing with 72 points, but there was something not quite for-the-ages about his 87 points. It seems ridiculous, but the fact remained that he didn't make the Ninety-Point Club, and that left the door open for the writers to consider a rare break with tradition. There wasn't a single new defenseman that made a sufficient impression, but with more than a decade having passed since the Calder was last granted to a goaltender, the voters had a live one in Tom Barrasso.

Goaltenders comprised a mysterious brotherhood within the sport. Traditionally they were drafted late, didn't get the big-dollar contracts of the scoring stars, and when they did win hardware beyond their own dedicated trophies, it was for the playoff MVP award, the Conn Smythe Trophy, which they tended to win in disproportion to the number of jobs they held in the league. No goaltender won the Hart Memorial Trophy, awarded by the writers to the player judged most valuable to his team, between Jacques Plante in 1962 and Dominik Hasek in 1997. Mike Liut of the St. Louis Blues had been a near miss in 1981, finishing second to Wayne Gretzky in Hart voting but winning the Lester B. Pearson Award, the MVP prize voted on by the players themselves.

In 1983, Housley had almost but not quite convinced the Calder voters that coming into the NHL straight out of an American high school and playing exceptionally well was worthy of the trophy. Barrasso's nomination in the very next year gave the writers a second chance to formally recognize not just a goaltender, but the potential of the U.S. high school system as a source of outstanding recruits.

Barrasso was no fluke. He played half of Buffalo's games (forty-two to be exact), sharing the starting job with the veteran Bob Sauve. He and Sauve were runners-up for the William

Jennings Trophy, awarded to the goaltenders on the team with the fewest goals against. And with the league's general managers deciding that Barrasso deserved the Vezina Trophy, which honors the league's finest goaltender, there seemed little chance that this Massachusetts nineteen-year-old would not win the Calder as well. He outpolled Yzerman, 242–203.

"You only get one shot at it, and I gave it my best one," Yzerman said to the *Detroit Free Press*'s John Castine. That was the extent of his public disappointment.

Ten years ago, there would have been no doubt that Barrasso had been the best choice for the 1984 Calder. Barrasso and Sauve won the Jennings in 1985, and Barrasso was runner-up for the Vezina twice in 1980s. He was named to the First All-Star Team in 1983–84, and to the Second Team in 1984–85 and 1992–93. Finally, he backstopped the Pittsburgh Penguins to two Stanley Cup wins in the early 1990s. By the time Barrasso was a Stanley Cup champion, Yzerman's career was in its most turbulent period, his future clouded by injury and incessant trade rumors. Twenty years on, Barrasso's win still looks deserved, but it no longer appears to have been an irrefutable statement on who among the rookie class of 1983–84 would accomplish the most in their careers.

Yzerman's near miss on the Calder also highlighted a yawning contractual gap. Gus Badali had negotiated a deal for Yzerman that called for a $25,000 bonus if he won the Calder, but didn't provide for any compensation if he was runner-up or was simply nominated. With a base contract of $70,000 in his first year, not enjoying some kind of Calder bonus was significant missed opportunity for Yzerman.

"You're *my* rookie of the year," Mike Ilitch told Yzerman even before the results of the balloting for the Calder were announced. Then he gave Yzerman the twenty-five grand anyway. Yzerman told Castine he was "shocked" by the bonus. "A simple 'congratulations' would have been fine." People looking for evidence of how much has changed in the relationship between NHL team owners and players need look no further than the cutting of that check and Yzerman's reaction to it.

Even after the Calder was handed to Barrasso and Yzerman got his bonus, the question of the greatest rookie from the 1983 draft class remained unanswered for many. Having chosen to play in the 1984 Olympics for Team USA, Pat LaFontaine only appeared in the Islanders lineup for 15 regular-season games. But in those games, he produced 19 points, with an incredible 13 goals. Fully aboard for the playoffs, LaFontaine put up another 9 points in 16 games as the Islanders ultimately bowed to Edmonton in finals, yielding the Oilers their first Cup win. Barrasso had the Calder, Yzerman had the best offensive effort of any rookie, but LaFontaine, in his limited appearance that season, had suggested where future stardom might actually be found.

FIVE

Nineteen was a Red Wings number looking for a good home. Sid Abel, who went on to become a Stanley Cup–winning captain, was one of three players to wear it in 1938–39 before he adopted his signature 12, and from then on, 19 was like a room in a boardinghouse whose tenant changed weekly. The only back it settled on for any length of time was that of Paul Henderson, who sported it for five seasons in the mid 1960s. Four different players used it in 1970–71, three different ones in 1973–74. In the nine seasons before Yzerman came along, thirteen more players passed through this numerical revolving door. Yzerman had worn the number in junior and there was no reason to deny it to him. When it was given to Yzerman in 1983, the parade of names stopped.

Without question, the number 19 will join Yzerman in retirement, taking its place in the rafters of Joe Louis Arena alongside the 1 of Terry Sawchuk, the 7 of Ted Lindsay, the 9 of Gordie Howe, the 10 of Alex Delvecchio and the 12 of Sid Abel. Unlike most of the other numbers, however, there's almost no chance of anyone else wearing 19 before the team moves to retire it. Only Howe's number was stricken from the roster as soon as he had finished playing for the Red Wings and was formally retired in 1972. Sawchuk's number waited thirty years; Lindsay's, thirty-four, Delvecchio's, twenty-seven; and Abel's, forty-three. The last jersey that Steve Yzerman wears in an NHL game will be one of the most desired artifacts of the modern NHL. A Red Wing in a 19 will be officially extinct.

The certainty that 19 should be retired was a long time coming. Yzerman wore it for fourteen seasons before 1997 Stanley Cup win sealed his place in Red Wings history. After his initial rush of success in 1983–84, when Yzerman was named to the NHL All-Rookie Team in addition to being runner-up for the Calder, he settled into becoming one more capable center in a league full of capable centers. He was a star in Detroit, but not in the league as a whole. He didn't make a top-ten scorers list, and wasn't voted onto the First or Second All-Star Team. Wayne Gretzky owned the First Team spot at center until 1986–87, and the Second Team slot in the first years of Yzerman's career was claimed by Bryan Trottier, Dale Hawerchuk and Mario Lemieux.

Yzerman was honored to be invited to join the Canadian team for the 1984 Canada Cup, and he beat out Denis Savard for a position, although it was debated whether Savard's purported groin injury or Yzerman's superior playmaking was the reason for Savard being cut. Regardless, he was on the squad, which was almost fatally riven by cliques of Oilers and Islanders, who had just met in the Cup finals—the younger Edmonton squad had finally ended the defending champions' playoff streak after fifteen consecutive series wins. Yzerman was a utility player and he saw minimal action. The Canadian team barely survived the round-robin, with a fourth-place 2–2–1 record, and with Yzerman not having produced a single goal, coach Glen Sather decided to scratch him from the lineup as he juggled forward units for the semifinal game

against the Soviets. Canada managed an overtime win to reach the
finals against Sweden, but by then Yzerman was a permanent
scratch. It turned out that Yzerman had been suffering from tonsillitis for more than a week, and there were suspicions that he had
been trying to conceal the ailment to stay in the tournament.

"I was amazed that he was able to function at all," Sather said
to the *Free Press*'s John Castine. "The doctor told me Saturday
[after the semifinal game] he had acute tonsillitis. Anybody I've
seen with that in the past, they've always been in bed for two
weeks. I don't know how he's had the stamina to be able to practice. And he played a couple games like that. He's a tough little
guy, who basically doesn't want to give up."

The ailing Yzerman was reduced to a spectator as Canada
downed the Swedes in two straight games. It would have been
inconceivable at the time that he wouldn't get near the Canadian
team again (in the tournament's reformatting as the World Cup)
for another twelve years.

In his sophomore season, Yzerman's goal tally retreated to 30,
although he led the team with 59 assists and tied Ron Duguay for
second place in points production, with 89, a slight improvement
from his rookie season. His linemate John Ogrodnick had a
career-best season of 55 goals and 105 points and was named to
the First All-Star Team. The team overall, however, retreated from
the gains of Yzerman's rookie season. Team scoring was up, but so
were goals against—Detroit was the fourth worst in that category.
Wins dropped from 31 to 27, points from 69 to 66, and the
team's record was the sixth worst in the league. By finishing third
again in the weak Norris Division, the Red Wings made another
playoff appearance, but the Chicago Blackhawks pushed them
aside in three straight.

After the 1984–85 season, Yzerman had sufficiently proved his worth to have his five-year contract reopened. He would now be paid $200,000 in 1985–86, rather than $95,000, as originally agreed, with paydays escalating from there. But in 1985–86, the Red Wings seriously lost traction.

Both the Wings and Yzerman were having a desultory season when they showed up in St. Louis in late January 1986. After fifty games, Yzerman had only 14 goals and 28 assists; John Ogrodnick was leading the Red Wings with 25 goals. Yzerman's plus-minus rating, minus-24, was a career low. Opposing them was one of the league's closest-checking teams, the Blues, who were having another strong season under coach Jacques Demers. Nick Polano had moved into scouting, and in his stead Brad Park (who had retired after the 1984–85 season, his future place in the Hockey Hall of Fame secure) was coaching the Wings. But Park was serving a suspension for his role in a bench-clearing brawl earlier in the month, and assistant coach Dan Belisle was in charge. The team and Yzerman were just beginning to show signs of a turnaround when, with the game barely under way, Yzerman collided with Blues defenseman Lee Norwood, breaking his collarbone. After losing the game 6–4, Belisle bemoaned the loss of Yzerman "at the top of his game."

"It's the first serious injury I've ever had," Yzerman said to Keith Gave of *Detroit Free Press*. "I had never broken anything before. . . . Finally, things were coming along. The team was coming and I felt I was finally coming around. Everybody had a pretty good feeling. I had a good feeling, too. It's kind of disappointing."

Yes, it kind of was for the Red Wings. Yzerman was expected to be out for at least six weeks. He never made it back into the lineup that season. Wins fell from an already anemic 27 to 17, points from 66 to 40. Having produced a franchise-record 313 goals in 1984–85, the team slid to pre-Yzerman levels of 266. Goals against, already their worst in franchise history at 357 in 1984–85, free-fell to 415—and the team needed five different goaltenders to surrender that many. Only Washington, in its debut season of 1974–75, had ever allowed more goals, and the 111 goals that Detroit gave up to power plays were a league record.

Not including Belisle, two different coaches, Brad Park and Harry Neale (who had coached Vancouver for six seasons), had tried and failed to produce anything close to a winning record or a promise of a turnaround. Under Neale, the Wings won eight of 35 games; under Park, they won nine of 45. After two seasons of playoff appearances, the Red Wings suddenly were back to being the Dead Things and cleaning out lockers at the end of the regular schedule.

For some players, the cleanout was permanent as Devellano tore apart the lineup. Ron Duguay had already been sent to Pittsburgh for Doug Shedden in March 1986; John Ogrodnick stayed until the middle of the 1986–87 season, when he was sent to the Quebec Nordiques in a six-player deal (which included Shedden) that landed Brent Ashton, Gilbert Delorme and Mark Kumpel. Steve Chiasson, a defenseman drafted fiftieth overall by Detroit in 1985, made the team and became a good friend of Yzerman's. A veteran Islanders center, Billy Carroll, whom Devellano had picked up in a trade with Edmonton in mid 1985–86, stayed for a half-season, the last games in his NHL career. Joe Murphy, taken first overall by Detroit in the 1986 draft, got a five-game look at the NHL in 1986–87; he would end up being traded to Edmonton and winning a Stanley Cup with them in 1990.

The most significant lineup change going forward was Devellano's decision to let go of his veteran right winger, Danny

Gare. The former Buffalo Sabres star was thirty-two, had appeared in more than 800 regular-season NHL games and had represented Canada in the Canada Cup tournaments of 1976 and 1981. His last Red Wings season was interrupted by injuries (groin and ankle) which cost him 23 games, and he produced only 16 points. Gare signed with Edmonton as an unrestricted free agent in September, but back problems ended his career the following March, before he had a chance to participate in what would have been his only Stanley Cup win, as the Oilers were stretched to seven games by Philadelphia in the 1987 finals.

Gare's departure also meant the team was losing the only captain it had had since Devellano became GM. The void raised a serious succession issue, which was also an immediate source of polite disagreement with the coach he had just hired.

To solve the team's coaching mess, Devellano was able to round up enough of Ilitch's cash to lure Jacques Demers away from St. Louis. The Blues were on a spectacular rebound from the death's-door days of 1983, when Ralston Purina had failed to win the NHL's permission to sell the club to a Saskatoon group led by Wild Bill Hunter. The team was now owned by Harry Ornest, and after winning just 25 games in 1982–83, the Blues, under Demers, had won 32 games in 1983–84 and 37 games in both 1984–85 and 1985–86.

Demers was an intensely emotional coach, given to show-boating histrionics behind the bench and calling soul-baring group meetings when a team was in a slump. His three seasons with the Blues were highly productive. Despite a losing regular-season record, Demers's Blues reached the Campbell Conference finals in 1986. Calgary appeared to have them salted away in game six of the series, with a 5–2 lead about halfway through the third period. But in what Blues fans would remember as the Monday

A baby-faced Steve Yzerman was drafted fourth overall by the Detroit Red Wings in 1983, shortly after he turned eighteen.

As Detroit's new general manager, Jim Devellano made Yzerman his first draft pick.

Weighing about 155 pounds, a lean Steve Yzerman was an outstanding rookie and a runner-up for the Calder Trophy.

Yzerman was well tutored in the two-way game by his junior coach, Dick Todd of the Peterborough Petes.

Yzerman confers with the superlative Sergei Fedorov, whose arrival in Detroit in 1990 helped relieve the longstanding pressure on the captain to carry his team offensively.

Playing on Yzerman's wing, Gerard Gallant became a Second Team All Star and a close personal friend.

Bob Errey was a linemate of Yzerman's in junior hockey and as captain of the San Jose Sharks delivered a stunning playoff blow to the Red Wings in 1994. He was acquired by the Red Wings the following year.

Yzerman drives to the net against the St. Louis Blues, watched by future Red Wings teammate Brett Hull. Yzerman's overtime goal against the Blues in game seven of the second round of the 1996 playoffs was a career highlight.

Yzerman looks for a hole in the defensive wall of Colorado goaltender Patrick Roy. The playoff encounters between the Red Wings and the Avalanche in 1996 and 1997 were among the most emotionally charged in recent league history.

Dave Lewis on Yzerman's evolution in the 1990s: "I think he still had to go through the process of being as strong defensively as you are offensively, of being a leader in that, regardless of your size, you're going to battle along the boards to get the puck out. You're going to block shots. You're going to drive to the net and get dirty, to score that goal. And you're doing it because you want everybody else to be doing it, because you know that that's the way you have to play to win."

At last: Yzerman celebrates Detroit's 1997 Stanley Cup win on the ice of Joe Louis Arena and on the streets of Detroit.

Mike O'Connell on Yzerman's leadership: "Some great players never understand what they have to develop into. And there are other players who have gotten it. . . . The sacrifices these players make change the game so that they win more. That's what you're trying to get to in understanding Steve Yzerman. Steve made that choice, and not all players make that choice."

Yzerman accepts the Conn Smythe Trophy as playoff MVP after the 1998 Stanley Cup win.

Yzerman in action against Finland (above) and Sweden (below) at the 2002
Olympics in Salt Lake City: an opportunity to avenge the heartbreak of Nagano.

A dream lineup: Mario Lemieux, Steve Yzerman and Joe Sakic share a gold-medal moment in Salt Lake City.

We did it: Yzerman leaps into the arms of Jarome Iginla after setting up Iginla's third-period insurance goal in the gold-medal game against the United States at the 2002 Olympics. Joe Sakic scored minutes later to provide a three-goal cushion.

Night Miracle, St. Louis rebounded to force overtime, win the game, and force a seventh game in Calgary. The subsequent loss to the Flames (who went on to lose in the finals to Montreal) didn't dampen fan or management enthusiasm for Demers.

Unfortunately for the Blues, three irresistible forces converged in the summer of 1986. Harry Ornest was a handshake guy who had never signed Demers to a contract. Demers was going through a divorce and had alimony and child support payments to think about. And Jim Devellano was in the market for a new coach in Detroit and had the combination to the Ilitch vault.

When people were surprised that Demers would willingly leave a serious contender like St. Louis for a basket case like Detroit, he made the least surprising response. "Very honestly, I went for the money," he wrote in a column he penned for *USA Today* during the 2002 playoffs. "They offered me an unbelievable five-year contract. But I also liked the fact that I had the strong backing of Mr. and Mrs. Ilitch, team president Jim Lites and general manager Jimmy Devellano. The Red Wings had gone through a lot of coaches. But Jim Devellano told me he was going to stick with me come hell or high water."

"We blew them out of the water," Devellano says of the contract offer, which was more than double what Demers was then making in St. Louis. "He didn't have to think about it." It was the Ilitch way: offer more money than any reasonable person could decline. It had worked on Devellano in 1982. It worked on Demers in 1986. It would work on Scotty Bowman in 1993.

Virtually the first key test of the working relationship between Devellano and Demers came from the agreed-upon cashiering of Gare, which produced the need to appoint a new captain. Demers wanted to give the responsibility to Yzerman, who had just turned twenty-one. No one in the history of the

NHL had ever been a team captain at Yzerman's age. (Technically, Brian Bellows had been the youngest player ever to serve as an NHL captain, having filled in temporarily at nineteen for the injured Craig Hartsburg for the last half of the 1983–84 season. Hartsburg, for that matter, was only twenty-three when he became Minnesota's captain in 1982.) And because of the broken collarbone, Yzerman hadn't even played three full seasons. "For Jacques, it was Yzerman all the way," says Devellano. "I questioned it."

While some organizations have allowed the captain's job to be put to a vote of the players, it has usually been the prerogative of management to make the appointment. In labor terms, the captain might be seen as a foreman rather than a union shop steward. Most fans regard it as an on-ice job—the guy who gets to argue calls with officials and lead by example. It's also seen as the position responsible for dressing-room pep talks. But leadership in professional hockey is a far more complex task than that.

The captaincy traditionally has fallen to an experienced player, not only one of the team's key members, but someone who has been around long enough to know what it takes to lead, and is able do so with authority. A glance at the ranks of the better-known captains of the Original Six era bears this out. In Montreal, Maurice "The Rocket" Richard didn't wear the "C" until his fifteenth season, when he was thirty-five. Jean Beliveau was thirty and beginning his ninth season. In more recent Canadiens history, Bob Gainey was twenty-eight and in his ninth season when he took charge in 1981. Detroit's own storied history told a similar tale. Ted Lindsay was twenty-seven and in his ninth season; Gordie Howe was thirty and in his thirteenth season.

Granted, these were dynastic clubs, with the luxury of succession plans and enough depth in de facto team leaders that the captaincy could be passed along judiciously. In the post-WHA NHL, talent was spread thin across a twenty-one-team league, and careful succession among deep rosters was no longer necessarily an option. The draft age had dropped to eighteen, and a new generation of young players was coming into the league, players who were either in dire need of leadership from veterans, or were more amenable to being led by someone their own age.

At the time, NHL teams were all over the map when it came to their captaincies. Some had two or even three players share the job, and Toronto didn't have a captain at all from 1986–87 to 1988–89. Quite a few captains around the summer of 1986, like Denis Potvin in Long Island, Dave Taylor in Los Angeles, Peter Stastny in Quebec, Dale Hawerchuk in Winnipeg, Rod Langway in Washington, Bob Gainey in Montreal, Ron Francis in Hartford, Ray Bourque in Boston, and, of course, Wayne Gretzky in Edmonton, were acknowledged stars as well as leaders. Still, many captains were role players: Lindy Ruff in Buffalo, Darryl Sutter in Chicago and brother Brian in St. Louis, Mel Bridgman in New Jersey, Dave Poulin in Philadelphia, Mike Bullard and Terry Ruskowski in Pittsburgh, and Ron Greschner with the Rangers.

Nevertheless, the league was on something of a youth kick—or more precisely, a young scoring superstars kick—in the appointment of captains. Rick Vaive had been named captain of the Leafs when he was twenty-two in 1981–82, when the corrosive relationship between owner Harold Ballard and erstwhile captain Darryl Sittler prompted Ballard first to offer to pay Sittler not to attend training camp and then strip him of the leader's role. Sittler got his trade wish and was sent to Philadelphia in midseason. (Sittler had inherited the captaincy from Dave Keon, when *his* feud with Ballard propelled him into the WHA in 1975.)

Wayne Gretzky was twenty-two when he was made captain of the Edmonton Oilers for the 1983–84 season. At the time of Yzerman's appointment, Gretzky's youthful captaincy was the league's best known, and other teams followed Edmonton's example of opting for both youth and star power. Dale Hawerchuk set the acknowledged record for youth, being twenty-one when Winnipeg named him captain for the 1984–85 season. If Devellano agreed to Demers's plan to appoint Yzerman, he would best Hawerchuk's record by one month. In 1987–88 another twenty-one-year-old, Kirk Muller, would get the job in New Jersey at the start of his fourth season (he was three months older than Yzerman was when he first wore the "C" on his jersey), while Mario Lemieux would assume the captaincy at twenty-two in Pittsburgh, in the middle of his fourth season.

But Gretzky was an exception to every rule of talent, and because Glen Sather was building his entire franchise around him, it was inevitable that he would take a formal leadership role in Edmonton, regardless of his age. Indeed, the entire Oilers experience was so freakishly unique that the Gretzky captaincy probably shouldn't have been an inspiration to other teams to follow suit. In any event, Gretzky, who had turned pro when he was only seventeen, wasn't rushed into the captain's role: Sather had given it Ron Chipperfield, then Blair MacDonald, then Lee Fogolin—who led the team into its first Stanley Cup final in the spring of 1983—before deciding Gretzky was ready to inherit the job from Fogolin, who stayed on with the team.

At the same time, Gretzky was being asked to lead an exceptionally young team. He didn't have a roster full of veterans, flighty superstars or troublesome fringe talents to corral. And with such a young team, he also didn't have much in the way of the often-incendiary ingredient called "players' wives" to deal with. Finally, the entire Oilers squad had Sather overseeing them, a former NHLer who served as a father figure to many players, Gretzky included.

There is no set blueprint for the job of captain. Whoever hopes to do the job well is supposed to know something about managing human beings, working between and with players and management, and not merely set an example on the ice, much less lead in points production. "You're looking for somebody to bring harmony to the dressing room," says Devellano. "They have to keep the players together, break down the cliques of old guys and new guys, and keep the wives from fighting. Organize a couple barbecues to get people together off the ice." And God help a captain if players start sleeping with each others' wives or girlfriends.

Devellano didn't think Demers's proposal to promote Yzerman was such a good idea—at least, not yet. He was bringing in more veterans—not just over-the-hill stars who might sell a few tickets to curiosity seekers, but experienced role players. He cut a deal that July with the Rangers for goaltender Glen Hanlon, who'd been playing in the NHL since 1977–78 and had been a teammate in Vancouver of defenseman Harold Snepts, whom Devellano had signed as a free agent in the summer of 1985. They were both players with enough experience and character to provide leadership. Most important, Devellano had just acquired Dave Lewis as an unrestricted free agent from New Jersey. He had drafted Lewis in 1973, and then shipped him to Los Angeles for Butch Goring on the eve of the Islanders' first Cup win. Lewis was then traded to the Devils at the start of the 1983-84 season, after serving as captain of the Kings for two seasons. His career was winding down, and Devellano had longer-term plans for him, in the coaching ranks. He was hoping that Lewis could serve as an interim captain in his last seasons before Yzerman, when he was judged ready, took over the official team leadership.

"I thought he was too young," Devellano says of Yzerman in 1986. "I suggested to Demers that he name Dave Lewis the captain. He had been the captain of the Kings, and had grown up in the tremendously successful New York Islanders system. I thought, for one or two years, he could be a 'bridge' captain."

Devellano's strategy—and his concerns—hearkened back to the way the Islanders' leadership had been structured in the franchise's formative years. While Devellano and Torrey were building a contender through draft picks, the captaincy was held by a gentlemanly old hand acquired from Boston in the expansion draft, Ed Westfall. The Isles then went through the debacle of the captaincy being turned over to a young star, Clark Gillies, who ended up finding the job too much to bear. Twenty-two when he was made captain in February 1977, Gillies had only been drafted in 1974 and was in the middle of his third season.

There had been previous attempts in the 1970s to make a young star into a captain. Defenseman Jim Schoenfeld was only twenty-two—the youngest in league history at the time—and beginning his third season when he got the job in Buffalo in October 1974 after the incumbent, Gerry Meehan, was traded to Vancouver. Injuries, mononucleosis and viral pneumonia plagued Schoenfeld's ice time over the next few seasons, and the captaincy passed to Danny Gare in 1977–78. More successfully in Philadelphia, Bobby Clarke took over the Flyers captaincy from an Original Six character player, Ed Van Impe, when he was twenty-three, during the 1972–73 season. Clarke had just come through the formative experience of the Canada–Soviet series that September, and he led the Flyers to two mid-decade Stanley Cup wins.

For Gillies, however, the captaincy weighed heavily through several disappointing playoff drives, culminating in a crushing failure in the semifinals against the Rangers in the spring of 1979, a year in which the Islanders had been strongly favored to win it all. The team had finished atop the league with 51 wins; Bryan Trottier won the Hart and Art Ross trophies, Denis Potvin the Norris, Al Arbour the Adams (for coach of the year). Five Islanders were named to the postseason All-Star teams—three of them, including Gillies, to the First Team. At the start of the 1979–80 season, Gillies announced that he no longer felt comfortable in the captain's role. Denis Potvin took over, and the streak of Stanley Cup wins began. The change in leadership wasn't the sole cause of the Islanders' transformation, but Gillies at least had the self-awareness to acknowledge that someone else needed to try to help the club to the Stanley Cup success so widely expect of them.

"Sometimes, being the captain is a burden," says Lewis. "Some players relish it. Some fumble it."

Astute clubs have always known that the captaincy should never be handed to a star player just because the "C" looks good on them, creating a stronger marketing vehicle for the team in the process. And even stars who are capable of serving in the role are sometimes passed over, in everyone's best interest. The accompanying responsibilities (most of which occur beyond the prying eyes of fans and media) can drag down the performance of a top player and do nothing for the team overall. Guy Lafleur steered clear of the role in Montreal in the 1970s; Bobby Orr and Phil Esposito were allowed to lead in their own ways in Boston while Johnny Bucyk played the official role. It was a good question in 1986 whether or not a captaincy could damage Steve Yzerman's young career.

Devellano says Demers agreed with him about Dave Lewis's leadership qualities, but nevertheless was adamant that Yzerman should get the captaincy right away. "Our franchise is going to be Yzerman," Devellano recalls Demers telling him. "You're building the team around him. Make him the captain."

"I did not pick Steve Yzerman to be captain because he was going to be the best player on the team—and he already was at the time," says Demers. "Because, how would you like to have Jaromir Jagr as your captain?" Demers says the inspiration to promote Yzerman came right after he was hired, at the entry draft in June 1986 in Montreal. "Who shows up at the draft," Demers says, "but Steve Yzerman?" It was a minor coincidence that Demers was the opposing coach when the broken collarbone had ended Yzerman's 1985–86 season. Yzerman had jumped in his car and driven from Nepean to Montreal when he got the news about Demers's hiring. "I said, 'Steve, what are you doing here?' And he said, 'I wanted to introduce myself to the new coach.'"

You had to know Yzerman to know that this was not some idle social call. Making small talk, Demers asked him what kind of summer he was having. "He said it was a miserable summer. 'I can't stand the kind of season we had.' And as I talked to him, he was low-key, not excited." (Demers says people still mistake Yzerman's inherent shyness for cockiness.) "But there was an immediate understanding from a kid who was just twenty-one that it was not acceptable for his team to play like that.

"So I thought about it. It was a very emotional decision." Demers spoke with Yzerman's father, as well as his junior coach, Dick Todd, to see if they thought he could handle the responsibility. He came away convinced that Yzerman could.

Todd doesn't recall the conversation he had with Demers. But by then, he had already witnessed Yzerman's growing appreciation of what it would take for the Red Wings to win. In the spring of 1985, with the Wings having been knocked out in the first round of the playoffs, Yzerman showed up in Windsor to watch Todd's Petes play the Spitfires in the Memorial Cup play-downs. The loss to Chicago had been demoralizing—a three-game sweep in which they went down 9–5, 6–1 and 8–2. Todd recalls: "He said to me, 'You've really got things the way you want them. You've got four balanced lines. You've got the team concept. That's the way you do things, isn't it?' Looking back, I can see that he really analyzed things. He realized that they were losing, and that it might be more fun to win, and that there were different ways that you could win. He'd started thinking about it then. Maybe it didn't happen for another twelve years, but I think that the concept of Detroit winning as a team was there in him."

"I had just come off St. Louis, where we had gone to the conference finals," says Demers, "and had Brian Sutter as captain, who was *dedicated* to his team." Brian Sutter had been made captain of St. Louis in 1979–80 at the start of his fourth season (before Demers was coach there), when he was just turning twenty-three. After speaking with Yzerman in Montreal, Demers was sure he was dealing with the same sort of dedication. "The Red Wings," he says, "meant a lot to him."

"Nobody's perfect," Demers says. "But he has such great qualities. I don't believe that because you're an athlete you should be a hero. But there's a guy you can say: he's a hero to a lot of kids. Because he's exemplary off the ice. His family, his girls, are a priority. He's dedicated to his profession, and loyal to a fault. With the Red Wings, it wasn't easy for him there at first, but he never asked to be traded."

Demers went to Jim Devellano, team president Jim Lites and Mike Ilitch with his request to make Yzerman the new captain. "When they hire a new coach and give you a five-year deal," he says, "it's not like they're going to shoot down the first thing you ask for. There was 'No, no,' but they showed confidence in my judgment. And Steve looked like a *boy* at the time." In an effort to look older, Yzerman began cultivating a week's growth of stubble.

Devellano says Demers knew there would be experienced players, like Lewis, Hanlon and Snepts, to lend Yzerman a hand. "And they did," says Devellano. "They were veterans, and they knew how to behave. Dave Lewis did a lot of things in those years without wearing the 'C.' I give Jacques a lot of credit for having the guts to make a young guy like Yzerman a captain in a locker room full of veterans."

So Yzerman became the Red Wings' captain. "Jacques made a good decision," Devellano says.

"You have to understand the state of the team," says Lewis. "When I got there, they hadn't made the playoffs, had gotten 40 points the year before, and they had some young players, along with this young, budding star. Jimmy and the organization had to make some changes. Jimmy wanted to bring veterans in because of their stability. They don't seem to get as rattled or as frustrated, as long as you have quality veterans." Lewis says Yzerman did turn to the veterans Devellano deliberately had surrounded him with— himself, Hanlon, Mike O'Connell, Snepts, Tim Higgins—for assistance and guidance. These were "players who had kicked around the league a bit and understood what the league was about," says Lewis. He notes that Hanlon is now a coach and O'Connell a manager, and that Gerard Gallant, although part of the younger crowd, has become a coach as well. Gallant also served as captain in Yzerman's stead for the last two months of the 1987–88 season when Yzerman was injured. Like Yzerman, he was quiet, an on-ice leader who had the respect of the league overall and could also provide leadership in the dressing room. "There was a good group of people that Stevie could draw on," says Lewis. "And he did draw on the people. We whispered in his ear when he wasn't sure what to do or when to do it."

Yzerman at least had been through the odd dynamics of the Peterborough Petes, where, because of the transition to a younger draft age, the youngest players also tended to be the most skilled and most valued. It was a situation not unlike that in Detroit, where the new recruits like Yzerman and Gallant were seen as the team's future, and many older players were in a position of having to defend their jobs and wonder what had happened to traditional dressing-room seniority.

The fact that Yzerman went on to be the NHL's longest-serving captain, and a team leader who would help bring three Stanley Cups to Detroit, would seem to make Demers's decision, as Devellano says, a good one. But not everyone is sure that Yzerman was a suitable choice. It wasn't a question of whether or not he deserved the job, but whether or not he deserved to be thrust into that role at that stage of his career.

"It was unfair," Mike O'Connell says flatly. The defenseman whose skills had so impressed Ken Linseman both in junior and the NHL had been sent by Boston to Detroit for Reed Larson in March 1986. His 1986–87 season, his first full one as a Red Wing, was also Yzerman's first season as team captain. O'Connell would finish out his playing career in Detroit in 1989–90 before moving into coaching the next season, with the San Diego Gulls of the International Hockey League. Today he is general manager and vice president of the Boston Bruins, an organization that is carefully grooming Joe Thornton, the league's first pick overall in the 1997 entry draft, to be the game's Next Big Thing, a scoring star who can also lead.

Thornton was twenty-three when he was made the Bruins' captain at the start of the 2002–03 season. (And Thornton chose to wear number 19 because of his admiration for Yzerman.) O'Connell can look back at Yzerman's earlier, youthful captaincy, which began when he was two years younger than Thornton, and wonder if the Red Wings appreciated what they were asking of him.

Being captain, O'Connell says, "is just really hard for a young guy, because he hasn't experienced enough. It's tough for a young player to understand that he has to concern himself not just with his own play, but with the play of everyone else on that team. It's not that young guys *can't* do it, but they just haven't been through enough to be able to see that maybe certain players aren't getting a fair shake from the coach, or may not be playing as well as they should, or are drinking too much. They haven't seen enough to know what is enough, and what isn't, in different situations.

"Whether it was tough for Steve, I don't know, but it was a lot to ask. I can't look back and say he did a terrible job, because he didn't. But to put a burden like that on someone that age . . ."

"It *is* unfair," Bob Errey agrees, to ask a player as young as Yzerman was to do the captain's job, and he repeats O'Connell's main point: "You haven't been through enough." Errey firmly believes that Yzerman may prove to be one of the greatest leaders in the history of the NHL, but that doesn't change the fact that he was asked to become a great leader when players his age usually were scarcely out of junior.

Errey spent a long time trying to find his own place in the professional game. While Yzerman was enjoying nascent stardom in Detroit, he was struggling to even earn a starting position in the NHL. After his first disappointing year in Pittsburgh, when his old Petes center was vying for the Calder Trophy, Errey spent the better part of two seasons in the minors. He finally secured a regular role with Pittsburgh in 1986–87, just as Yzerman was becoming an NHL captain, and he did it by retooling himself as a defensive forward. Despite having been touted by the Penguins as a scoring machine when he was drafted, Errey's marketable skills lay in the defensive game that had been drummed into him by Dick Todd. As a forward, "It's not easy just to play defense," he says. "And I was smart enough to realize that I wasn't going to make it scoring ten goals a year."

Errey showed heart, and hustle, and what's been called a terrier-like determination to come up with the puck in the opponent's end. And he showed a commitment to backchecking and shot blocking that was rare in the Penguins lineup as a championship team began to gel around Mario Lemieux. He played a widely acknowledged role as a dressing-room leader on the model of Yzerman and Gallant, and as a workhorse who covered the offensive rushes of stars like Lemieux and Paul Coffey (while chipping in 20 goals a season himself) as the Penguins won back-to-back Stanley Cups in 1991 and '92.

After signing as a free agent with San Jose in the summer of 1993, Errey became captain of the Sharks. He was twenty-nine years old, had been in the NHL for ten years, and had just won a pair of Stanley Cups with Pittsburgh.

Becoming captain, Errey says, "was better for me at that point. I was also voted in by my peers. I had a lot to draw on, and reflect on. There were the two Stanley Cups, but also all that had gone before that. There's a learning curve that comes with being with so many players and so many coaches.

"As a captain," Errey explains, "you're almost an 'in-between,' someone between a coach and a player. The coach will ask you things he wouldn't ask any other player—how he should deal with this or that situation. You have to have a pretty good feel for players."

In Pittsburgh, he'd been exposed to an array of quality players who demonstrated leadership, for the team's depth in that department went far beyond Mario Lemieux's captaincy. The Penguins had Ron Francis, one of the game's great stars and class acts; they had Paul Coffey, who had won three Cups with Edmonton before being traded away as a cost-cutting measure; they had Rick Tocchet, who had reached the Cup finals against Edmonton with Philadelphia in 1987 and was a member of Canada's winning Canada Cup squad in 1987 (and again in 1991). And they had Bryan Trottier, who had already won four Cups with the Islanders and was one of the game's great two-way players.

Errey learned from all of them en route to becoming a team leader in San Jose. Compared to Errey, Yzerman was grossly unprepared, in his life and game experiences, for the difficult challenge of being what O'Connell calls "a young man who is expected to lead a group of twenty highly compensated people."

"I agree with that," says Gerard Gallant of the idea that asking Yzerman to assume the captaincy was unfair to him. "At that time, Stevie was a quiet guy. He was a great guy in the dressing room, but with all the other stuff outside of the room, it was really tough for him. It's tough on anybody, and not an easy job for a young person to do. But we were in a transitional time as a team. We'd had a lot of older guys like Danny Gare and Darryl Sittler, who were at the end of their careers. And a lot of new guys were coming in, seven or eight in two or three years. There weren't a whole lot of 'medium' guys, players in the middle of their careers, to make captain. Jacques was an emotional guy, and once he'd made his mind up, that was pretty well it.

"Everybody was gung ho for it. It was, 'Stevie's a young kid, he's going to be here for a long time, and that's a great thing.' So they figured, 'Steve's been here for a couple years, and it's time for

a change of leadership.' At that time, it seemed like a great decision. But a year or two down the road, I'm sure they would have
said, 'Well, it would have been great to have a guy with a little
more experience to put that burden on.'

"It didn't affect him," Gallant emphasizes. "It's just that our
team wasn't that good at the time, and that was frustrating for
him. And how do you bring him in to mold the veteran guys, to
tell them to pull their weight and get it going? It was really tough
on him in that situation, but he handled it very well."

Demers discounts the idea that he might have been asking
too much of Yzerman. "My thinking at the time was the same as
Mike O'Connell's: Was I putting too much a burden on him? But
actually, I didn't, because he took off with that responsibility. He
led us to the playoffs that year." Demers says he was conscious of
Yzerman's age, but notes that maturity isn't automatically indi-
cated by a player's birth year. "Vincent Lecavalier at eighteen was
a very mature guy." He names a player he had in Detroit who at
twenty "was not mature. Steve Yzerman at twenty-one was way
ahead of his time."

It was Lecavalier who broke Yzerman's record for youngest
NHL captain when he was named captain of the Tampa Bay
Lightning near the end of his rookie season in 1999–2000,
shortly before he turned twenty. Lecavalier was fully aware of
whose record he was breaking. "I've always liked what Steve
Yzerman has done in Detroit," he told John Kreiser in an article
published in *Hockey Digest* in February 2001. "Steve's always been
great on and off the ice. Any player would be proud to be like
Yzerman." However, Lecavalier's youthful reign lasted only two
seasons in Tampa Bay.

The period in which he assumed the captaincy was difficult
for Yzerman personally. The lineup changes Devellano made after

the debacle of 1985–86 may have gained him levelheaded veterans who could help him, but this also cost him some friends. Fellow center Claude Loiselle and right winger Lane Lambert, young guys who had broken in with the Red Wings at the same time he had, were shipped out in midsummer trades in exchange for experience. For Loiselle, Devellano received right winger Tim Higgins, who had already played nine seasons with Chicago and New Jersey; Lambert was part of the multiplayer deal that brought in Glen Hanlon. (Among other newcomers was Lee Norwood, the player who had broken Yzerman's collarbone. He was brought in at Demers's behest in a trade in August 1986.) Not particularly outgoing to begin with, Yzerman reacted to the changes by withdrawing. "Our team wasn't close at all," he would tell Austin Murphy in a *Sports Illustrated* profile published in the February 8, 1988, issue. "After practices and games, everybody went their own way, and so did I."

"I don't think you should make young guys captain just because they're your best guy," says Errey. While the criticism is not leveled specifically at the Red Wings, he feels it's important to understand a captain's time-consuming duties away from the rink, which few fans appreciate—and which not all team front offices appear to appreciate these days, as they choose captains based more on fan popularity than the actual job description.

For instance, captains have an obligation to ensure that newcomers are properly settled into their new community and are made to feel as much a part of a team as can be managed in a business in which trades mean good friends are here today, opponents tomorrow. Skills like these may sound trivial, even demeaning to the stature of a celebrity athlete, but mastering them is absolutely critical to the captain's job of creating a cohesive team that is capable of fulfilling its objectives on the ice.

"You have to know how to welcome players when they come into the organization," says Errey. "Even the captain's wife has different responsibilities than the wives of other players. There are families that have to be made happy. New players ask the captain everything. He's the guy they think is going to give them the reliable information. It's, 'Who's your dentist? Who's your doctor? Where are your kids going to school? Who's your realtor? Where do I buy a car? Where do I rent one? Who do I trust in that regard?' Honest to God, it's a whole list of things that *anyone* asks when they come into a community. It really is amazing, everything that has to be answered. And for hockey players, moves are certainly often more temporary. Everything's quick. You get in there, and you have to get the family moved in, figure out the school district . . ."

Yzerman was not a family man when he took over the captaincy. He was young and single, driving a sports car, living in a condo in the well-off suburb of West Bloomfield, about twenty miles northwest of downtown Detroit, a pretty township of lakes, recreational areas and golf courses (which he frequented). He kept in close touch with friends and family in Nepean, who would come to Detroit to keep him company, and he became engaged to Lisa Brennan, who was attending Algonquin College back home in Ottawa, during the 1987–88 season. There were no kids underfoot yet (there would be three daughters, the first of them born in 1994), no experience with school boards or pediatricians to draw on. But Lord knows he did his best to be welcoming and accommodating as a team captain in his first seasons in the role.

Lewis can remember discussing with Yzerman what they should do about a team Halloween party, and agreeing together that Lewis, who was married with kids, should have it at his house. Mike O'Connell personally experienced Yzerman trying to do the right thing on a club which was not always cohesive, and which started to (again) go south in the win column after an initial flush of success under Demers.

Around Christmas 1990, during O'Connell's last season with Detroit (and in the professional game), his wife was expecting and the family wasn't able to attend the Red Wings' traditional family skate. "Steve called my house and said, 'Listen, Mike, I know you and Rose are expecting any day and you've got people in. Do you want me to take your kids to the skating party?'" Having their six-year old son, Greg, go with the team captain sounded like a great idea. "Rose goes, 'Greg, Steve Yzerman's on the phone. He's going to pick you up and take you to the skating party.' And Greg says, 'I don't want to go. I don't even *like* Steve Yzerman.'"

Mike O'Connell still laughs at the memory of his son's obstinacy. "And *of course* he liked him. He was just lazy and didn't want to go. I said, 'Greg, any kid in Detroit would give their left eye or their left arm to hop in a Porsche with Steve and go skate around with him.' So Greg went, and he had a great time.

"Steve thought that way. He knew I couldn't go. He knew I liked going to those things and bringing the kids."

"He's always been thoughtful," says Gallant. "As good a guy as he is on the ice, he's a great guy off the ice. My family grew up with him. Steve and Lisa are the godparents of my first daughter, Melissa. When new guys were traded to us during the season, Steve would say, 'You come live with me until your family is settled here.' Paul Coffey [who was traded to Detroit in January 1993] lived with him for a year, and Steve Thomas is with him now [in the fall of 2003]. He *cares* about people. Other guys will be, like, 'How ya doin', nice to see ya, hope you'll get settled in here.'"

That aspect of Yzerman has never changed. Dave Lewis notes how, on the 2003 U.S. Thanksgiving weekend, Yzerman personally looked after two new Red Wings, Jamie Rivers and Mark Mowers, who had no family in town. Yzerman's own family had gone to Florida, so he took Rivers and Mowers to a Detroit Lions football game and then to Oakland Hills Country Club for a Thanksgiving dinner. "Steve figured, 'These guys are young and nobody's here with them,' so he grabbed them and said, 'Come with me,'" Lewis says.

"Steve is a thoughtful guy and the Red Wings are his team," says Gallant. "And when people become part of that team, he wants to make sure everything is taken care of with them. He's just a quality person."

Demers remembers the duties Yzerman had to struggle with away from the rink, the Halloween parties and the rest, and acknowledges their importance. But he has no regrets about having made Yzerman captain when he did. Yzerman, he says, "is the greatest player I've ever coached, and I've coached guys who are in the Hall of Fame. We had a real solid rapport. Steve is not the kind of guy who's going to suckhole a coach, trying to get favors. He would defend his teammates [in front of me]. And if he wasn't happy with the way a guy had practiced, he'd tell him, but he wouldn't make a scene so everyone in the building would know.

"The greatest contribution Steve Yzerman has made as captain of the Red Wings has been on the ice," says Demers. "Some of the greatest captains of the Montreal Canadiens, like Bob Gainey, who was very respected, were made on the ice. Steve Yzerman *led* this team, like any good captain does." It's an echo of the leadership by example that Dick Todd saw Yzerman and Errey provide in Peterborough while still in their teens. "I've been fortunate in my career to have had absolutely solid captains, like

Brian Sutter, Guy Carbonneau, Mike Keane," Demers adds. "I have seen the captains who rah-rah—'Keep your fucking head up, you fucking guys, practice harder!'—and do not produce."

And so Yzerman stepped up to the proverbial plate to meet the challenge of leading a troubled team, while striving to establish a career that was only three seasons old and that had already been interrupted by one serious injury. The next few seasons were full of wildly contradictory moments for him—celebrated on one hand, ignored or vilified on another, with people (even some within the Red Wings organization) increasingly wondering if he had the mettle to lead a strong team to a Stanley Cup victory. Clark Gillies had shown the good sense to get out of the heavy traffic of the captaincy and still contribute to the string of Cup victories that the Islanders did enjoy. With Yzerman, there would never be any doubt that he saw himself as the captain of the Red Wings, and only the Red Wings. He would have to find out if his own team was willing to let him keep trying to lead them to a championship.

SIX

"We needed somebody to come in and make a big impact," Jim Devellano says of the decision to hire Jacques Demers. "And he sure as hell did."

For a few seasons, Jacques Demers proved to be the necessary tonic for the Red Wings' woes. Demers became the first (and so far the only) person to win the league's coaching award, the Jack Adams, two seasons in a row, as Detroit rebounded from the wretched performance of 1985–86 to finish second, and then first, in the Norris Division. In those two seasons, the team's points improved from 40 to 93, rising to the fourth-best record in the league, and goals for were boosted from 266 to 322 (third best), as goals against receded from 415 to 269 (sixth best).

In considering the reputation that the team had before he arrived in the summer of 1986, of being fractured by cliques and "selfish" play, Dave Lewis counsels: "Older players who worry about their jobs feel that young players are taking them. Jimmy decided to bring in a different group of veterans. And that group's mentality was, 'Well, this is sort of our last real chance. Let's rally around each other and let some of these young guys play and see what we can get done.' It was a pretty good run for a couple of years."

That pretty good run took the Red Wings to the third round of the playoffs in both 1987 and 1988. A new rivalry was born (or, rather, a very old Original Six one revived) with the Toronto Maple Leafs, as the two teams twice met in the opening round. Detroit squeezed by Toronto in seven games in 1987, in six in 1988. In the division finals, the Wings handled the Blackhawks in four straight in 1987, the Blues in five in 1988. Both playoff runs delivered them to the doorstep of the Edmonton Oilers for the conference finals. And each campaign ended with a 4–1 series loss to the Oilers, who went on to win their third and fourth Stanley Cups. But the Red Wings gave the Oilers a legitimate scare, playing a close-checking game and showing no respect for the unwritten no-go zone around Wayne Gretzky. Time and again, the Oilers had to pull out a win in the final minutes of play.

Had the Red Wings been able to get by the Oilers, they would have made their first Stanley Cup finals appearances since the spring of 1966, but no one, not even the Red Wings themselves, really thought that was possible. "Steve and I talked about it all the time, how good it would be to win a Stanley Cup," says Gerard Gallant. "The first seven years we were there, we had no chance to win the Cup, and we knew that."

In those years, says Gallant, "Steve was the key offensive guy on our team, a superstar. And he had to get a lot of points for us to get better. We didn't have a whole bunch of Fedorovs. Steve never, *ever* cared about getting fifty goals, or seventy-five goals. He just cared about winning, and when our team wasn't winning in the first years, it was frustrating. Many nights, we'd go for pizza after the game, after getting beaten 10–3 by Minnesota, and talk about it. But each year we'd build on what we'd done, and it got to be a little more fun, like when we lost to Edmonton in the semifinals two years in a row. The team was getting better and

Steve was getting better. He was playing a more complete game. He was starting to block shots and do all that stuff. Not stuff he didn't do before, but he knew that for our team to take the next step, he'd have to do things like that."

Jacques Demers emphasizes that Yzerman was already doing the two-way job when he coached him in the late 1980s that people would only begin to credit him with when he was a Stanley Cup champion in the late 1990s. "Steve was on the first unit of penalty killing. He blocked shots. When Steve started winning Stanley Cups, he was surrounded with better players. He carried the Red Wings for years."

When John Ogrodnick was traded away in 1987, a spot opened for Gallant on Yzerman's left wing. For Gallant, those seasons were the pinnacle of his career. "We were the best of friends, and he was just a pleasure to play with. He enjoys playing the game, and that's what's made him a superstar and such a character player. I was the type of guy who went to the net hard, who picked up pucks in the corner. Steve was the kind of guy who could find you all over the ice. He was so crafty with the puck, making the great plays and great passes. If I got the puck from the defenseman and got it to the middle, he'd be there. He *always* knew where to be. The best thing about him was that he wasn't a guy who was just going to play the middle of the ice. He'd forecheck and work in the corners. It wasn't like he thought, 'I'm the superstar on this line, so get me the puck.' He bumped, he banged, he worked both ends of the rink.

"I probably played with him for five years, and watched him perform, in and out, every night. He wasn't just a straight scorer or point getter. Every night, he'd bring his game to the table. And he was never going to bitch at you. Some nights are off nights. You don't play as well, and that's part of the game.

But he wasn't going to come over to you and say, 'You're slipping.' He'd blame himself."

For a time, the pair had Bob Probert on their line, "a physical guy who kept people off Yzerman's back. But Steve was never intimidated by guys shadowing him. If you shut down Yzerman then, you shut down our team. But he battled through it every night."

Gallant produced more than 70 points in 1986–87 and 1987–88, and in 1988–89 had a career-high 93 points, which earned him a position on the Second All-Star Team. He was the first Red Wing to be named to an All-Star team since John Ogrodnick made the First Team in 1984–85. It was telling somehow that two of Yzerman's left wingers had now been named All-Stars, but not Yzerman himself.

After having his third season shortened by the broken collarbone, Yzerman's offensive production began to pick up. The 1986–87 season was another typical Yzerman outing: 31 goals, 59 assists, 90 points—not much different from his first two seasons. But in 1987–88, when he and Gallant clicked, Yzerman had a fifty-goal season, with 102 points in all, which he amassed in only 64 games. No sooner had he scored his milestone goal, in a game against Buffalo on March 1, 1988, than his season was finished by an injury that would stalk him for the rest of his career.

The fiftieth goal came in The Joe at 3:26 of the second period, in front of 19,418 ecstatic fans. Yzerman fired a backhand past the Sabres' Tom Barrasso, and the building, and the Wings bench, erupted. Jacques Demers leapt atop the bench and began applauding; his teammates pounded the boards with their gloves. It was only the fourth time in Red Wings history that a player had scored fifty goals in a season. Mickey Redmond had done it twice in the early '70s. Then there was John Ogrodnick, with Yzerman's help, in 1984–85. But no one on the team had reached the mark as quickly as Yzerman had just done.

Yzerman collected the historic puck—and flung it into the audience, horrifying Demers. His coach went after the puck, trading another one, plus an autographed stick, with the cooperative fan who caught it. "I was so proud of [Yzerman]," Demers told Keith Gave of the *Detroit Free Press* after the game. "I made him my captain, and he never once failed me. He never even came close to failing me."

Demers by then was sounding like a man delivering a eulogy. Because, eleven minutes after goal number fifty, the euphoria that had gripped The Joe shifted to abject despair as the team's captain and star was helped from the ice. Trainer Jim Pengelly was supporting Yzerman under one arm; assistant trainer Larry Wasylin held him up by the other. Yzerman's right skate wasn't touching the ice. His season was finished, his career in jeopardy.

It scarcely bears mentioning that hockey is a dangerous game. The world's fastest team sport, played on ice, with full contact permitted and encouraged, presents near-infinite opportunities for injury. A study by the University of Michigan Medical School of twenty-two Junior A players, published in April 1999, found eighty-three separate injuries among them in just one season. Even with players wearing helmets, visors and mouth guards, the study found that the greatest number of injuries—42 percent—occurred to the head and face, with 27 percent to the upper body and 31 percent in the lower body.

The Michigan study also identified some trends in how—or when—injuries are sustained that are now widely accepted. The authors found that, in addition to players in general being twenty times more likely to be injured in a game than in a practice, injuries clustered in definite temporal patterns. They happened more often near the end of a period, near the end of a game, and overall in the first half of the studied season. The inescapable conclusion was that conditioning was an important factor in avoiding injury. Players who began the season in top physical shape, and could maintain a high level of conditioning, could avoid the fatigue that placed them at much higher risk for getting hurt. Yzerman had played sixteen NHL seasons by the time the Michigan study revealed the link between stamina and injury avoidance, but his long-standing commitment to off-season training and in-season conditioning had already paid off in a lengthy career with mercifully few serious injuries.

Many hockey injuries, such as cuts to the face (or a broken nose, as Yzerman experienced in his rookie NHL season) are treated quickly enough that the player might not even miss a shift. Muscle bruises and other aches might send a player out of a game early, but are often healed in time to allow them not to miss a subsequent game. The types of injuries that cause professionals to sit out games have a particular distribution of sore points.

The list of NHLers out of action at the 2003–04 Christmas break provides a sobering variety of ways in which a player can sustain damage grave enough to force him to miss at least one game. There were 109 players on injured lists at the break, not counting a handful of "personal" (generally, substance abuse) cases. With twenty-one players dressed for any game in a thirty-team league, this translates into a theoretical "time lost" injury rate of 18 percent. About two dozen different injury types appeared, including a case of the flu. Hands, fingers, thumbs, elbows, jaws, eyes, thighs, necks, ribs, wrists, backs, and pelvic areas all took a beating. By far the most common injuries were to the shoulder and knee (17 percent each), followed by groin (10 percent), ankle (8 percent) and concussion (6 percent). This snapshot of the midseason wounded jibes with the general medical wisdom about hockey's more serious injuries. The game exacts a steep toll on shoulders and knees, and a further toll on brains through concussions.

Among the litany of ways for a player to be seriously hurt, only a few are considered career killers. Shoulders are prone to separation and ligament tears through upper-body collisions, but they are generally repairable. Ankles get beaten up through slashes and shot blocking, but they, too, heal. So do the mangled fingers, bruised ribs and pulled groin muscles. Concussions have recently begun ending careers because those involved with the game have become sufficiently enlightened about the long-term effects of repeated brain injuries that players now choose retirement before serious damage sets in. The loss of an eye can finish a player, but an already rare occurrence has been made even more rare by the increased use of protective visors. (When Yzerman nearly lost his left eye to an errant puck in the 2003–04 playoffs, he vowed to begin wearing a visor.)

Historically, the most likely things to finish off a hockey player are bad knees. Hockey knee injuries are in a class of their own, distinct from those seen in football and soccer. In turf-sport knee injuries, ligament damage—whether a sprain or a complete tear—is usually caused by twisting, when the foot is firmly planted in the turf and the leg and body above the knee are wrenched. While this kind of injury, which primarily damages anterior cruciate ligaments—the ACLs—does occur in hockey (a serious ACL tear in November 1995 was the trigger for Pavel Bure's knee problems), it is far more common to see injuries to the medial collateral ligament (MCL), which among other things serves as the main restraint against inward motion of the shin bone (tibia) on the thigh bone (femur).

As with a slalom racer carving a turn on the inside edge of a

ski, a hockey player's MCL endures particular strain as the skate
blade digs into the ice to produce forward thrust. The strain is
compounded by hits on the outside of the knee, which drive the
knee sideways, and these hits are even more dangerous when the
joint is flexed, as it typically is while skating. The MCL is the
knee's line of defense against buckling inward, and it doesn't often
tear completely, although it can be torn, along with the ACL, in
a twisting type of injury.

The real career-ending damage comes not from the injuries
suffered by ligaments, but the cascading effect on the knee's
internal structure. As anyone familiar with the downward trajectory of Bobby Orr's playing career knows, hockey players are susceptible to damage to the articular cartilage on the bones that
form the knee joint, and to the connective tissues—the menisci—
which are crescent-shaped pads between the tibia and femur on
the inside and outside of the knee. The cartilage and menisci can
degenerate through the general wear and tear of athletics, but the
deterioration can be exacerbated by injured ligaments, particularly if slackness sets in.

As it happened, when Yzerman did seriously injure his knee
on March 1, 1988, it was not a textbook hockey calamity, nor a
sports calamity in general—it was more like something a car accident would produce. He had come up with the loose puck in the
left corner of the Sabres' end of the rink and made a drive for the
net. Buffalo's rookie defenseman Calle Johansson tried to slow
him down; the two men became tangled, and then piled into
Barrasso as well. Yzerman went down awkwardly; Johannson
thought that perhaps Yzerman had stepped on his stick. However
he got there, his right knee took the full impact of his collision
with the Sabres' left goalpost.

Barrasso didn't think Yzerman had hit the post very hard,

"but he hit it at a bad angle." Play stopped with Yzerman writhing in pain and trainer Jim Pengelly making a desperate sprint across the ice in sneakers. The Red Wings franchise was in agony in front of a capacity home crowd which, until this moment, had been enjoying the buzz of Yzerman's fiftieth goal (as well as his fifty-second assist), in a game that was headed toward Glen Hanlon's third shutout of the year, in a season that was promising the team its first-ever Norris Division title.

Yzerman would be gripped by a case of the what-ifs. "I keep saying to myself, 'Why did you go to the net? Why didn't you cut back?'" he told the *Free Press*'s Curt Sylvester. "But injuries are part of the game."

"My heart went from where it was supposed to be down to my toes, and I think it's still there," Jim Devellano confessed to the *Free Press*'s Keith Gave after the game. Never one to mask his emotions, Demers declared himself to be in shock. But the coincidence of the fifty-goal performance and the injury didn't surprise him. "That's fate," he declared cryptically and with a trademark emotional flamboyance. "I believe in fate, and it came true tonight."

The impact with the Sabres goalpost spared Yzerman's ACLs and MCLs, instead tearing his posterior cruciate ligament, which is located in the center of the knee and prevents the shinbone from flexing too far backward.

Yzerman was hustled to Madison, Wisconsin, for an appointment with the knee specialist Dr. William Clancy, who after performing an arthroscopic examination confirmed the initial diagnosis of a severed PCL.

"He's a terrific kid," Clancy told Gave. "There was absolutely no fanfare about him. He's a very intelligent, articulate and charming young man. Detroit has a lot to be proud of. It's a real pleasure to deal with intelligent individuals like him because they have to make the decision. . . . They have to overcome all the emotion and pressure to make a decision that's appropriate."

Giving Yzerman an "excellent" prognosis for a full recovery, Clancy advised that the knee be repaired through rehabilitation rather than reconstructive surgery, which in the case of a PCL injury is a major procedure. If you're going to tear a knee ligament, you'd rather it be the PCL than the ACL. An athlete can compensate for a torn PCL through muscle-building physiotherapy. Treatment would require anywhere from six to twelve weeks, making it *just* possible that Yzerman would recover in time for the playoffs. After returning to Detroit, he showed up for the next home game, his knee locked in a brace, to watch from Mike Ilitch's private box.

After two weeks in the brace, the physiotherapy began. Yzerman traveled with the team, working out in hotel gyms. He dropped $1,000 taking his teammates to dinner in Los Angeles. He stewed about the lack of immediate results from his physio regimen.

And he missed the rest of the regular season. The team continued to perform, with Gerard Gallant filling in as interim captain, easily winning the Norris Division by 17 points over St. Louis; their 93-point effort was the fifth best in the league. The Red Wings again reached the conference finals, for another matchup with the Oilers, the defending Stanley Cup champions. Yzerman was able to dress for three games, and contributed four points, but the Wings lost their second consecutive semifinal series to the Oilers, in five games. Once past Detroit, Edmonton swept the Boston Bruins in the Stanley Cup finals. It was the closest Detroit would get to the finals for seven seasons.

It's a matter of debate as to whether or not full reconstructive surgery would have saved Yzerman any pain and agony down the road. The Red Wings had gathered a full dossier of medical opinions before deciding their star captain could best be served by physiotherapy, a course with which he agreed. Players live with the pain of a deteriorating knee for a lot of reasons. For one thing, many of them simply can—and Yzerman counts among athletes who appear to have an almost inhuman pain threshold. But the knee is also a finicky thing, to be treated wherever possible with strength training and braces rather than surgery. And the prospect of knee surgery gives any athlete pause; it can cause the loss not only of weeks of play, but of an entire season. Knee problems are considered so career-threatening that surgery can signal to the management ranks that you are vulnerable, less valuable. Some players never quite recover their old form after they go under the knife.

As it turned out, almost thirteen years would pass after the goalpost collision before Yzerman was forced to turn to a surgeon for help.

In 1988–89, the season that followed the knee injury, Yzerman became a de facto superstar, registering 65 goals and 155 points. He made the top-ten scorers' list for the first time, finishing third in points behind Mario Lemieux and Wayne Gretzky, and third in goals, behind Lemieux and Gretzky's Los Angeles linemate, Bernie Nicholls.

And yet.

There was something out-of-sync about Yzerman's stardom. He was producing points at a furious pace, leading the Red Wings to their best playoff results in two decades. He also represented Canada at the 1985 World Championships in Prague, earning a silver medal, and he had been good enough in his rookie season to be invited to join Team Canada for the 1984 Canada Cup. But his pride was wounded by his failure to make the 1987 Canada Cup roster. Team Canada was coached by Mike Keenan, who had just taken Philadelphia to the Stanley Cup finals against Edmonton, losing in game seven. "Iron Mike" was a disciple of the old-school Scotty Bowman style of autocratic management. He had a surfeit of talented centers to choose from for the Canadian squad, and Yzerman turned out to be surplus material. The 1987 tournament may have been the best ever held; the teams were especially strong, and on the Canadian squad Keenan was able to test-drive Wayne Gretzky, Mario Lemieux and Mark Messier, all of whom were natural centers, as one frightening forward line. (It was a Gretzky breakout in the dying moments of the third game of the best-of-three finals against the Soviets that produced one of the sport's most memorable goals, a drop pass from the Great One to Mario Lemieux, the Next One, who then rifled a wrist shot over the shoulder of Soviet goaltender Sergei Mylnikov.)

Yzerman fell between the cracks of talent: not a superstar like Gretzky, Lemieux or Messier; also not so outstanding that he could avoid being cut in favor of Mike Gartner, Doug Gilmour or Dale Hawerchuk. Nor could he outmuscle and outhustle role players like Brent Sutter of the Islanders and Claude Lemieux of the Canadiens, at least in Keenan's eyes. Canada recorded perhaps its most memorable victory of the tournament's history without Steve Yzerman.

Yzerman nevertheless had rebounded from the rejection by Keenan to produce his first great season, the 102 points in 64 games, and then rebounded from his knee injury. The Red Wings got better as he did, and he responded to the vote of confidence Demers gave him in making him captain. The additional responsibility gave him more incentive, larger goals beyond improving his own game.

The 1988–89 season saw Yzerman make a spectacular breakthrough into the narrow circle of hockey superstardom. For several years, the official imprimatur of "The Greatest" had wavered between Wayne Gretzky and Mario Lemieux. The league had

been through this before, when Gretzky broke into the NHL and
Marcel Dionne was entrenched as the official Best Player There
Is. It took a few seasons for the consensus to shift from Dionne to
Gretzky, and it later took a few seasons for that same consensus to
move from Gretzky to Lemieux.

The actual shift can be tracked by three idiosyncratic barom-
eters: the Hart Memorial Trophy, the Lester B. Pearson Award,
and All-Star Team selections. The Hart is one of the NHL's oldest trophies, having been introduced in 1926, while the Pearson
didn't come along until 1971. The Hart has an odd criterion: it is
not simply the league MVP award, but rather the award for the
player "adjudged to be most valuable to his team." Why try to
decide if one player is more valuable to the Maple Leafs, for
example, than another player is to the Blackhawks? One suspects
that the conditions have less to do with an individual's importance to a particular team's success than they do with a league not
wanting back in 1926 to name one player better than everybody
else and create a salary headache in the process. It was left to the
new NHL Players' Association to create such an unequivocal
award with the Pearson. Named for the former Canadian prime
minister and Nobel Peace Prize laureate, the Pearson is dedicated
to the league's outstanding player. Period.

Between the awards, there is also the important difference of
who decides upon the recipient. Like the other individual NHL
player awards, the Hart is voted on by the professional hockey writers, who have long agonized over the peculiar criteria of the Hart
and haven't necessarily followed the same strict logic every season.
The writers also choose the First and Second All-Star teams. The
Pearson, on the other hand, is a peer award, voted on by the members of the players' association. While the Hart continues to have
the greatest cachet, perhaps because of its longevity, the Pearson is

the purer award in terms of its criteria; the fact that the players themselves award it should also count for something.

When Steve Yzerman broke into the NHL at eighteen, the shift from Dionne to Gretzky as the game's premier star was complete. Gretzky had been named to the First All-Star Team at center every year since 1980–81, and the writers had also decided to grant Gretzky virtual ownership of the Hart beginning in 1980. The players themselves held off in jumping on the Gretzky bandwagon. Dionne earned the Pearson for the second straight year in 1980, and then goaltender Mike Liut got it in 1981. But beginning in 1982, the Pearson fell in sync with the Hart, which was also in sync with the First Team All-Star berth for centers. Throw in the Art Ross Trophy for the scoring race, and Gretzky was making a clean sweep of the major silverware.

The consensus first crumbled in 1985–86. Gretzky won the scoring race and the Hart again, as well as the First Team All-Star berth, but the players diverged from the sportswriters and named Mario Lemieux, for the first time, the game's top player by giving him the Pearson. After that, the two sides appeared to agree on the seesaw battle between Gretzky and Lemieux. Gretzky regained the dominant position in 1987 by taking the Hart, Pearson, Art Ross and First Team honors, and in 1988, when Lemieux won the scoring race (and the Art Ross) for the first time, all the major prizes swung his way: the Hart, the Pearson and the First Team berth.

In 1988–89, the symmetry was again lost, but in a new way. The players and writers didn't just disagree on Lemieux and Gretzky, as they had in 1985–86. This time, there was a three-way split.

Jacques Demers had been lobbying incessantly for Yzerman to be considered for the Hart. Even in 1987–88, when Yzerman's season was cut short by the knee injury, Demers had pushed for the Hart for his captain, arguing that he had led them to the division title—to no avail, as Yzerman finished a distant fourth in voting, behind Lemieux, Grant Fuhr and Gretzky. Demers knew the deal, that sportswriters cast the ballots. And it was obvious, given the recent waffling between Gretzky and Lemieux, that the voters were divided and, in no small measure, confused about the purpose of the award. During the 1988–89 season, in whatever city the Red Wings were playing in, Demers again talked up Yzerman as deserving the prize, on both possible counts: he was the most valuable to his team *and* the greatest all-round player in the league.

For a while, it seemed as if the lobbying was paying off. In mid March, the *Detroit Free Press* polled twenty-six of the sixty-three writers who would cast ballots, and found Yzerman to be the favorite. A Chicago writer vowed to vote for Yzerman "because he's so valuable in all three zones. From inside the red line, he does a lot of things the other two don't do." A Montreal writer said Yzerman would be his choice "because he guided the team through a hellacious year. And he's had a tremendous year, as far as I'm concerned." But the difficulty of deciding between Yzerman, Gretzky and Lemieux was summed up by a Hartford writer: "I'm having a terrible time deciding. If you vote for the best player in the game, which we did when Gretzky won it all those years, you have to go with Lemieux. If you vote for the guy who means most to his team, then Yzerman should win. Gretzky has had a big impact in Los Angeles, but I think Yzerman's out-played Gretzky in many ways this season."

Mario Lemieux won the scoring race for the second straight season, his 199 points placing him well ahead of Gretzky's 168 and Yzerman's career-high 155. The writers named him to the

First All-Star Team at center, and gave Gretzky the Second Team spot. But in a landslide, with 40 of 63 first-place votes (compared with Lemieux's 18), they gave the Hart to Gretzky, who had led the Kings to a 23-point improvement in the regular season and upset his old team, the Oilers, in the opening round of the playoffs. Yzerman received just five first-place votes.

In an echo of Mike Ilitch's decision to give Yzerman his Calder bonus in 1984, Penguins owner Edward DeBartolo Sr. presented Lemieux with the $100,000 bonus a Hart win would have earned him. Regardless, Lemieux was unrestrained in his disappointment. "Nothing in this league makes sense," he complained. "In the past, they gave it to the best player or top scorer. I don't know why it should change. . . . The facts are there."

"I went around the league, promoting [Yzerman] as the MVP," says Demers. "And they gave it to Gretzky. And did you see the players Gretz had playing with him?" It didn't help that Yzerman was his own worst enemy when it came to promotion. "Steve never sold himself," says Demers. "He was low key, quiet"—those perennial descriptors of Stevie Y—"and he just wanted to play the game. He refused so many interviews because he just wanted to be a hockey player."

Nevertheless, Yzerman's peers went in an entirely different direction than the writers, and chose a brand new face for their league MVP. They gave him the Pearson. And while Lemieux's bitterness over playing second fiddle to Gretzky boiled over into the press, Yzerman collected the Pearson without personal fanfare. Two days before the awards were handed out, he married Lisa Brennan. His priorities clearly were elsewhere that summer.

The league had not seen such a schism in the major hardware department in the past decade. While Mike Liut's Pearson win in 1981 was a respite in the duel between Dionne and Gretzky for top honors, Liut was also a First Team All-Star in 1980–81 and was named the starting goaltender for Team Canada in the 1981 Canada Cup tournament. This time around, the players had completely broken away from the writers by elevating an entirely different star with the Pearson in 1989. Steve Yzerman had never won anything: not the Calder, not a scoring title, not a position on either All-Star Team, not a Stanley Cup ring. He hadn't made the cut for Team Canada in 1987, nor had he been included in the NHL All-Star Team that played the Soviets at Rendezvous 87 in Quebec City. While he had made his first of five consecutive appearances in the league's annual All-Star Game in 1988, the hockey writers could not bring themselves to vote him onto the First or Second Team. To this day, Steve Yzerman has not been a postseason All-Star.

The collapse in Hart support for Yzerman in 1988–89 can be attributed in large part to the failings of the team he was expected to lead. His Red Wings had topped a weak Norris Division, but had retreated from 93 points to 80; goals against had ballooned from 269 to 316; and the lowly Chicago Blackhawks, with the fifth-worst regular-season record in the NHL, knocked them out of the playoffs in six games in the opening round, in spite of Yzerman's five goals and five assists. The 'Hawks delivered a true coup de grace in game six, humiliating the Wings by a 7–1 score. After the early playoff exit, Yzerman and Gallant signed on for the Canadian team at the World Championships in Stockholm. There, Canada won another silver medal as Yzerman finished third in scoring on the team, behind Brian Bellows and Dale Hawerchuk, with 11 points in 8 games.

The Pearson award brought Yzerman to a professional crossroads. He had won the respect of his peers, if not the unequivocal admiration of the writers, by demonstrating dimensions of his game that scoring stats, as good as they were, could not alone describe. He had rebounded from his initial knee problems, and had played through the pain of other, less publicized injuries. (Demers would recall Yzerman enduring an injured foot in a playoff series which caused him to discard a sock soaked in blood between every period.)

The Pearson raised the ante on what was expected of Yzerman, going forward, particularly after the playoff collapse against Chicago. It also led, inevitably, to increased expectations on Yzerman's own part, vis à vis his contract with the Detroit Red Wings. The players had not yet agreed among themselves, via the players' association, to make all contracts public knowledge in order to promote salary parity, so hard numbers on deals were impossible to come by. Mario Lemieux got a new five-year deal in Pittsburgh said to have a base value of $2.4 million per season. That left him trailing Gretzky's $20 million over eight seasons, but Lemieux wasn't grousing—his anger over not getting the Hart evidently had passed. Lemieux said that, "with what [Gretzky has] done for hockey over the years, he deserves a little bit more money."

Yzerman's negotiations didn't go nearly as smoothly. Not only was his agent, Gus Badali, unable to settle with Detroit management before the start of training camp, but talks stretched on until the start of the 1989–90 season. Yzerman had completed the fifth year of a seven-year contract that was paying him about $400,000 annually. Badali was looking for $10 million over five years, and it was believed that he settled for $1.2 million a year for five seasons. Despite the Pearson award, when it came to remuneration Yzerman was still not seen to be in the same league as Gretzky and Lemieux. And he understood that he had more to do, to prove himself. He didn't want to discuss the contract's details, but volunteered to the *Free Press*'s Gave, "I've got to play a little harder to earn it to prove I'm worth it." This, after a season in which he produced a franchise-record 155 points. "I can't guarantee that I'll be worth the money I'm getting, but I'll try. They made a commitment to me by offering me that contract. I have to make a commitment to them now. It's not okay if I don't."

It was plain what Yzerman had to do next to justify his salary, which the Red Wings promised was the third highest in the league. Great players who are also captains are expected to be great leaders, and without a championship to show for that leadership, their greatness will have to suffer the presence of an asterisk.

"When you first come into the league as a young player, you want to establish an identity—what kind of player you are," says Dave Lewis. "That's a primary goal of any young player. And then, in terms of career progression, you want to reach a level where stardom's important, if you're that kind of player. You want to play in All-Star Games, things like that."

Players who have established their presence, he notes, then say to themselves: "I've made it. Now what can I do?" A lot of them simply continue piling up points, collecting bonuses and counting their All-Star Game appearances. It's a good way to make a living. But for the players who aspire to more, the next accomplishment to reach for is pretty obvious, and in many ways so much more difficult than scoring goals that make the nightly highlight reels. "Once you get to a certain level, the next most important thing—really, the most important thing—is winning. And Steve learned that what he had to do to win, was to not be anything other than a winner."

That might sound terribly simplistic—to win, you have to be a winner—but it's one of the hardest lessons to learn in team sport. Because becoming a winner, as Lewis emphasizes, means being *nothing but* a winner. It's what you leave out of your game and out of your ego that makes the difference and brings you a championship.

Yzerman had done exceptionally well to crack the upper echelon of stardom by hauling himself above Gretzky and Lemieux in Pearson voting in 1989. But he would have to do much more to achieve wider regard from fans and, yes, the writers. Gretzky had four Stanley Cups in Edmonton, and was doing his utmost to bring one to Los Angeles. Lemieux was about to win a pair of Cups in Pittsburgh. Mark Messier was also about to secure his status as a championship leader. Already a multiple winner with the Oilers, now that Gretzky was gone from Edmonton, he would lead the Oilers on his own to another Stanley Cup in 1990, and then do it again with the Rangers in 1994. Yzerman was just beginning a streak of 100-plus point seasons, but ultimately his ability to lead Detroit to playoff success was going to be the measure of his greatness.

In an expanding league, there would be many, many talented players who just wouldn't be in the right place at the right time ever to hoist the Cup over their heads. Great players often find themselves trapped in the wrong franchise. They are able to meet those personal goals, of establishing themselves in the elite ranks, of playing in All-Star Games. But so often they realize, almost too late, that they have no hope of ever being a champion and can't extricate themselves from their circumstances. Demanding a trade won't produce the desired result if the right team isn't willing to deal for them.

For a player appointed a team leader, on a team whose owner was determined to spend any amount necessary to create a winning organization, to not ever win would be a sign of personal failure. Giving Yzerman the captaincy at such a young age might have been an unfair burden, but it had been in his nature to accept it, and now he had to make something of it. He was not the kind of player who would be satisfied, when his last game was behind him, with an assortment of individual achievements. His decision to fling his fifty-goal puck into the crowd at The Joe left little doubt of that. If he were to finish his career as the highest-scoring center in the history of the Red Wings, something fundamental would still be missing. The goals, hundreds as they might be, would have added up to nothing.

For Yzerman to become a champion, he would have to lead. But he also needed a team that could be led. "In the mid 1980s to the early 1990s, we didn't really have a Stanley Cup–caliber team," says Jim Devellano. "I'd take some of the responsibility for wanting him to score a lot of goals and assists. We had to sell tickets, and his contract was incentive based. But it wasn't the approach needed to win a championship."

Even as Yzerman was winning the Pearson, the Red Wings were changing. Key ingredients had been coming together even as he was receiving the award. They would give the Red Wings and Yzerman more to work with. But they would also change the dimensions of Yzerman's role, and even cause the Red Wings to question whether Yzerman still had a role.

The initial revival of the Red Wings under Jacques Demers, when a group of young players banded together with veterans to see how far they could take things, deflated entirely in 1989–90. Following the shocking loss to the Blackhawks in the opening round of the 1989 playoffs, Yzerman found himself leading a hockey club that could no longer win. He had another outstanding season, his 62 goals ranking second highest (after Brett Hull) in the NHL and his 127 points placing him third overall in the scoring race for the second consecutive season. But the Wings themselves settled to the murky bottom of the Norris, with 28 wins. The team had stopped responding to Demers's emotional leadership, except occasionally in the wrong way. Demers was convinced that referee Brian Stewart had it in for the Red Wings—and himself personally— and was persecuting them with unwarranted penalties. That season, Yzerman received two ten-minute misconducts from Stewart for arguing his calls. In a game against the North Stars on January 13, 1990, Gallant ran amok after Stewart waived off a Detroit goal late in the game, saying that a player had been in Minnesota's crease, then handed the Wings enough penalties to leave them playing three-on-five hockey until the final buzzer. After Detroit lost 6–4, Gallant tried to go after Stewart. While being held back by a linesman, Jerry Pateman, he threw a punch that connected with Pateman. While it did seem that Gallant's punch struck the official accidentally—as he tried to hit a Minnesota player— Gallant nonetheless received an automatic three-game suspension.

Yzerman's 1989–90 misconducts were not the last that he would receive after losing his composure with a referee. Early in 2003–04, Yzerman was levied two twenty-minute misconducts for his vociferous objections to calls against Detroit in one brawl-filled game against the Nashville Predators. During the 1987–88 campaign, Yzerman's mother told *Sports Illustrated* that Steve and his father "are quiet, subdued and keep a lot to themselves, but occasionally they explode."

Detroit's sorry effort in 1989–90 left them out of the playoffs for the first time in four seasons. When the Red Wings had last missed the playoffs, in 1985–86, Jim Devellano hired a new coach. This time, he went one better: Devellano bought Demers out of his contract, allowed himself to be kicked upstairs to a senior vice presidency, and recruited Bryan Murray to serve as both coach and general manager.

Murray had compiled one of the strongest coaching records in the NHL during the 1980s with the Washington Capitals, beginning in 1981–82. But with the Capitals struggling in 1989–90—with only 18 wins in 46 starts—Caps general manager Dave Poile replaced Bryan Murray with his own brother, Terry Murray. In hindsight, Detroit's decision to give Murray both the coach and general manager's jobs was surprising. Washington under Murray had turned a string of regular-season successes into playoff disappointments. In 1983 and 1984, the defending Cup champions, the Islanders, eliminated the Capitals. In 1985, the Islanders again knocked off the Capitals, who had finished third overall in the regular season. In the next two seasons, the Rangers and then the Islanders again took turns snuffing out Washington's Cup hopes. In 1988 and 1989, the job was inherited by New Jersey and Philadelphia. In eight seasons, the Capitals had never got past the second round.

The Red Wings thought that Murray, with the added clout of the general manager's job, could get Detroit into the final round. The team did recover from its regular-season disaster of 1989–90, as wins climbed to 34, then to 43, then to a franchise-record 47 in 1992–93. But every spring brought another playoff reversal. In 1991, the Red Wings had the Blues painted into a corner, down three games to one in the opening round. St. Louis came back to win three straight and eliminate the Wings. In 1992, Detroit won the Norris Division and topped the Campbell Conference with the league's third-best record, but then required all seven games of the opening round to get rid of the North Stars, who had finished 28 points behind them. After that, the Blackhawks, who had finished 11 points behind Detroit in the Norris (with 63 fewer goals) disposed of Yzerman and company in four straight. In '93, the Red Wings concluded their best season ever, breaking the 100-point barrier and leading the league in total goals (369). But in a matchup with their more defensive-minded Norris rivals, the Toronto Maple Leafs, Detroit lost in seven games in the opening round after winning the first two games.

The seventh-game loss to the Leafs, which occurred right in The Joe, was devastating to Yzerman. It would be said that he sat alone in a room in the back of the arena, crying for hours.

Losing in the playoffs "was almost like a sickness for Bryan," according to Devellano. (In 2003, the Anaheim Mighty Ducks, under general manager Bryan Murray, would reach the Cup finals against New Jersey—and lose in game seven.) Ilitch and Devellano decided to keep Murray on as general manager, but replace him as coach. Ilitch suggested that they hire Mike Keenan, whose Blackhawks had eliminated the Red Wings in 1989 and 1992, reaching the finals and losing to the Penguins in the latter year. Like the Red Wings, the Blackhawks had been a playoff bust in 1993, having been swept in the opening round by St. Louis. Keenan had been serving as Chicago's general manager in 1992–93—the coaching playoff loss belonged to Darryl Sutter—but was nevertheless available.

Devellano, wanted nothing to do with him. Although Ilitch had already discussed personally with Keenan the possibility of coming to Detroit, Devellano talked Ilitch out of pursuing him any further. "I wasn't threatened by Mike Keenan. I just didn't think that it was the proper direction for this organization to go." Keenan's mentor and role model was Scotty Bowman, who was coach and general manager of the Buffalo Sabres when Keenan was coaching the Sabres' AHL farm club, the Rochester Americans. Bowman "is the only coach today who gets away with an authoritarian style," Devellano has observed. "Keenan tries, but can't."

There was also no love lost between Keenan and Devellano's star player, Steve Yzerman. In addition to the playoff defeats Keenan had inflicted on the Red Wings, the coach had cut Yzerman at the Team Canada training camp in 1987—and again in 1991, infuriating Yzerman.

Getting sent home in 1991 was a low point for Yzerman, and it came at a confounding period of his career. His treatment epitomized the massive contradictions in his stature at the time. The player who had never been voted to an All-Star Team had been recognized as the league's greatest player by his peers in 1989. And in 1990, Yzerman had again turned out dutifully for Canada's World Championship team. He ran away with the team's offensive production, piling up nineteen points in ten games (Theoren Fleury was the next most prolific Canadian, with eleven points), and while Canada finished fourth, out of the medals, Yzerman was named the tournament's top forward. He had now played for Canada at four World Championship tournaments: three senior and one junior. The Worlds were not a glamour event for NHLers like Yzerman. Fans didn't pay nearly as much attention to that tournament as they did the Olympics or the Canada Cup. But he had never refused Hockey Canada's request for his services when Detroit's playoff schedule (or lack thereof) allowed him to attend. He showed up and did the job, and after his first serious problems with his knee appeared in 1988, it was clear that every extracurricular tournament he appeared in thereafter was placing his professional career at risk.

But in the fall of 1991, he failed to make the cut for Team Canada. Most galling was that, when Mario Lemieux's bad back made him unavailable, Keenan passed over a proven pro like Yzerman in favor of Eric Lindros of the Oshawa Generals. The much-hyped Next Big Thing, who had just been drafted by the Quebec Nordiques, had not played, as Yzerman had, in the

World Senior Championships, and wouldn't even begin his NHL career until 1992–93.

Yzerman's dismissal was a painfully drawn-out process. He survived training camp, but then was parked on the team's taxi squad. Both he and Theoren Fleury—the lone fifty-goal scorers on the Canadian team—watched in street clothes as Canada produced a 2–2 tie with the unheralded Finns in the opening game. George Gross wrote in the *Toronto Sun* that it was "difficult to fathom that a Steve Yzerman was sitting in the stands" during the uninspiring game against Finland.

Asked to comment on his status, Yzerman tried to bite his tongue. "I better choose my words carefully. I don't know what I am right now. I'm disappointed. I think I've proven myself. I feel I should be playing. But I'm not playing and that's their decision. I wasn't told the reason why."

For the next game, against a strong U.S. team, Yzerman was again a healthy scratch. Canada won, and Keenan moved to finalize his taxi squad. In deciding to use the spot occupied by Yzerman for a spare defenseman, he sent the Red Wings captain packing. Yzerman had just completed, in the words of the *Detroit Free Press,* "the most humiliating week of his celebrated pro career."

For all the complaining about his choice to cut Yzerman, and his other lineup decisions that favored checking over pure goal scoring, Keenan knew the proof would be in the results. "If we win, there won't be second-guessing after that. That's the way it goes. We felt we had a good balance in scoring."

As it turned out, Canada did win—never losing a game— and swept Team USA in the best-of-three finals. It didn't help Yzerman's cheering section that the teenaged Lindros turned in one of the team's better efforts, scoring three goals and two assists and playing an effective physical game.

Yzerman had also been sucked into the rampant speculation over where Lindros might actually end up playing in the NHL. Lindros had no interest in playing for the small-market Quebec Nordiques, and even though he was drafted by them, he was making it clear he wouldn't actually report. A junior player had no legal obligation to sign with an NHL club. If he and the club couldn't come to terms, the team's rights could be allowed to expire and the player would re-enter the draft. But in the meantime, the player wasn't playing and the NHL team knew it would end up with nothing to show for its draft pick. With Lindros prepared to delay his professional career by playing on Canada's Olympic team (the next games were in Albertville, France, in 1992), it was left to the Nordiques to trade Lindros's rights to a franchise that he would agree to play for, and receive something substantial in return.

In the speculation over where Lindros might end up, Detroit was floated, and the possibility of Yzerman being sent to Quebec as compensation was in the air in the summer of 1991. The league was on a power-center kick: Pittsburgh had just won the Stanley Cup with Mario Lemieux—all six-four and 225 pounds of him—leading the way. The previous season, Mark Messier had led the Oilers to their fifth Cup. Big men with playmaking skills, stickhandling ability and a scoring touch were rare treasures, and teams, Detroit included, wanted them. At the 1990 draft, the Red Wings had dealt their way into possession of the third pick overall and chose Keith Primeau, a six-foot-four center who had just produced a league-leading 57 goals and 127 points for the Niagara Falls Thunder of the Ontario Hockey League. Still eighteen when Detroit introduced him to the NHL in 1990–91, he only produced 15 points in 58 games, and spent half of 1991–92 with the Wings' Adirondack farm team as the parent club brought him along more slowly.

But the Wings had also just finished their first season with Sergei Fedorov. At six-one and 200 pounds, Fedorov, who turned twenty-two halfway through the season, had dazzled. He was everything the Red Wings could have asked for: an effortless, powerful skater, an astute playmaker, a dangerous shot and a forward who didn't have to be told what backchecking was. His 79-point effort topped all rookies, just as Yzerman's 87 points had done in 1983–84. And like Yzerman, he lost out in Calder voting to a goaltender—in Fedorov's case, to Ed Belfour of the Blackhawks.

At this point, the Red Wings had in Fedorov and Primeau a pair of centers who were stronger than Yzerman, bigger than Yzerman and younger than Yzerman. Eric Lindros was dangling before them, and Mike Ilitch had the budget, the trade bait and the Stanley Cup ambitions to make a deal possible. But the opportunities in the market for star centers didn't end there. None other than Pat LaFontaine was available from the New York Islanders.

Being chosen by the Islanders right before Yzerman in the 1983 draft had given LaFontaine the chance to play with some of the most accomplished players in the league. And while the trip to the 1984 Cup finals proved to be the Islanders' last, the team still turned in solid regular-season finishes and determined playoff efforts. In 1987, LaFontaine was front and center in one of Bryan Murray's pre-eminent playoff nightmares. The Capitals were locked in a game-seven struggle on home ice in the Patrick Division semifinals against LaFontaine and the Islanders. Tied at two goals apiece at the end of regulation time, the clubs struggled through an epic of overtime hockey—four extra periods in all. The Islanders' Pat Flatley would recall LaFontaine repeatedly yelling, "Who's going to be the hero?" during the intermissions as the team tried to recuperate in the dressing room. The hero turned out to be LaFontaine himself, as he drilled a slapshot from the blue line past Bob Mason of the Capitals just before 2 a.m. on Easter morning.

Heroics like that aren't easy to forget. And it wasn't easy to forget that LaFontaine was the player that Detroit had coveted at the 1983 draft, the hometown hero whose drafting by Bill Torrey had left Devellano to opt for Yzerman. In 1989–90, LaFontaine came through with his first fifty-goal season (54 in all, with 105 points), and he managed 85 points in 1990–91 despite the fact that the Islanders, so recently a proud dynasty, were rapidly coming apart. In the summer of 1991, with Eric Lindros in play as well, LaFontaine wanted off Long Island.

Many trade rumors are little more than people in the league or in the press speculating about who would make a good swap for whom. Jim Devellano wasn't privy to any serious discussions to send Yzerman to Quebec City for Lindros. Doing such a deal was firmly in Murray's bailiwick as GM. But Devellano doesn't deny that there were serious discussions between Murray and the Islanders about LaFontaine.

Rumors were so persistent about Yzerman going to either Quebec City or Long Island that the captain felt compelled to address them. He nixed any thought that he would tolerate a move to a troubled franchise like the Islanders, and wasn't any more willing to play in Quebec City than Lindros was. He did his best to emphasize that his objections to the Nordiques didn't have anything to do with the French-Canadian culture. Instead, he complained about high taxes on income and gasoline.

Detroit didn't end up dealing for either Lindros or LaFontaine. Lindros went to Philadelphia, while LaFontaine landed in Buffalo.

After being cut from Team Canada in September 1991, Yzerman gave in to another public outburst. After the humiliation of being cut from the team at camp in 1987, Yzerman said he only agreed to attend the 1991 training camp because Alan Eagleson had guaranteed him a spot on the squad. Eagleson flatly rejected this, and added the only player to whom he guaranteed a spot on the squad was Wayne Gretzky.

That in itself was an interesting admission by Eagleson: that Gretzky alone was issued a "Get Past the Tryouts Free" card. Given his stature, it's probably not surprising. Gretzky was considered the greatest player ever, and he had just demonstrated his staying power by winning the scoring race and being voted to the First All-Star Team. (The Pearson and the Hart went to a dual citizen, Brett Hull, who would play for Team USA in 1991.) But it also perpetuated the idea that Gretzky held some kind of unspoken special status in the game. He was considered a no-go area when it came to rough play (no one broke his nose with a crosscheck in his rookie season, the way Behn Wilson did Yzerman's), and Demers had been frustrated by his inability to convince the press that they should give the Hart to Yzerman in 1989, rather than to Gretzky for the umpteenth time.

On balance, the press that Yzerman generated in the summer of 1991 ran overwhelmingly against him, not with him. He spoke so rarely to the media, and now this. It wasn't as if Yzerman had sprinkled a trail of bon mots through his career, cultivating a marketable public persona, before letting these complaints slip. The public had no clear perception of who the guy was, beyond being someone who scored goals and was paid well. Standing in stark isolation, his complaining words came dangerously close to serving as a snapshot of the kind of person he was. He sounded petulant and spoiled: a wealthy young athlete who didn't want to spend more than he had to for the fuel in his Porsche, and who thought he was so great that, unlike Lemieux, Messier, or any number of other stars, he didn't have to submit to tryouts at the Team Canada camp.

It's not the impression he would have wanted to leave. With Team Canada, he genuinely believed that he was being welcomed back after the snub of 1987, assured of being included. He had no interest in being dumped by Iron Mike a second time, and he was apoplectic when it happened. As for the potential Nordiques deal, it's likely he was simply trying to refuse a trade to a small-market team while at the same time avoid offending francophone fans. He had, after all, committed himself to Detroit as a team and to greater Detroit as a place to start a family. And he had just acquired American citizenship (without relinquishing his Canadian one). So, in objecting to Quebec City, he chose to offer Quebec's high tax rate as an excuse. It would have been better for him had he just emphasized his desire to play and live in Detroit. He wouldn't have been the first professional hockey player to blanch at drawing his salary in Canada, never mind in Quebec. When Brian Bellows was being coveted by the entire league before the 1982 draft, his agent, Alan Eagleson, bluntly advised the Canadian clubs not even to bother drafting him, because his client—a Canadian—wasn't interested in being a Canadian taxpayer.

Yzerman's American citizenship was understandable given the tax realities of his residency and, as a newly married man who would be starting a family, the nationality of his kids. Still, one had to wonder if the persistent slights from Keenan's team selection process would compel him to take advantage of his status and show up with Team USA the next time out. Bryan Trottier, Tony Esposito and Brett Hull, all Canadian born, would play for Team USA. It wouldn't happen; his identity as a Canadian was never in doubt.

The year 1991 saw Yzerman reach what was probably the lowest point in his career, less as a player than as a public figure. Not much of a public figure to begin with, Yzerman, like a turtle who had poked his head injudiciously out of his shell, withdrew again after the unhappiness of that summer. He would dutifully answer the media's questions about his play or how things were going with the Red Wings (and he was getting better at this with every season) but essentially he was back to being a hockey player. When he didn't make an All-Star Team—an annual oversight that had become as traditional for the NHL as serving turkey is on Thanksgiving—he would brush it off. Things like that, he would always say, didn't matter to him. More and more, he made it clear, in case people hadn't figured it out already, that winning did.

Thanks to Jim Devellano's imprecations, Yzerman dodged the bullet of having Mike Keenan as his new coach. But the one he did get, Keenan's mentor, Scotty Bowman, would test him sorely. It is still up for debate whether Bowman changed Yzerman for the better, or whether Yzerman did it himself, in spite of the ordeal that Bowman put him through.

SEVEN

Scotty Bowman was not Jim Devellano's first choice to coach the Red Wings after the string of playoff failures under Bryan Murray. The guy he *really* wanted was Al Arbour.

Devellano, Arbour and Bowman went way back together, to the St. Louis Blues of the late 1960s and early 1970s, when Bowman was coach and general manager, Devellano was chief scout, and Arbour was an old reliable on the blue line who had bounced in and out of the minors playing for Detroit, Chicago and Toronto during the Original Six days. When the league doubled in size in 1967, new employment opportunities were created at all levels of the NHL, and the expansion gave each of these three men their big breaks. In Arbour's case, it was a steady job on an NHL roster when his career should have been all but over. He'd been in the league since 1954, but for most of the previous two seasons, as Toronto's property, he'd been in the AHL with the Rochester Americans. Bowman put him to work in his customary role as an old-school, stay-at-home blue-liner. Late in the 1969–70 season, Bowman had Arbour coach two games, then turned the bench over to him for 1970–71.

With twenty-two games to go and the Blues struggling, Bowman decided to take the coaching reins back from Arbour to finish out the season, but he made it clear the job would be Arbour's again. The Blues had reached every Stanley Cup final in its first three years of operation, but in the spring of 1971 they were eliminated in the opening round by Minnesota. Bowman was fired, and immediately landed on his feet as the coach of the Canadiens. Arbour, improbably, was kept on by the Blues, even though Bowman's determination to have him coach was widely understood to be a reason he got the chop. Arbour coached thirteen games in 1971–72 before he, too, was let go, as was Devellano. When Devellano was hired as chief scout of the New York Islanders by Bill Torrey, he was able to convince Torrey that Arbour would make a good replacement for the Islanders' original coach, Phil Goyette, who had won only six of forty-eight starts and been temporarily replaced by Earl Ingarfield.

When Arbour took over the Islanders bench for 1973–74, an unprecedented coaching run began. No one had ever coached as many NHL games with the same team as Arbour would with the Islanders. He steered them through their four successive Stanley Cup wins, and even with the team's strength fading in the latter half of the 1980s, Arbour was still astute enough to give Bryan Murray's Washington Capitals a great deal of grief in the playoffs. Arbour retired after the 1986–87 season, but was coaxed back for 1988–89 as the team's prospects began to slip. The club missed the playoffs three times in the ensuing four seasons (and lost Pat LaFontaine to Buffalo), but reversed the slide in 1992–93 with a forty-win season and a strong playoff run. Those playoffs brought Arbour's Islanders up against Scotty Bowman's Penguins.

Which brings us to Bowman's erratic career trajectory after his eight celebrated seasons—and five Stanley Cups—with the Canadiens in the 1970s. He had left Montreal for the big job of general manager in Buffalo in 1979. The Sabres' owners, the Knox family, very much wanted him to coach as well, but Bowman took the new job understanding that he could replace himself as coach and focus on managing. He never did find someone to take his own job: a string of pinch hitters—Roger Neilson, Jimmy Roberts, Jim Schoenfeld, Craig Ramsay—tried and failed to coach the Sabres under Bowman. The coach who should have succeeded him, Mike Keenan, fouled up the succession plan when he jumped from coaching the Sabres' AHL farm team in Rochester to take an NHL posting with Philadelphia. Meanwhile, Bowman's aggressive rebuilding effort was coming under heavy criticism. More seasons passed without a championship, after the strong lineup Bowman inherited was broken up. He traded away experienced talent for draft picks, and when those draft choices failed to create a younger, winning club in short order, he wore out his welcome.

Time proved that many of Bowman's draft picks were in fact good ones, but these teenagers often needed more time to reach the point of being NHL regulars than the Knoxes were willing to give. By the fall of 1986, Bowman was finished in Buffalo. The Sabres had missed the playoffs in 1985–86, after Bowman took over the coaching job from Schoenfeld halfway through the season. After giving the coaching job to Ramsay, taking it back, then giving it to him again, Bowman was fired.

Bowman spent the next few seasons doing color commentary for *Hockey Night in Canada,* waiting for the break that would return him to the work he really desired.

That break came from Craig Patrick, the general manager of the Pittsburgh Penguins and the son of Lynn Patrick, who had hired Bowman in St. Louis. Craig had also played junior hockey for Bowman with the Notre-Dame-de-Grace Monarchs of Montreal's Metropolitan league. Patrick got the Pittsburgh GM job in 1989, and in turn immediately hired Bowman as his director of player development and recruitment. Bowman was essentially a roving scout, working out of his home in suburban Buffalo, helping Patrick make a contender out of the Penguins, who despite the presence of Super Mario Lemieux, could not find their way into the playoffs.

The Penguins' turnaround was extraordinarily rapid, if uneven. The team had missed the playoffs for the sixth consecutive season in 1988, reached the Patrick Division finals a year later, missed the playoffs again in 1990, and won the Stanley Cup in 1991. The Penguins had barely been able to celebrate their victory before they were laid low by the death, from brain cancer, of their beloved coach, "Badger Bob" Johnson. The loss of the upbeat, collegial Johnson opened the door for Bowman to return to coaching. He guided the Penguins to a second Stanley Cup in 1992, and was back behind the bench for another try in 1992–93.

The Penguins had managed to win two Stanley Cups with fairly ordinary regular-season results, and even their playoff runs had been roller-coaster rides. In 1992–93, Bowman drove them to a regular-season title. To his critics, his determination to finish first overall with the Penguins looked eerily similar to the way he pushed the Buffalo Sabres to first overall in his inaugural run with them in 1979–80. With the Sabres, injuries on the hard-driven team brought their playoff run up short; with the Penguins, it was Al Arbour's Islanders. The teams met in the division finals, and Pittsburgh's 32-point advantage in the standings counted for nothing. At 5:16 of overtime in game seven, a shot by David Volek beat Tom Barrasso (Bowman's celebrated 1983 draft pick back in Buffalo) and ended Bowman's quest for his seventh Stanley Cup as a coach.

That win propelled Arbour into the Wales Conference finals, where none other than Jacques Demers was waiting for him. Fired by Detroit in 1990, Demers had just completed his first season as the Montreal Canadiens' coach after a two-season hiatus in broadcasting. Demers took the Canadiens past the Islanders in five games to meet and defeat Wayne Gretzky and the Los Angeles Kings in the finals. It was a spring chock-full of what-had-beens and might-have-beens for Jim Devellano. The coach he had fired for missing the playoffs in 1989–90 had just taken a team that was less accomplished than his Red Wings of 1992–93 to a Stanley Cup win, while the Red Wings had been sidelined in the opening round by the Leafs. Scratch any idea, however, of bringing back Demers. He was now the toast of Montreal, and in any event there was no going back for the Red Wings. But the Patrick Division finals had showcased two true powerhouse coaches, the most successful of the 1970s (Bowman) and the 1980s (Arbour). They were also the winningest coaches in the history of playoff hockey. Arbour's record of 114 postseason wins was surpassed by Bowman when his Penguins defeated the Capitals in game three of the division semifinals in the spring of 1992. Either man would make a fine bench boss for the Red Wings.

It was just that Devellano preferred Arbour. He came with less baggage. Arbour was a paternal figure not given to angry outbursts, icy aloofness, or mind games. Bowman, on the other hand, had a legendary reputation for baffling and alienating some players while motivating most of them, regardless of whether they loved or hated him. His behavior was unpredictable—calculatedly so, many felt (or at least hoped). He specialized in keeping selected players off balance, uncertain of their security. Some wondered whether he had adapted sufficiently to command respect in a new era of millionaire athletes, in which players expected not only to be told what to do, but *why*.

Devellano approached Arbour first, and was turned down. Arbour had been settled on Long Island for a good twenty years; he was going to coach the Islanders for one last year and then move into a front-office job. He wasn't interested in starting all over again in a new city with a new team. So Devellano turned to Bowman, whose future in Pittsburgh was, if not gloomy, at least uncertain after the recent playoff letdown. Ilitch used the same strategy on Bowman as he had with previous hirings: he threw lots of money at him. Bowman was making about $300,000 as the Penguins' coach and director of player development. He could make $800,000 a year, with a $100,000 signing bonus, if he signed a two-year contract just to coach Detroit.

The money was certainly an important factor in Bowman's decision to come to Detroit. He would end up earning more in his first four years in Detroit than he had in all of his professional career to date. But Devellano also knew that money had not been his sole motivation for job changes in the past. After Bowman was fired in St. Louis, he was offered the general manager's job in Los Angeles, and turned it down in favor of the lower-paying coaching job in Montreal. Most significantly, Bowman had turned aside a package in 1979 that would have given him ten percent equity in the Washington Capitals, choosing instead to work in Buffalo. In both instances, Devellano saw Bowman making a career move that placed him in a position to win. Bowman could see the talent in the Canadiens system in Montreal in 1971, just as he could see it in Buffalo in 1979 (even though he was about to trade a lot of it away to get high draft choices).

And the talent in Detroit in 1993 was self-evident; it was just that no one had figured out how to make a winner out of it. The franchise was also coming through some rough seasons. And it wasn't just the playoff shortfalls. The ten-day strike by the players' association in the spring of 1992, which delayed the start of the playoffs, had disillusioned Red Wings owner Mike Ilitch; some saw his attention wandering from hockey as he returned to his first sporting love by acquiring baseball's Detroit Tigers that summer. As Ilitch's passion for hockey appeared to wane, people were pointedly wondering if Steve Yzerman, the franchise player of a franchise slipping in the affections of its deep-pocketed owner, had the ability ever to lead the team to postseason success. In 1992–93, Yzerman produced 58 goals and 137 points, an output exceeded only by 1988–89's superlative 155 points. But in the playoffs, his points production had again fallen below the pace he'd set in the regular season. There had been six points in seven games in 1991; eight in eleven in 1992; and seven points in seven games in 1993. Sergei Fedorov had outproduced him in the last two playoffs, with ten points in eleven games and nine points in seven games. In the summer of 1993, Bryan Murray, concerned that goalie Tim Cheveldae wasn't enough of a "money player," was floating Yzerman's name as trade bait as Detroit sought a more experienced playoff goaltender. No trade was completed; the next season, the bulk of the goaltending duties went to Chris Osgood, a Detroit draft pick (fifty-fourth overall) in 1991. Another trade rumor involving Yzerman had come and gone. But in 1993–94, the spotlight would continue to point away from him as, for the first time since 1985–86, Steve Yzerman did not lead his team in scoring. As had happened during the playoffs of 1992 and '93, he would again be upstaged by Fedorov.

On October 27, 1995, the Central Red Army invaded Calgary's Saddledome. Their uniforms were the familiar red and white, but the winged wheels in the center of their chests was not a recognized

Soviet sporting motif. A lot happens in a few years when an Evil Empire crumbles. Five former members of the Central Red Army team, fixtures of the great Soviet Olympic and World Championship clubs, were roaming the ice against the Flames within the first two minutes of play. At center was Igor Larionov; at right wing, Sergei Fedorov; at left wing, Vyacheslav Kozlov. Backing them up on defense were Viacheslav Fetisov and Vladimir Konstantinov. And on the bench, behaving like a general who'd got his hands on the enemy's top-secret laser cannon, was Scotty Bowman.

It was the first time that five Russian skaters had occupied the ice at the same time for the same team in the NHL. You could not help but look upon this spectacle and imagine that it was more than symbolic, that it signaled a major shift in the game in general and the Red Wings in particular. Bowman had just acquired the final member of this unit, Larionov, three days earlier when he traded Ray Sheppard to San Jose. Never mind the people watching from the stands; the Red Wings watching from the bench, including captain Steve Yzerman, were witnessing the dawning of something new and, for some of them perhaps, a little intimidating, within their own ranks, although Yzerman personally had enormous admiration for the Russian players.

The Red Wings had been crushed by the New Jersey Devils just a few months earlier in the Stanley Cup finals. Heads had rolled, and more would follow. The Wings now on the ice were some of the most gifted athletes ever to lace up skates. Six years earlier, when Yzerman was winning the Pearson award, the scene would have been considered beyond possibility in even the most wildly divergent of parallel universes. But the groundwork for the Russians' arrival actually dated back to that summer when Yzerman won his Pearson.

At the 1989 entry draft, Detroit's director of player personnel, Neil Smith, made a last, dramatic, plunge into the talent pool for Detroit. Just before the 1990 draft, he would accept the post of general manager (and, in another year, become president) of the New York Rangers. In 1989, in his final appearance at the Red Wings draft table, Smith—working with Ken Holland, the former minor-league goaltender who had become Detroit's chief scout of amateur talent, and Christer Rockstrom, the Red Wings' European scout—decided to make a move on overseas talent. Detroit's first two picks, Mike Sillinger (eleventh) and Bob Boughner (thirty-second) stuck close to home and were nothing special. But at fifty-third, the Wings took Nicklas Lidstrom, a nineteen-year-old defenseman for Vasteras in Sweden's Elite League. Having found a future winner of multiple Norris Trophies in the third round, Detroit then collected a future Hart, Pearson and Selke winner in the fourth round when they claimed Sergei Fedorov, seventy-fourth overall. And then, way, way down at 221st, the Wings secured the rights to Konstantinov.

At the same draft, in a move that sparked some controversy, the Wings almost, but didn't quite, get Pavel Bure. Smith would later say that the Wings wanted to take Bure with their fifth pick, ninety-fifth overall, but league officials told them he wasn't eligible. Instead, Detroit took Shawn McCosh from the Ontario league. He would prove to be a career minor-leaguer whom Detroit traded away the next summer to Los Angeles. It later turned out that Bure was in fact draft eligible, and Detroit prepared to choose him with their next pick, at 116th, but he was spoken for by Vancouver with the 113th pick overall. Despite Detroit's protests, the Canucks' selection of Bure couldn't be undone. The what-ifs surrounding the prospects for the Red Wings in the 1990s, and perhaps for Yzerman, are mind-boggling.

The draft would have a profound impact on the NHL of the 1990s, as a handful of teams showed the nerve or the prescience to devote draft picks, even late ones, to Eastern Bloc talents that would shortly prove to be available. In addition to Detroit's (and Vancouver's) gambles, Edmonton took Anatoli Semenov 120th; the Islanders, Vladimir Malakhov, 191st; Minnesota, Arturs Irbe, 196th; the Rangers, Roman Oksiuta, 202nd; and Winnipeg, Evgeny Davydov, 235th. The Communist grip on Czechoslovakia was just a few months away from being broken in the bloodless revolution that, among other things, sprang loose such imminent NHL stars as Jaromir Jagr and Dominik Hasek. There was no way to predict that event, or the ultimate failure of Gorbachev's attempt to reform the Soviet system without causing the absolute collapse of the union itself, but both developments paid immediate dividends to teams who, in the previous few years, had placed longshot bets by using picks, however late in the proceedings, to secure the rights of these Eastern Bloc players.

Players living behind the Iron Curtain were still a risky choice at an entry draft in 1989. Some Soviet players were being allowed to emigrate and play in the NHL, but only after their best years had been bled from them. Fedorov in particular would have seemed unlikely to arrive in Detroit any time soon. He had just finished inflicting (along with linemates Pavel Bure and Alexander Mogilny) a 7–2 drubbing of Canada at the World Junior Championships in Anchorage, Alaska, to clinch the gold medal for the Soviets and send Canada down to fourth overall.

Of course, there were ways other than haggling with state sports systems to get star athletes out of eastern European countries. Mainly, you had to smuggle them out, through clandestine defections. This had been going on in the NHL for several years. Most famous among those early cases were the defections of

Czechoslovakia's Peter and Anton Stastny in 1980, which brought them to the Quebec Nordiques. The Red Wings helped Fedorov get into the West by engineering his defection at the Goodwill Games in Seattle in 1990. By 1990, enough Soviet players were finding their way into NHL lineups that the Red Wings had the confidence to select Kozlov forty-fifth overall. He joined the team prior to 1991–92. The veteran Fetisov, who had lobbied for his own release from the Soviet system in 1990, was acquired from New Jersey in April 1995.

Many more lineup changes had occurred on the Red Wings since 1989, and the club had also undergone a major front-office shakeup. Yzerman was a rare constant. Unfortunately, the other constant during the first half of the 1990s was a playoff disappointment every spring. Failing to reach the Cup finals in the late 1980s, when the team didn't honestly expect itself to get there, had been bearable. But the early nineties were different.

With Bowman's hiring, the coaching staff had solidified into a talented triumvirate. Dave Lewis continued to focus on defensive responsibilities as an associate coach, while Bowman brought in his own man, Barry Smith, to serve as an associate coach in offensive matters. Smith had been an assistant coach under Bowman late in his Buffalo tenure, and joined the Pittsburgh coaching staff in 1990–91, when Bowman arrived as director of player personnel. A Buffalo native, Smith had considerable experience in Europe, with coaching stints in Sweden, Norway and Italy.

On paper, Scotty Bowman and his coaching squad didn't do any better in 1993–94 than Bryan Murray had the year before: Murray won 47 games to Bowman's 46. Murray's Wings scored 369 goals and allowed 280; Bowman's Wings scored 356 and allowed 275. Bowman at least was able to overtake Mike Keenan's

Blackhawks in the standings. While Murray's Wings had 103 points to Bowman's 100, Detroit under Murray had finished second to Chicago in the Norris Division and fifth overall, while in 1993–94 the team won its division and finished with the league's fourth-best record.

But there was no difference in the playoff results. Murray's Wings were eliminated in seven in the opening round by Toronto. Bowman's Wings went down in seven at the first opportunity, to the San Jose Sharks. The loss under Bowman in 1994, however, was far more shocking. Toronto at least had been a close division rival of Detroit, finishing just four points behind them. The Sharks were 18 points behind Detroit, having labored to a losing record.

The NHL had changed its playoff format beginning with 1994. Rather than allow fans to follow the season's divisional rivalries logically into the playoffs, the league in its wisdom decided that the opening round should feature cross-divisional pairings. The whole conference and divisional structure had also been overhauled. Gone were the Campbell and Wales conferences and the divisions named after Jim Norris, Conn Smythe, Charles Adams and Lester Patrick, to be replaced by geographic names. And Detroit, which had played in the Norris Division of the Campbell Conference with Chicago, Toronto, St. Louis and Tampa Bay in 1992–93, was now in the Central Division of the Western Conference, with Toronto, Dallas, St. Louis, Chicago and Winnipeg. Rather than face the very capable St. Louis Blues in the first round, as would have been the case under the 1993 playoff system, the new format linked the Red Wings with San Jose. What seemed like a blessing for Detroit proved to be a curse.

The Sharks were a most unlikely threat to Detroit's Cup ambitions. Established in 1991 via a convoluted transfer of part of the Minnesota North Stars franchise, San Jose missed the play-offs in its first two seasons, and the 1992–93 campaign ended with just 11 wins in 84 games. It was hard to think of a worse team to sign on with than the Sharks, but that's precisely what Bob Errey did in mid August of 1993 as a free agent.

As bad as things looked, there were bright spots. For starters, the Sharks were moving out of their temporary first home, San Francisco's aged Cow Palace, into a brand new arena. There was a new coach, Kevin Constantine, who wanted to stress defensive discipline, which was the kind of game Errey knew all about. The Sharks also had an outstanding goaltender, Arturs Irbe, whom Minnesota had chosen 196th overall in the 1989 draft. A Latvian who had played for Dynamo Riga and the Soviet national team, Irbe had played 49 games over the previous two seasons, and he earned the starting job for 1993–94, playing in a league-leading 74 games. The Sharks had another Latvian alumnus of Dynamo Riga, defenseman Sandis Ozolinsh, taken thirtieth overall by San Jose in the 1991 draft and a standout in 1993–94 with a 64-point effort. And there were two other Soviet phenoms, Igor Larionov and Sergei Makarov. Two-thirds of the famed Soviet KLM Line of the 1980s (the "K" was Vladimir Krutov, who had a one-season stint with Vancouver in 1989–90 before retiring), they had found it difficult to adjust to the NHL. In June 1993, San Jose acquired Makarov in a multiplayer deal from Calgary via Hartford. Larionov had turned in three undistinguished seasons in Vancouver before opting to play in Switzerland in 1992–93, and San Jose picked him up on waivers in October 1993 so that he could be reunited with Makarov.

After going winless in their first nine games of the season, the Sharks, with a defense-first strategy from Constantine and leadership from their new captain, Errey, compiled a respectable

33-win record, which still left them third in the Pacific Division and well behind Detroit in every statistical measure. Detroit had far and away the league's top offense, with 356 goals, which was 104 more than San Jose scored. Even allowing for the strong defensive performance of the Sharks, who allowed only 265 goals to Detroit's 275, the Red Wings should have been able to employ their superior speed, skill and firepower to use San Jose as a sparring partner in preparation for the heavier going of later playoff rounds.

But the regular season was a poor predictor of their playoff matchup, particularly the 1–11 record San Jose had compiled in its franchise history against the Red Wings. And the regular season had ended for the Red Wings on a jarring note in a game against Dallas. Yzerman sprained the medial collateral ligament in his left knee and was scratched for the first four playoff games. Keith Primeau tore a shoulder rotator cuff, and while he dressed for the San Jose series, he was largely ineffective. Sergei Fedorov, who had suffered a slight concussion near the end of the season, was dressed for the Dallas game rather than resting, and he took another hit that may have affected him in the playoffs.

The Sharks surprised Detroit with a 5–4 win in the opening game at The Joe. Immediately, the Red Wings were paying the consequences for Bryan Murray's failure to secure a clutch playoff goaltender. Efforts to bring in Bill Ranford from Edmonton had come to nothing. Chris Osgood, a twenty-one-year-old rookie, had started half of Detroit's regular-season games, but he wasn't considered sufficiently prepared for playoff hockey. To that end, Murray had secured Bob Essensa from Winnipeg in early March, giving up his other regular goaltender, Tim Cheveldae. A chance to acquire Grant Fuhr from Buffalo had been turned down because the Wings would have had to surrender both Essensa and

Keith Primeau. Come the playoffs, Essensa lost Bowman's confidence after the opening-game loss to the Sharks.

Benching Essensa in favor of Osgood, Bowman seemed to get the Red Wings pointed in the right direction as they won the next two games 4–0 and 3–2, and were leading game four, 3–1. Then the Wings somehow fell off the Detroit wheels. The Sharks rebounded with three unanswered goals to take game four, then scored on their first two shots at Osgood in game five, for which Yzerman rejoined the lineup. Bowman went back to Essensa, who let in four of his own, and San Jose wrested the series lead back from Detroit with a 6–4 win.

Facing elimination, Bowman switched goalies again, back to Osgood, and Detroit demolished the Sharks 7–1 at The Joe, chasing Arturs Irbe from the San Jose net after the sixth goal. This was also the first game in the series in which Yzerman scored. The teams reconvened on Detroit's home ice for the deciding match. Irbe was back in net, and San Jose grabbed a 2–0 lead. Detroit came back to tie it, and with less than seven minutes left in the game, with the score tied at two, overtime loomed.

By then, friction had begun to build between Bowman and some of the Red Wings, notably Paul Coffey and Dino Ciccarelli, who were frustrated by Bowman's insistence on playing defensive hockey rather than the more wide-open game that earned them the 7–1 blowout in game six—in the process, playing to San Jose's strengths.

As overtime threatened, the Sharks were playing their usual smothering checking game, often using only one forechecker while the rest of the skaters hung back and clogged up the neutral zone. Osgood left the Detroit net to play the puck. Bob Errey was forechecking, and Osgood fired a clearing pass up off the glass and around the boards, only to have it bounce toward San

Jose center Jamie Baker. "I didn't think it was going to settle down," Baker would tell the *Toronto Star*. "But it did at the last second. I saw someone—it turned out to be Bob—and I just wanted to get the puck over to him."

Errey saw the pass coming from Baker, thought instinctively of trying to tip it, and had a split second in which to change his mind. What if he knocked it over the net? So he got out of the pass's way and watched the forty-five-footer carry right on into the empty net. Osgood hadn't been able to get back into the crease in time.

The clock showed six minutes and thirty-six seconds left in the game. Plenty of time for Yzerman and the Wings to regroup and get a tying goal. But the goal didn't happen. Irbe was impenetrable, and Baker's pass into an empty net proved to be the game and series winner. The fans in Joe Louis Arena had just seen the Red Wings exit the playoffs for the second season in a row with a game-seven loss on home ice. But this time, the team advancing at their expense paled in comparison to the Maple Leafs of 1993.

Bowman stormed off the Red Wings bench without congratulating the winning coach, Kevin Constantine, or any of his players. Igor Larionov was confused and insulted. The Russian veteran had assisted on the first two San Jose goals and was expecting gracious congratulations. "How come Scotty Bowman did not shake our hands?" he asked after the game. "He has deep respect in Russia, Scotty Bowman. But tonight was something different."

Osgood cried openly in the Detroit dressing room. "I'm sorry, I'm sorry, I'm sorry," he said. "I hope these guys stick by me next year."

Paul Coffey tried to make it clear to journalists that the loss wasn't Osgood's fault. "We shouldn't have been in a position where the goal should have mattered," the *Star* reported. "We should have had four or five goals. And there was more than six minutes still remaining in the game."

As with the 1993 game seven loss to Toronto, the 1994 upset was said to leave Yzerman again alone in The Joe, in tears, long after everyone else had cleared the building. The defeat cast a horrible pall over him and the Red Wings overall. Rumors were still alive that Mike Ilitch, fed up with building labor strife, would sell the franchise. A lot of jobs looked precarious. "We had a lot of individual players who didn't step up," Keith Gave of the *Detroit Free Press* reported Murray saying. He was waiting to meet with the coaching staff before deciding what changes to make.

As it turned out, Bowman wanted a thorough overhaul. Gave reported that Bowman presented Murray with a list of at least eleven players he considered expendable, and Yzerman and Coffey were among them. Yzerman was saying nothing about his status (or about the loss), but Murray was happy to volunteer to the press the details of his postseason meeting with the captain. "I asked Steve about [a possible trade]," Gave reported. "He, like a lot of our key guys, feels that a change or two among the core group of guys is probably necessary. He said, 'I'm not sure, Bryan, what's best for me or what's best for the team. I'd just like to get the job done here.' But Steve Yzerman would not be shocked if I went to him and said, 'Steve, I'm going to try to move you to another team.' He understands we have to think about everybody now." The only player Murray considered untradeable was Fedorov.

On June 1, Murray made it official: he was ready to entertain offers for Yzerman. "I will talk about him now," he told Gave. "We have to see what Steve Yzerman might bring in the market." Murray had fielded queries from Calgary, Washington and New York over the years, but said the possible deal for LaFontaine was the last time the captain had been a serious trade subject. Murray was looking for a defenseman and/or a big winger.

And two days later, Murray was looking for a job. Ilitch fired him, and sent his assistant, Doug MacLean, packing as well. Murray was shocked and bitter. He felt that Detroit hadn't stuck with him long enough to allow his draft picks to come along, and he made it clear that he'd had no say in the hiring of Bowman as coach. Ergo, the failure against San Jose belonged in Bowman's bailiwick, not his. It didn't matter. Ilitch bought out the final year of Murray's contract and then presided over several weeks of intense maneuvering to redefine Detroit's front office. Bowman was widely believed to have the inside track on the general manager's job, but he didn't quite get it, mainly because he didn't altogether want it. Bowman desired control over the roster, but not all the paperwork. He was named director of player personnel, which gave him the authority to negotiate trades and contracts, while he continued to serve as coach, but deals would still have to cross Ilitch's desk. At the same time, Ken Holland was promoted to assistant general manager, although there was no actual general manager to assist. Jim Devellano, meanwhile, was expected to supervise the hockey operations from his vice presidency's position.

Bowman moved quickly to declare that Yzerman would not be traded. And the coach attended Paul Coffey's wedding that summer, which might have been a gesture of rapprochement— but who ever knew, really, with Scotty. Bowman's assurance that Yzerman was off the auction block was not widely embraced as a sign of renewed affection for the highly paid star (a new contract at the start of the 1993–94 season had raised his salary to about $3 million). He was an expensive package to unload, and in addition to the MCL sprain that cost him the opening four games in the San Jose series, a herniated disk in his neck had kept him out of the first twenty-three games of the 1993–94 season. After the playoff loss to San Jose, Yzerman had gone to Los Angeles for surgery, which left his head immobilized in a "halo" for about six weeks. He wasn't exactly the picture of desirability. It would be better for Detroit to wait for him to heal, get back on skates in October, and see how things shaped up—whether Yzerman could play well enough to lead the Red Wings, or merely well enough to attract a workable trade offer.

Bowman refused to comment on speculations about lineup changes, vowing he was "not interested in running this team through the media," according to the *Free Press*'s Gave. "We don't need to make wholesale changes." It was clear, however, that either by acquiring new players or changing the skill sets of the ones he had, Bowman intended to lower Detroit's goals-against average.

Within the culture of the game, Errey's performance as captain of the Sharks' run in 1994 ranks as one of the more inspired efforts in recent playoff history. His team almost pulled off another upset in the second round, extending Toronto to a full seven games. Errey is probably known in knowledgeable circles for this feat as much as he is for winning two Cups with Pittsburgh. They certainly did not forget him in Detroit. Scotty Bowman had traded him away from Pittsburgh in the spring of 1993 to Buffalo, knowing he would be eligible for free agency that summer. Those enthusiasts of the what-if game can wonder what Pittsburgh might have been able to do in 1993 if they had still had the defensive role player in the lineup. Instead, he was allowed to mosey on to San Jose via Buffalo, where he helped Kevin Constantine inflict a postseason calamity on Bowman in his first season as Detroit's coach.

The ultimate compliment a team can pay an opposing player is to make a deal for him after he's done them damage. A dozen games into the 1994–95 season, Scotty Bowman got his hands back on Errey relatively cheaply, giving up a fifth-round pick in the upcoming draft. (In October 1995, Bowman also brought Igor Larionov, whose hand he had declined to shake, in from San Jose in exchange for Ray Sheppard, who had played on Yzerman's right wing.) After twelve years apart, Errey and Yzerman were linemates again.

The deal for Errey was made on February 8. The new season was only a few weeks old, as a lockout of players had almost caused the entire season to scrapped. (Technically, the 1994–95 season was really the 1995 season, since play didn't start until January 20. A forty-eight-game schedule had been drawn up to salvage the season after a new collective bargaining agreement was struck.)

The lockout may have saved Yzerman's bacon as a Red Wing. With the game in labor limbo, the momentum toward a possible fall 1994 trade evaporated. And in the new year, everyone was playing hurry-up hockey, simply trying to complete a shortened season. There would be plenty of time to reassess Yzerman's future after the lockout-shortened season—and his latest playoff performance—was over.

Errey joined the Red Wings on the road, in Edmonton, and Yzerman sat down with him in a restaurant to welcome him to the club and back into his playing life.

"He just wanted one thing," says Errey. "A Stanley Cup."

It was just the two of them, reunited linemates from Peterborough whose careers had followed such dramatically different trajectories. Errey was the scoring prodigy who turned out not to be the scoring star, and who had struggled for several seasons to carve out a niche in the NHL. He was never going to be an All-Star, a Hart contender or a Pearson winner, but once he had figured out where he belonged, and demonstrated his worth, he had become a champion in Pittsburgh, a respected role player in the Penguins' back-to-back wins. Players with far more natural talent than Errey spent entire careers in search of some greater satisfaction, and never achieved what Errey had. Looking at Errey's 1993–94 record in San Jose—30 points in 64 regular-season games, 5 points in 14 playoff games, a plus-minus of minus-11—it's hard to imagine that this assemblage of numbers belonged to somebody who knew something about winning. But people who couldn't see that didn't understand team sports, didn't understand that role players like Errey brought intangibles of attitude and experience, above and beyond their other skills, which did not translate readily into statistics. They were often the glue that bound great clubs together and tipped the balance of power normally thought to be the exclusive preserve of the acknowledged stars.

Errey had been privileged to play, and win, with many great players in Pittsburgh, and the Penguins had benefitted from the presence of players who had already won elsewhere: Paul Coffey in Edmonton, Joe Mullen and Jiri Hrdina in Calgary, and Bryan Trottier on Long Island. By the time Trottier got to Pittsburgh, his days as a scoring machine were over, but he knew it, and his defensive skills had allowed him to stretch his career in new directions, with new opportunities for success.

"Trottier was a guy who *knew* how to fit in," says Errey. "He was older, and he just knew where his spot was. Some players never know their role. They just never figure out what the hell they're doing."

Trottier's role had been to help everyone win, together. He'd never lost the desire to keep winning. After his second Stanley

Cup win with the Islanders in 1981, Trottier had declared, "I wish everyone who played hockey could know the feeling of winning the Stanley Cup. You win it once and you get greedy. You want to keep on winning it."

Errey had also become greedy from playing and winning. It was what had kept him dragging San Jose, an expansion club with a losing record, through two playoff rounds and almost reaching the conference finals. Now he had been brought to Detroit by Bowman, and he wanted to win again.

And Yzerman? He just wanted to win, period. Yzerman was the prodigy who had proven to be the prodigious scorer, who had accepted the responsibility of leading an NHL team at a young age, but who had not been able to figure out, despite his own talents and the resources provided to him by the Red Wings organization, how to become a champion—how to get an entire team to work toward that goal of winning in the playoffs.

Time was beginning to run out on Yzerman, and he knew it. Not just as a Red Wing, but as a professional hockey player. During the season he recorded his 600th assist and 1,100th career point and played in his 800th regular-season NHL game. There was nothing wrong with Yzerman's skills, and in fact as a player and a leader he was becoming better, more well rounded, every year. But injuries had a way of interfering with ability. He had now suffered injuries to both knees. He had missed those twenty-three games at the start of the 1993–94 season because of the herniated disk in his neck, which had driven him under the surgeon's knife. He'd already seen his linemate Gerard Gallant's career derailed by injury, his spine no longer able to withstand the punishment of the game.

The problem had first surfaced for Gallant in March 1990, when a back injury cost him the balance of the season. "I'd always had a bit of a bad back, but nothing I'd miss games over. Then one day in Montreal, we were just doing a morning skate, and I reached out for a pass a little funny. Something popped back there, and from that point on . . ."

Back spasms plagued him in 1990–91, so much so that he was no longer Yzerman's regular winger. "For a year they couldn't really find anything wrong, and then I went through surgery." Removal of a bone spur in his back in March 1991 left him off the roster in the playoffs.

The fact that Gallant had to have a bone spur operated on at the age of twenty-seven illustrates the debilitating effects of a professional hockey career. Bone spurs are a common human affliction, but they generally don't appear until old age, after a lifetime of spinal degeneration. As disc material wears out, the ligaments holding the spine together loosen, and to combat the resulting excess motion, those ligaments thicken. With time, the ligaments can calcify, creating the spurs. Gallant was a young man whose chosen career had delivered sufficient blunt trauma to give him the spinal column of an old man.

More lost games followed for Gallant—to a strained back, a hand injury, the flu. The left winger who had been a 93-point All-Star in 1988–89 had been so quickly reduced to seasons of 30 points or less, his appearances interrupted by one debilitating ailment after another. "After surgery," he says, "that was pretty well the end. I played, but never at the same level as before. I lost probably 25 percent of my game." By the summer of 1993, Gallant was done in Detroit and trying to extend his career by signing as a free agent with Tampa Bay. Two back sprains in 1993–94 limited him to 51 games and 13 points. After just one game with Tampa Bay in 1994–95, Gallant's NHL career was done.

There's nothing inherently fair in the way professional sports careers do or do not unfold. But the way Gallant's career ended, just when he was hitting stride as a marquee player, seemed a particular injustice. He had overcome his status as a late draft pick to demonstrate his worth in the game. He had shown talent, dedication and unquestioned leadership, all the things one could expect of a player. And none of it was going to matter when his back rapidly betrayed him.

Gallant and Yzerman never lost touch, speaking on the telephone every few weeks. "When I went to Tampa Bay, Detroit was very good. They had their Fedorovs and Kozlovs and Lidstroms. Steve was getting maybe 80 points now, and he's making the team play more defensively, and if he's blocking shots, they've all got to block shots." Gallant watched as Yzerman's career gathered the craziest contradictions. "He goes from winning the Pearson to supposedly not being a good leader. Now, he's one of the greatest leaders in the history of the National Hockey League. Stuff like that blows you away."

The loss to Errey's Sharks in the spring of 1994 had seriously stunned the Red Wings. After the series of playoff disappointments under Murray, the switch to Bowman hadn't solved anything. A large portion of the blame began to be focused back upon the lineup, and ultimately that blame was Yzerman's to confront. There was something missing in the will of this team to achieve, and he was striving to grasp what it was about the team, his own game and his leadership that might be wanting.

This made Yzerman's meeting with Errey in Edmonton more than the usual welcome a team captain extends to a new player. The two men who had last played together in Peterborough as teenagers were now veterans, and Yzerman was beginning to morph into an Errey. Errey had been forced into a checking game by the realities of his skill set. Yzerman, on the other hand, was adopting a more defensive role because he chose to. Even though he could still score goals, it was becoming clear to him that if he ever wanted to get his name on the big trophy the way Errey had, he had to play more defensively, and so did the team. Having produced 58 goals and 137 points as recently as 1992–93, Yzerman had put his days as a scoring phenomenon behind him. In the lockout shortened, 48-game 1994–95 season, Yzerman would produce just 12 goals.

"I asked him, 'What does this team need to win a Stanley Cup?'" Errey recalls. "And he said, 'I don't know. You tell me. You've won Stanley Cups.' I didn't expect that. We had a couple beers that night. I started telling him what I thought Stanley Cup teams had to have. It was one of the greatest conversations I've ever had."

It wasn't as if Steve Yzerman had decided that the secret to winning lay exclusively with Bob Errey. He was debriefing Errey the way he'd been buttonholing people for years. "He was a very intense listener," Mike O'Connell recalls of his time with Yzerman in the late 1980s, "almost to the point of making you uncomfortable when you were talking to him. He's all into listening to what the person is saying, and digesting it. That gives people a sense that he's quiet, or not as engaging as they'd like, but he is. He focuses on the person he's dealing with and the issue at hand, and he takes it all in."

"What makes him a good captain is he's a good listener," says Errey. "He can draw from other people and their experiences and then form his own opinion. He's not afraid to ask the tough questions. He doesn't feel he's above everybody else. He respects and values other people's opinions."

And so, over beers that night in Edmonton, Yzerman listened as Errey explained what it took to win in the NHL, in the opinion of someone who'd done some winning and had laid on the latest, and perhaps the greatest, humiliation the Red Wings had experienced in their troubled playoff history.

There is no single blueprint for success. Different teams have won in different ways. Errey talked about how in Pittsburgh they'd had to get it together defensively. A version of the left wing lock system of forechecking was used, and so Errey, a left winger, became a key player.[1] In San Jose, they'd had strong goaltending in Arturs Irbe and a good defense. Detroit had obviously had big problems in goal, one of the failings that made Bryan Murray vulnerable to being ousted. In late June 1994, Bowman made what would prove to be a critical trade, sending Yzerman's friend Steve Chiasson to Calgary to get Mike Vernon, who had won the Cup with the Flames in 1989. He would split the netminding duties with Osgood in the new season. The Red Wings also loaded up on more experienced defensemen: Bob Rouse, Mike Ramsey and Slava Fetisov.

But it was also important to have forwards who would pay attention to both ends of the rink. Bowman had been addressing that, too, since the San Jose stunner, picking up utility forwards like Errey, Doug Brown and, later in the 1994–95 season, Stu Grimson. These moves didn't let the big guns off the hook, though. "You didn't need guys who scored fifty goals but didn't do other things," Errey argued. A team also had to show discipline, particularly against a more powerful club, and stay out of the penalty box. "It should be the least talented team taking the undisciplined penalties," says Errey, "but in the San Jose–Detroit

---

[1] See page 232 for a description of the left wing lock.

series, it was the other way around." Indeed, Sergei Fedorov was lucky not to have been tossed out of game seven after cross-checking defenseman Jayson More in the first period.

Perhaps the most important point that Errey stressed was this: "You learn through losing. And you learn as a group. You ask yourselves, 'What are we *not* doing?'" Nothing better demonstrated the ability to learn from losing than San Jose's response to the thrashing they received from Detroit in game six, which sent the series into a winner-take-all final tilt. Many clubs in San Jose's position, inferior in almost every way on paper, would have been inclined to accept that drubbing as a reality check, a disciplinary correction from the Red Wings. If the NHL was a wolf pack, the Wings were the alpha male. The Sharks might have tucked their tail between their legs at the first crescendo of the fans' cheers in Joe Louis Arena, collected the inevitable loss, and congratulated themselves for having extended a powerhouse club to all seven games. Instead, they won 3–2 and went on to almost pull off the same upset against the Leafs.

"They'd beat us 7–1, and then we won 3–2," says Errey. "What do you learn from that? *Winning is winning.*" There's no cumulative score in playoff hockey. A 3–2 win is worth every bit as much as a 7–1 blowout. Detroit didn't garner extra style points for game six. And if someone pastes you 7–1, you might as well have lost 1–0 in overtime. Either way, you lost. You learn from it. You go win the next one, and remember that, just because the other guys won by six, you don't have to. And what if you're on the winning end of a thrashing like game six? "If you beat someone 7–1, that doesn't mean you'll win the next one," says Errey. "There's no resting on laurels."

In Pittsburgh, Errey had won Stanley Cups on a team that scrambled and scrapped every step of the way. Despite the brand name stars like Mario Lemieux, Kevin Stevens, Mark Recchi and Jaromir Jagr, Pittsburgh hadn't been a dominant force in the regular season. While the team won the Patrick Division in 1990–91, its 88 points would only have been good for third in any other division. In 1991–92, it produced another middling effort, 87 points, which did leave them third in the Patrick. But while the Red Wings were making early playoff exits after vying for the overall regular-season title, the Penguins were forging ahead from one adverse playoff situation to another. New Jersey had them down two games to none, then three games to two, in the opening round in 1991. But where Detroit let a three-games-to-one advantage over St. Louis slip away, Pittsburgh won against the Devils in seven. After handling Washington in five, the Penguins found themselves again down two games to none, against Boston in the conference finals. They came back with four straight wins. In the finals, they lost the opening game at home, against Minnesota, and fell behind two games to one. They responded with two wins to put Minnesota on the ropes for the first time in the series. In a crucial sixth game at home, Minnesota withered in an 8–0 Pittsburgh romp, the most lopsided Stanley Cup–winning game ever.

In the 1992 playoffs, Pittsburgh again started slowly, losing its first two games against Washington in the first round. After the Capitals put them on the brink of early elimination by taking a 3–1 series lead, Pittsburgh won the next three games. In the division finals, the Penguins fell behind two games to one against the Rangers, then won in six. After that, it was smooth sailing, as they swept Boston in the conference finals and Chicago in the finals. The Penguins' regular-season record in 1991–92, with its winning percentage of .544, was one of the poorest in the history of Stanley Cup champions. But no team had swept its final two series en route to a Cup win, the way the Penguins had, since the Oilers in 1983. Ironically, when the Penguins did produce an outstanding regular season, in 1992–93, they didn't get past the division finals.

Pittsburgh's recent successes taught another lesson about play-off hockey in the NHL. The league was in a new era of parity. In the 1970s and '80s, the league had been dominated by dynastic teams—the Canadiens, Islanders and Oilers—which turned strong regular seasons into Stanley Cup wins. But beginning in the late 1980s, a disconnect set in between the regular season and the playoffs. Calgary, in 1989, had been the last team to convert a regular-season title (the President's Cup) into a Stanley Cup win. The Oilers who won under Mark Messier in 1990 were a pale imitation of the offensive crush the team had been known for in the mid 1980s. Gretzky and Coffey were gone, and compared with their first Cup-winning season, scoring was down by 131 goals and wins by 19. Calgary, Boston, Buffalo and Montreal all had better regular seasons. But the Oilers still had a critical mass of players who knew how to win in the postseason, and after a scare from the Winnipeg Jets, who took them to seven games in the opening round, Messier and company made a workmanlike job of bringing a fifth championship to Edmonton.

In 1993, Jacques Demers managed a similar postseason triumph with the Canadiens, who were far from shabby but had finished behind Pittsburgh, Boston, Quebec, Chicago and Detroit. They also rolled up a record seven consecutive overtime wins in the course of their playoff run, a clue to the club's sheer tenacity. The Rangers appeared to reverse the trend by finishing first overall and winning the Cup in 1994, but this proved to be a one-season anomaly. And even at that, the Rangers barely survived their seven-game final series against the Vancouver Canucks, who had finished 27 points behind them.

The trend of recent years suggested that the successful teams had some special capacity for the rigors of the postseason, since success wasn't at all predicted by how well they did in the regular season. It didn't help the NHL's stature that the regular season's results were being rendered essentially meaningless. The league was running a six-month, 84-game round-robin tournament with an increasing number of teams. A new wave of expansion had been launched in 1990, with the NHL determined to grow from twenty-one to thirty teams within a decade. An almost fifty-percent increase in the number of teams and players brought a corresponding decrease in their familiarity with each other. With schedules weighted to emphasize divisional play, many teams scarcely met in the regular season, and even if they did play each other more than once or twice, the results might not count for much in predicting playoff outcomes, because team lineups went through so many changes because of trades, injuries, call-ups and demotions. Whatever team emerged from the March trade dead-line with the strongest, healthiest lineup could ignore their regular-season results, provided they had a group of individuals who could navigate four grinding rounds of confrontations, one opponent at a time. In the regular season, a team could suffer a thrashing from a tough opponent, then bounce back by playing a weaker one two nights later. In playoff hockey, the same set of SOBs was waiting, night after night. Physically, mentally, tactically, clubs had to recuperate quickly from a bad game, before a series became unsalvageable.

Yzerman was the captain of a team that could win the battles of statistics, but not a battle against a nominally inferior club like San Jose. A team with 82 points had thwarted the ambitions of a team with 100. Detroit had the star coach and the star players. San Jose had the right people working together at the right time.

It didn't matter that the Sharks were subsequently unable to get past Toronto. What mattered was that Detroit would keep on coming up short against other teams who had the right people at the right time, even for just one series, if it didn't solve its postseason problems. Inevitably, Yzerman was whispered about as one of the postseason problems, a star player who hadn't elevated his game in the playoffs.

"I think it was a real struggle for Steve to get to the finals, with the expectations people had for him," says Dave Lewis. "There was always that question of a lack of leadership in Steve. You can't really prove your leadership until you win. Players you're playing with will buy into it, but other people won't. That was a battle for Steve that people tend to forget about. Besides his performance on the ice, there was the big question of: Is his leadership enough to guide the team to a Stanley Cup? I'm not saying that's fair, but that's the way things were perceived, and perception was reality."

EIGHT

Out of life's school of war: What does
not destroy me, makes me stronger.

The nineteenth-century German philosopher Friedrich Nietzsche came up with those bon mots in his quest to define the qualities that allow the "Superman" to rise above the common herd. Next to "God is dead," the words express his most enduring idea. At the least, they comprise the one Nietzschean statement quoted by everyone from drummers in eighties big-hair metal bands facing a reunion tour of Japan to stockbrokers girding themselves to answer a few questions from the Securities Exchange Commission about insider trading. It was also the one comforting thought that the Red Wings could conceivably cling to after being swept by the New Jersey Devils in the 1995 Stanley Cup finals. During the final game, a fan in Brendan Byrne Arena had held up a sign for the Red Wings that read: WELCOME TO HELL. He didn't know the half of it.

It had taken Steve Yzerman twelve seasons to reach the Stanley Cup finals. He was the captain of a team that had domi-nated the regular season (with 70 points in 48 games), and that had the weight of media opinion and the betting line behind it. Yet where there was supposed to be an affirming triumph in which all previous playoff demons were banished, the Devils and their raucous corner of Hades delivered abject humiliation, maybe even a taste of eternal damnation. Yzerman personally hadn't contributed a single point in the entire series. His team was so bad in game three, falling behind 5–0 before the game was half done, that Scotty Bowman told the assembled media afterwards that his players shouldn't bother taking a shower because they hadn't worked up a sweat. Bowman called the 5–2 loss "the most embarrassing and humiliating loss I've ever had. It's totally unacceptable to play like we did. It's an embarrassment to the NHL in what is supposed to be their showcase series."

Where was Mr. Nietzsche when Yzerman and the Red Wings needed him? The philosopher had an undeniable way with deeply resonating ideas about achievement. Nietzsche churned out numerous pearls of Teutonic warrior wisdom that the Red Wings would be in dire need of learning before they could begin to consider the upside of not actually having been killed by the New Jersey Devils.

Professional hockey, while having been as familiar to Nietzsche as the didgeridoo (the man died in August 1900), now seems purpose-built as a proving grounds for steely musings. The ways of sport and the art of war are rhetorically inseparable. What makes for great generals, makes for great captains. What makes for great armies, makes for great teams. Winning sports championships has become a Nietzschean pursuit that requires sacrifice, courage and the ability not only to define goals, but to know how to pursue them and to lead others in that pursuit.

We have reached mastery when we neither
mistake nor hesitate in the achievement.

Mistakes? Hesitation? Too many to count in that series with New Jersey. Like the shortened regular season itself, and Detroit's breakneck pace in the opening three rounds (taking only fourteen games to amass twelve wins), the finals seemed to happen all too quickly once the Red Wings found themselves at a disadvantage. They were playing an opponent that wasn't supposed to have the strengths that it did. (They were also playing a team they knew nothing about. Because interconference play had been scrapped in the lockout-shortened season, Detroit and New Jersey hadn't met in 1994–95, and they'd never before met in the playoffs.) New Jersey was dismissed by many as a plodding team of big men who survived through defensive dullness. But they turned out to have far more going for them than the neutral-zone trap, which bogged down swift opponents in the middle of the rink. In midseries, Detroit defenseman Paul Coffey marveled that, back in his Oilers days, they would skate away from opponents who tried to hit them. But these guys would hit the Red Wings, and then skate them down so they could do it again. And they could score when they wanted to. Coming into the series, in fact, the Devils had averaged more goals per game in the playoff run (3.4) than Detroit had (3.14). And they'd allowed fewer goals—1.8 versus 2.0.

Greatness means leading the way.

The top-performing center Detroit had going into the finals was not Yzerman or Fedorov, but Keith Primeau. His contribution was larger than his points production suggested: the big man was playing an exemplary two-way game. But in the second period of game one, Devils defenseman Scott Stevens caught him with a check from behind that sent his back into spasm. He left the game to rest in a hyperbaric chamber that traveled with the

Red Wings, and was a scratch for game two. When Primeau left the game, Fedorov and Yzerman had to be double-shifted. Detroit had already been held to twelve shots in the first two periods. In the third, the team had just one shot as it lost 2–1. Fedorov and Yzerman chipped in a total of two shots on net the whole game.

"Our team doesn't change much with Keith gone," Yzerman said after the loss. "We just need someone to come in and do the job." But it wasn't him. When another reporter asked him if the Wings would miss Primeau, Yzerman, in a more honest assessment, quipped, "Well, we don't have another six-foot-five, 230-pound center to throw in there."

Yzerman was already hobbled by his troublesome right knee, which locked up in their second-round series against San Jose (a sweep that avenged the opening-round upset of 1994). In the finals, Yzerman was simply not a factor. No points, no impression made on the Devils. "I thought we'd be able to persevere and get through their defensive shell," he said after the series. "Obviously, we weren't able to do that."

Character is determined more by the lack
of certain experiences than by those one has had.

The final series was a throwback to the last playoff series Errey and Yzerman had played together as juniors in Peterborough, against the Oshawa Generals. And they even had John MacLean, their old Generals opponent, facing them in the Devils lineup. The Generals had been bigger, tougher, and they had been expected to win by manhandling the Petes in the opening round of the OHL playoffs in 1983. They did some manhandling, but they also proved to have more going for them in terms of all-around skill and, most important, discipline.

"Talentwise, the Petes are at least on par, if not better, than Oshawa," Mike Brophy complained in the *Peterborough Examiner* after the Petes dropped the first two games, "but their desire to win, their sacrifice, has been less than impressive." Yzerman was named player of the game in game one; but after another loss in game three, Brophy wrote: "Peterborough's top shooters . . . have been checked by Oshawa, but not to any degree. Some—notably center Steve Yzerman—seem to be stuck in neutral. Yzerman has just one goal and one assist in three games." He would rebound with three points in the final game, but it was a losing cause as the Generals recorded a sweep. Now a dozen years later, another big, tough team had kept Yzerman from postseason success, and left observers questioning his playoff fortitude.

The great epochs of our life come when we gain the courage to rechristen our evil as what is best in us.

"I'm the most hated man in hockey," New Jersey Devils captain Claude Lemieux crowed after completing the sweep of Detroit with another 5–2 win, "and I have my name on the Conn Smythe Trophy."

The guy voted the most valuable player of the 1995 playoffs would sign with Colorado as a free agent, and in the course of eliminating Detroit in six games in round two of the '96 playoffs, would sucker punch Vyacheslav Kozlov and smash Kris Draper's face into the top of the boards at the Detroit bench, right in front of Yzerman. Sometimes, nice guys do finish last. Learning to embrace their inner evil was something many players had learned to do in the course of becoming winners—just ask Ken Linseman. Not everyone had to do it, and many of those who did do it would have preferred not to, but the ones who did often prevailed. Those who weren't about to embrace their inner evil would have to figure out how to smother the evil mojo of their opponents.

Many are stubborn in pursuit of the path
they have chosen, few in pursuit of the goal.

Great teams and their leaders have to learn how to win. And once they have learned, they often demonstrate an ability to go on winning, reaching a higher level than their regular-season record or individual statistics suggest they should. They learn by understanding that if they're in the game to win, they have to be willing to change the way they play. If what they are isn't what's required, then they become what is necessary, individually and collectively. Never mind the path: focus on the goal.

And therein lay Yzerman's sole hope for retribution after the 1995 loss. His greatest strength has been his capacity for engineering change, first in his own game, then in that of his teammates. Mike O'Connell reiterates some of the basic points Dave Lewis has made on how a young star establishes himself in the league and then shifts his priorities.

"With the top leaders," O'Connell explains, "there are different stages in their development. The young player coming in has to establish himself, in what he does and what's he's strong at. And that takes time. That's why Steve was racking up 130, 140 points per year. All of a sudden he realizes, 'Well, I can do this. Now, what's next?' At that point, when Steve realized, 'This is all great, all these points, but really, I'm not winning,' that's when the transformation comes, turning a really top player into a leader. It's when they realize they'd be better off getting ninety points and taking more defensive face-offs, being more responsible, playing the full sheet more. They become aware of the full sheet, and the ramifications of not playing the full sheet: you lose. Yzerman obviously became one of those players. Whether it was through Bowman's assistance or the people around him or just his own development, he finally said, 'Screw this. I'm tired of losing and scoring 130 points. I want to win and I don't care if I score 130 points or thirty points.'"

"It came to the point with Steve where he didn't need to score fifty goals," Bob Errey chimes in. "It didn't get him a championship. He had to ask himself: What am I doing to help my team defensively? He was always a great player, but he was never going to go down as a great champion, a great leader. Now he's going to go down as one of the greatest captains and leaders of all time."

When did that transformation come with Yzerman? There was no great divide in his career, with mountains of points on one side and defensive tenacity on the other. Yzerman did not simply wake up one morning and decide, "Today I'm going to be a completely different player." Yzerman had been trained in the two-way game in Peterborough, and those who played with him and coached him in Detroit in his early years insist the defensive skills were already there and on display when he was having seasons that put him in the highest reaches of the scoring race. But people who know him well also generally agree that 1995 was, for several reasons, a kind of tipping point, a fulcrum on which his entire career proved to be balanced. The ordeal by fire of the tumultuous, bloody and even hateful playoff matchups between the Red Wings and the Colorado Avalanche in 1996 and '97 are sometimes seen as the fundamental catalyst in Detroit's capability to finally win the Cup in 1997, and then win repeatedly. But Dave Lewis places the most important event back in June 1995, when the Devils destroyed whatever postseason credibility Detroit had managed to amass in the first three rounds.

And the criticism had been brutal. Bob McKenzie's assessment of the Red Wings after game four was typical. "The only trap evident last night was the one that we all fell into this spring," he wrote in the *Toronto Star*. "That is, the widely held belief that the Red Wings, weak-willed and dismal playoff failures the last two years, were finally made of much sterner stuff. Now we know they're not."

"Before going into the finals," says Lewis. "I called Steve, and we talked. We felt we were playing so well that we were going to win a Stanley Cup. And as it turned out, we lost in four straight. And I think the lesson learned there, and which he never forgot and I never forgot, was that you can be very good and so close, but you're *still* four games away. And we didn't get it done. I think that went very deep to the soul of Steve. We made changes in the organization, and a couple of years later we ended up winning. I think that was—I don't know if it was a defining moment, but a moment you don't forget as an athlete."

Jacques Lemaire, the coach of the Devils who had once played for Scotty Bowman as a Cup-winning Montreal Canadien, had in fact telegraphed a root cause of Detroit's impending fate during a press conference before game one of the final series. He was comfortable in the underdog's role. "If everyone keeps telling you how great you are," he suggested at a pre-series press conference, "maybe you believe it and forget how much hard work it took to get there."

For a player like Yzerman, being swept by New Jersey after finally reaching the Cup finals after so many seasons of trying was not unlike watching Chris Osgood throw away the puck late in the third period of game seven against San Jose in 1994. You're down by a goal and there's only about six minutes left on the clock. If you don't figure out something soon, you're going to lose, and you won't get another chance to win. Yzerman by then was acutely aware that, as capably as he was playing, careerwise time was not on his side. "He thought in 1995–96, that this was the end of his career," says Errey. "At that point, every year was going to be his last year, his last chance to win the Stanley Cup."

Yzerman had good reason to consider every season as his last. When his right knee locked up in the second round of the 1995 playoffs, it was a worrying sign that his body might not be able to keep pace with his ambition. A lockup is a classic sign of damage to the minisci, the knee's shock absorbers. Minor tears can be alleviated with a muscle-strengthening program, but more serious damage inevitably leads to surgery. Without the surgery, as the minisci break down, so too does the cartilage shielding the ends of the bones. Loose bits of an injured meniscus alone can cause excruciating pain.

A sense of one's professional mortality has a way of focusing the mind, and Yzerman's goal became truly singular: win the Cup. But he wasn't interested in winning it just anywhere. After the disappointment of the New Jersey series, Yzerman did not begin casting his eyes about for another vehicle to deliver him that success. He was not Ray Bourque, asking to be traded after an entire career in Boston so that he could have a chance to win with Colorado on the eve of retirement. Yzerman already had most of the necessary ingredients to win in Detroit. Ever since being invited to Detroit to check out the Red Wings organization before he was chosen in the 1983 draft, he had committed himself to winning in Motor City. But he came close to not getting a second chance.

The departure of Bryan Murray in the summer of 1994, just two days after saying he was prepared to entertain trade offers for

Steve Yzerman, did not end the trade rumors surrounding the captain. Nor did the assurances made by Bowman, immediately after Murray's departure, that Yzerman was not on the auction block. In August 1995, two months after the loss to New Jersey in the Cup finals, Yzerman's name was being heard as a possible inducement to get the Rangers (where former Red Wings director of player personnel Neil Smith was in charge) to hand over Mark Messier—a bigger, brawnier center than Yzerman, four years older (and that much closer, it would have seemed, to retirement) but a proven winner, possibly what Detroit needed to get the Stanley Cup with one solid shove in 1996. That deal never happened, but in September a much more serious discussion was held between the Red Wings and the Ottawa Senators.

"There were two times in Steve's career when there were definite trade possibilities," says Jim Devellano. The first involved the possible swap for Pat LaFontaine. The second was the deal with Ottawa, which involved protracted negotiations right before the start of the 1995–96 season.

Three meetings were held in three different places: in Windsor, Montreal and finally Denver. The principal figures were Randy Sexton, the general manager of the Senators, and on Detroit's side, Scotty Bowman and assistant general manager Ken Holland, whose knowledge of draft prospects was critical to shaping any package.

The motivations behind the deal were multiple. First, Bowman was willing to let Yzerman go. In Devellano's words, "Scotty was not particularly enamored of Steve's two-way play." But while it's true that Yzerman had not had anything close to a standout series against New Jersey, Yzerman's agent, Larry Kelly, still cannot seriously believe that Bowman actively wanted to get rid of him. "There clearly was a time when there was so much smoke that there had to be some substance to [the trade rumors]," says Kelly. But he sees the Ottawa talks in the broader context of Bowman's relationship with both Yzerman and Fedorov. The idea that Bowman might have been unhappy enough with Yzerman's two-way game to actively want to trade him "shocks me," says Kelly. "There was a time after Fedorov came in that I recall Scotty, who was a master at playing one player off against another, really did challenge Steve, and almost elevated Fedorov above Steve. I don't think anyone ever questioned Steve's ability to play defense. And Steve just took the bull by the horns and made it very clear who was the premier player on that team."

Fedorov's arrival unquestionably had changed the complexion of the Red Wings. He was an outstanding talent, gifted offensively and defensively, and in 1993–94 he broke through as a superstar, finishing second in the league in total points and third in goals, as well as second in plus-minus. His trophy haul was unprecedented. Not even Gretzky ever managed to win the Frank Selke Trophy (for best defensive forward), the Hart Trophy, the Pearson Award and the First All-Star Team berth at center in one season. *The Hockey News, The Sporting News* and *Hockey Digest* all named Fedorov the player of the year. In terms of celebrity wattage, he vastly outshone his team captain. It was also the first season since 1985–86 in which Yzerman did not lead his own team in scoring, finishing behind Fedorov and right winger Ray Sheppard. Although Yzerman's points production was down in part because he had missed twenty-six games with a herniated disc, it was nevertheless the beginning of a change in Yzerman's career.

The Ottawa trade also had the appearance of being a Plan B for the Red Wings, an alternative to the one alleged to have been in the works to acquire Messier. Instead of Messier, Detroit would replace Yzerman with another big power forward, Alexei Yashin. Given Detroit's enthusiasm for Russian talent, the desire to obtain Yashin would not be out of character. But the impetus for the deal, in hindsight, makes much more sense when Ottawa is placed in the driver's seat. It wasn't so much that Detroit wanted Yashin, or wanted to be rid of Yzerman. It was more likely a case of Ottawa both desperately wanting Yzerman *and* desperately wanting to avoid paying Yashin what he was demanding. While doubts about Yzerman's ability to bring Stanley back to Detroit were enough to allow the negotiations to occur, it was Ottawa's eagerness to bring home a favorite son that kept the teams enmeshed in discussions.

The root of Ottawa's desire to have Yzerman was no different than Detroit's wish to draft hometown boy Pat LaFontaine back in 1983: the name of the game was filling arena seats. Yzerman was a product of Ottawa's minor hockey system, with friends and family still in the area. As a season-ticket draw, Yzerman would be impossible to surpass, and the Senators had a lot of tickets to sell. In the first three seasons of the franchise's history, beginning in 1992–93, the Senators had played their home games in the Ottawa Civic Centre. It only had 10,500 seats, but the Senators were so bad that they had trouble even filling that modest facility. Come January 1996, the team was due to move into its permanent home, the newly built, 18,500-seat Palladium (now the Corel Centre) in suburban Kanata.

There had been delays in finishing the new arena, and the team did not shine with either managerial or on-ice competence. At the expansion draft in June 1992, the Senators lost their list of available players and twice tried to draft people who weren't on offer. And at the entry draft that followed, the Senators, choosing second overall, selected Yashin, a strapping eighteen-year-old with Moscow Dynamo who would prove to have talent, but also major contractual baggage.

The Senators took another promising center, Alexander Daigle, in 1993, when they selected first overall. Randy Sexton, a real estate man serving as Ottawa's general manager, rewarded the teenager with a five-year, $12.5 million contract. Daigle had produced 137 points in 53 games for the Victoriaville Tigres of the Quebec Major Junior league in 1992–93; as impressive as that production might have been, the contract struck the rest of the league as totally outrageous and a sure trigger to inflate rookie salaries as agents for other youngsters looked for similar deals.

The Daigle contract, predictably, also had immediate repercussions with the Senators' other young star, Alexei Yashin. Only a last-minute effort got his signature on a contract he was happy with before the start of the lockout-shortened 1994–95 campaign, but when the season ended, the problems resumed, and Yashin refused to report to training camp. It would be September 2001 before Yashin's extended contractual disputes with Ottawa were fully resolved—by sending him to the Islanders—but as early as the summer of 1995 it had already occurred to Sexton that the most efficient way to deal with Yashin might be to trade him.

And so the stage was set for the traveling negotiations with Detroit. The principals were the proven star whose ability to bring a championship to Detroit was being questioned, but whose marquee value in Ottawa was sure to help fill the new arena in January, and an obviously gifted young Russian who had an additional gift for contractual squabbles. If Yashin went to Detroit, he could play with a club full of talented Russians, and for an owner whose dismay with hockey in the wake of the 1992 walkout had evaporated in his desire to see a Stanley Cup win. Mike Ilitch was, as always, willing to pay the top salaries in the league to people who could help achieve that goal.

And a player of Yashin's caliber did represent the sort of compensation the Red Wings would demand before entertaining the notion of giving up Yzerman. There would have to be "something immediately very good to replace Yzerman," says Devellano. A "bundle for the future," in the form of draft picks or young players, could also be part of the package, but there would have to be someone of comparable value *right now,* to help finish the job of winning a Stanley Cup. Looking at the Senators' lineup at the time, Yashin was the only logical "someone." Daigle was too young, and, as it would turn out, overhyped as a future star; he would end up being traded to Philadelphia in January 1998. The Senators' first-overall pick in the '95 draft, Bryan Berard, could conceivably have become part of the deal, but Ottawa was hamstrung by the fact that he had walked out of training camp that fall when Sexton didn't offer him a contract. The Rhode Island–born defenseman, like Brian Lawton a product of Mount St. Charles High School, instead remained in junior hockey with the Detroit Whalers of the OHL, and Ottawa ended up trading his rights to Long Island in January 1996.

The worst-case scenario for Yzerman was not to have an injury end his career prematurely before he had a chance to win, as was the case with his friend and linemate Gerard Gallant; it was to be dealt away to another team and have to watch the Red Wings win without him, while he was in his prime. Dave Lewis had been through it, and it was not pleasant.

"Personally, there was obviously a lot of emotion," Lewis says of his trade from the Islanders to the Kings just weeks before his old team won its first of four consecutive Stanley Cups. "I was disappointed I did not win the Cup with the Islanders. It took me another seventeen years to win a Cup, so I guess it did help me persevere. But I was so excited that they won, because I had gone through the struggle with them in the seven years I was there. There was so much pressure to win, and nobody thought they could ever win. I felt part of at least the mindset, if nothing else. And the players actually called me from the locker room after the final game."

It was heartfelt and generous of the Islanders to do that for Lewis. But that was a phone call Steve Yzerman never wanted to take. *Hey, we won finally. Wish you were here.*

It has been said, even by people close to Yzerman, that he killed the Ottawa trade. But Kelly says he had no knowledge of any particulars of a deal, and did not act to turn it down at his client's direction. And Devellano is adamant that there was never a deal to kill. Extended discussions of a possible deal—yes. An actual deal—no.

"Names and draft choices were bounced around for a long time in the meetings," says Devellano. Sexton flew to Denver for a meeting with Bowman on October 6, in a last-ditch effort to strike a deal before Detroit opened its season against the Colorado Avalanche. "At the end of the day, the truth of the matter was Ottawa could not afford to pick up Yzerman's contract. It was high, and in U.S. dollars. They actually expected us to still pay some of it."

Regardless of whether or not Yzerman ever killed a deal that was never in fact completed, he was adamantly opposed to leaving Detroit for Ottawa. Even without his attachment to Detroit, Ottawa's chaotic state and dreadful record would have horrified him, although the team's fortunes were due to improve. An immediate management overhaul included the arrival of Jacques Martin (who had scouted Yzerman for the Petes) as coach. The Senators missed the playoffs again in 1995–96, but a season later they improved from 18 wins to 31. With time, the team began to be talked about as a Stanley Cup contender, in much the same way that the Red Wings had been in the early 1990s—and when their playoff drives repeatedly came up short, they also began to be labeled playoff choke artists, in much the same way that the Red Wings had been. Fans who suffered through the seemingly endless melodrama surrounding Yashin's contract can be forgiven for wondering if things might not have turned out far more happily, far sooner, if the Senators hadn't tried to get Detroit to pick up part of Yzerman's salary and had just brought their favorite son home, whether he wanted to come or not.

In any event, there probably would never have been a trade, because in Detroit the buck stopped with owner Mike Ilitch. Scotty Bowman could negotiate a trade, but he'd still have needed Ilitch's approval, and there's no guarantee he ever would have agreed to let his captain go.

"When Steve knew he had a chance to win the Stanley Cup, it was so disappointing for him when he lost," says Gerard Gallant, recalling the 1995 series. "He kept battling, and there were trade rumors, and rumors that he wasn't a great leader. He just shook that stuff off. He wanted to win the Stanley Cup with Detroit. He didn't want to go to Ottawa or somewhere else to win it. He wanted to finish the job, and he wanted it so bad."

And the Detroit fans wanted him to finish the job, too. Star players experience widely differing relationships with fans. In a city like Montreal in the 1950s, 1960s and 1970s, the culture of winning was so deeply ingrained that players faced daunting expectations of continued excellence. It was considered a privilege to wear the *bleu, blanc et rouge,* and the tremendous sense of obligation came right along with the prestige of doing so. By the 1990s, when stars like Eric Lindros and Alexei Yashin started playing hardball about where they were willing to play and the amount they were willing to play for, fans responded by taking a colder, more calculating view of them and holding them up to almost ruthless expectations. In the absence of goodwill on the players' part, fans began to display no patience for subpar performances or anything less than playoff success.

But even in this poisoned environment, a relationship can still develop between a player and a team's fans in which the fans beg for success as much for the player's sake as their own. They want a player to achieve the completeness of a champion, to fulfill the admiration they have for him. It's an unusual form of empathy and adoration, and it doesn't come along very often. Doug Gilmour, the captain in Toronto during the early 1990s, was a rare example. Many fans streaming into Maple Leaf Gardens would have willingly donated blood if it would have helped Gilmour lead the Leafs to a Stanley Cup title. The longing of Leaf fans for a follow-up win to their 1967 title is legendary, yet this desperation never translated into impatience with Gilmour or dissatisfaction when his efforts came up short of a Cup parade.

It was no different with Steve Yzerman in Detroit. The fans in The Joe were overwhelmingly in tune with Yzerman's own ambitions, to stay in Detroit and finish the job of winning he'd taken on in 1983. After the Yashin trade talks, a bond solidified between fans and captain. They embraced his loyalty, didn't question his ability or determination, and treated him as the people's player, with management (particularly Bowman) and even other Red Wings players consigned to a separate category of supporting characters who were not always necessarily on Yzerman's—or their—side.

When Yzerman stepped back onto the ice of Joe Louis Arena after the negotiations that would have sent him to Ottawa collapsed, he was greeted by a chorus of chanting fans, who shook the building with a rhythmic *Stevie . . . Stevie . . . Stevie.* At the same time, they booed Bowman.

"We need Yzerman. I won't trade him," Bowman would pledge. And the Red Wings would reward Yzerman with a new four-year contract in 1996 that was meant to ensure he ended his playing days in Detroit.

Bob Errey agrees wholeheartedly with the idea that his linemate occupied a unique place in the fans' affections. "They just loved Stevie. Steve *was* Detroit. The fans wanted a championship for Stevie. Maybe for Steve and themselves and not even anyone else on the team."

NINE

GERARD GALLANT'S PHONE RANG. IT WAS JUNE 1997; Gallant was back home on Prince Edward Island, his playing career having been over for two seasons. He was beginning a fresh chapter in his hockey life, as a coach. After injuring his back one final time in a practice with the Detroit Vipers of the International Hockey League in November 1996, he had returned home and taken over the bench of the Summerside West Pontiacs of the Maritime Junior A league. Gallant had just completed his first full season as Summerside's coach, finishing with a flourish in May: the team had hosted the Royal Bank Cup, the national championship of Tier II Junior hockey. After going 1–3 in the round-robin, the West Pontiacs came through in the playoffs and won the title with a 4–3 defeat of the South Surrey Eagles.

Gallant had finally won something, and he was on his way to a string of upwardly mobile coaching jobs that would see him become head coach of the NHL's Columbus Blue Jackets in 2003–04. On the other end of the phone was a friend who was trying to finally win something as well. Steve Yzerman was deep into another playoff run with the Red Wings—so deep that it was promising to end on a high note. The Wings were leading the Philadelphia Flyers three games to none in the 1997 Stanley Cup finals.

Detroit had a seeming stranglehold on the series, as Scotty Bowman's close-checking game and line-matching skills had placed his opposite number, Terry Murray, without any obvious options. Bowman had also stuck with Mike Vernon as his starting goaltender, even after pulling him twice in favor of Chris Osgood earlier in the playoffs, while Murray waffled between Garth Snow and Ron Hextall in the finals. The Red Wings were playing with the sort of machinelike efficiency that had been their undoing in 1995 at the hands of New Jersey. No one could imagine the Flyers rebounding to win four straight games, or the Red Wings falling apart at this stage. Such a collapse had happened in the finals only once—ironically, to the Red Wings, in 1942—and this year's edition appeared to be the least likely squad to repeat such ignoble history.

Yzerman and Gallant had spoken quite a bit on the phone throughout this postseason, and now Yzerman thought they should wind it up by speaking in person. "Turk, why don't you come on up to Detroit?" Yzerman proposed. "I know you'd like to be here when we win the Cup."

At thirty-two, Yzerman could sense the victory at hand, and he was gathering family and friends around him to share in the success he had chased for fourteen NHL seasons. It was important to him that an old linemate and friend, who hadn't been able to make the full run with him, could at least share in some of the experience of winning.

But Gallant refused the invitation. "We're both superstitious. I said, 'Steve, I'd love to be there, but I'm not moving until you've won the thing.' I didn't want to be part of them losing somehow, of Philly coming back and winning four straight."

So he stayed home and watched on TV. And once the Cup was securely in Steve Yzerman's hands, Gerard Gallant went to the mainland for a party Yzerman had organized to express his thanks for the contributions so many former teammates had made to help him turn the Dead Things into a championship team.

Asked if he remembers this gathering, Dave Lewis says, with a laugh, "There were a *lot* of parties after we won."

Few NHL clubs that are good enough to earn multiple championships actually begin their streak of titles as soon as they're thought to be capable of doing so. The regular-season titles tend to come first, and the playoff successes follow. More often than not, there is a period of losing, and learning from what doesn't kill them. It makes key players stronger, more aware of their own roles and their obligation to the team overall. It finds other players wanting, or makes them expendable in the cause of filling holes that failure exposes.

The Red Wings lost two Cup finals in the late 1940s before squeaking out a seventh-game, double-overtime win against the upstart New York Rangers. Once they'd put that cliffhanger behind them, they completed a run of four Cup wins in six seasons. The Toronto Maple Leafs lost two finals in 1959 and 1960, and were knocked out in five games in the semifinals (by Detroit) in 1961 when they were capable of going all the way, before reeling off three straight Cup wins and adding a fourth in 1967. The Boston Bruins had to live and learn through a pair of losses to Montreal—first in the 1968 quarterfinals, then in the semifinals—before they won it all in 1970 and '72. They might have gone on winning had the arrival of the WHA not cost them key players like their goalie, Gerry Cheevers. The Islanders struggled famously in the late 1970s to turn their regular-season successes into a decent playoff run. Until they finally did it, in 1980—the first of four consecutive Cup wins—many people had written them off as a team of individual stars who didn't know how to win as a group in the postseason. The Edmonton Oilers went through a less trying initiation but they nevertheless had to be swept in their first finals, by the Islanders in 1983, to learn from a veteran team about defensive discipline and personal sacrifice. A famous story is told, of members of the losing Oilers team seeing the Islanders tending to their wounds with ice packs in their dressing room after sweeping Edmonton. These Oilers recognized that nobody in their own dressing room looked as beat-up as the Islanders did. The lessons they had yet to learn, but which the Islanders were all too aware of, included the knowledge that to win, you had to be willing to pay a high personal price.

It was Dave Lewis's experience as an Islander in the late 1970s that gave him faith in Yzerman's ability to prove the doubters wrong about his leadership and his capacity for playoff hockey. "He got better every year, and he improved in all areas. He improved in his outlook on the game, in what is needed to win, in how he can complement players, how he can make players around him better. Whether it was in a weight room or on a stationary bike or doing drills when he practiced skating, that's the Steve Yzerman I saw improving. I saw the Steve Yzerman of points and skill and playmaking go through a phase that all the great ones go through. Mike Bossy and Bryan Trottier, they came in with the Islanders and were criticized for not winning big games. Then all of a sudden, things happened. You learn, you grow, and you get an understanding of what it takes to win."

From the outside looking in, Yzerman's leadership ability wasn't ever obvious. He didn't have the *rah-rah* mentality.

Sportswriters looking for news of a stirring, to-the-battlements dressing-room speech by Stevie Y largely went wanting. Maybe the guy just didn't have what it took.

But within the organization, there was no doubt that the Red Wings were Yzerman's team. "Steve blocks more shots than anyone on that team," says Errey. "He's a leader in all facets of the game. He can be as physical as you want him to be out there. He doesn't take crap from anyone. And he didn't have a problem, when I was there, going up to a top offensive player on the team and saying, 'What are you doing?' You don't have to be a captain to be a leader. He was the leader, regardless of the letter on his sweater. He had a lot of leeway, and could take a forty-goal scorer behind closed doors and tell the guy what was needed from him. He had no problem getting into a player's face and telling him what he thought."

"Steve wasn't the kind of guy who was going to yell at someone and say, 'You were a dog tonight,'" says Gallant. "When it got to the point where someone had to be talked to, to be told, 'If we're going to win, you've got to be better,' he would do that. He wasn't going to rant and rave.

"When Detroit started to win championships," Gallant stresses, "it was all about Steve. It wasn't about you getting 45 goals or 103 points for the team that season. It was about guys sacrificing offensive production, and maybe sacrificing a little bit of salary they could have gotten somewhere else, to win. That's what it was all about, and he was the leader of that group."

Spend any time thinking about the transformation of Steve Yzerman from a great player into a great champion, and you will end up thinking about Scotty Bowman as well—about how important he was to Yzerman's evolution.

A professional hockey club's dressing room is still a closed shop, and there is a code among players which holds that (except for positive events) what goes on in there, stays in there. Yet there's no question that there was, at times, antagonism between Yzerman and Bowman. In a documentary produced by the CBC on Yzerman in 2002, his teammate Brendan Shanahan allowed, "For a guy who had really earned the right to a certain amount of respect, there were a couple of years he was treated poorly for a team captain." In the same documentary, the *Detroit Free Press* columnist Mitch Albom quipped, "Bowman ended up here long enough that he let go of picking on Steve Yzerman and he started picking on everybody else."

Scotty Bowman is best thought of in the same vein as a theater or film director who is concerned only with the end results of the production, and doesn't particularly care what kind of private and public torment the actors have to go through as he shapes a perfect ensemble performance. He spent his entire career keeping people off balance, challenging their comfort zones. Many players need this. Some players don't respond with anything more than frustration and contempt. Some, on whom it works, hate it while it's happening but appreciate it later. And some just chalk it up to the game being a business and Bowman having his role and they having theirs.

The Red Wings had appeared to be coming apart at the seams in the midst of the disastrous 1995 series against New Jersey. Paul Coffey, who was on the ice for five of the first six New Jersey goals, was pleading publicly for the team to pull together and work as a group, while Bowman was accusing them of turning in the most embarrassing performance of his career. Forward Shawn Burr, who was the second most experienced Red Wing on the team after Yzerman, having played his first games in

1984–85, exploded in public when he was scratched for game three, a move Bowman defended because he felt Burr wasn't producing enough offense. "All year they're preaching good defense and now, all of a sudden, they want me to score goals," the *Toronto Star* reported Burr as saying. Bowman also accused Burr of having handed a dropped stick back to New Jersey's Scott Neidermayer in game two, a charge he later retracted. But Bowman still traded Burr to Tampa Bay that August. Safely ensconced as a Lightning, Burr excoriated his old coach to the *Tampa Tribune*. "He's the most disrespectful man I've ever met. He's just a mean man with no social skills. You can't argue with his success as a hockey coach, but the way he treats people? That's not right. There's a difference between not getting close to a guy and treating him like scum. And Scotty, as far as I know, treats everyone like scum."

The animosity extended beyond the playing ranks. Jim Devellano, who had hired him, respected Bowman's ability to get results, but their personal relationship became essentially nonexistent after Devellano felt Bowman was saying one thing to the press about his future plans following the 1997 Stanley Cup win and another thing to him.

Bob Errey was coached by Bowman both in Pittsburgh and in Detroit. He was also unloaded by him twice—from the Penguins in the spring of 1993, then from Detroit in February 1997, when he was placed on waivers by Bowman and returned to San Jose. He helped Canada win a world championship in 1997, then played his last NHL season, 1997–98, with Dallas and (after a multiplayer deal right before the trade deadline) the Rangers. He spent the next season with Hartford in the American league, and when his former coach in San Jose, Kevin Constantine, was hired to coach the Penguins for 1999–2000, Errey attended Pittsburgh's training camp but didn't make the cut. His professional career was officially over, and he moved into the broadcast booth, providing color commentary for Penguins games for Fox Sports. After he left Detroit, Errey said of Bowman: "A man that doesn't respect people should not be given any respect." Today, he declines the opportunity to say anything at all about Bowman.

Back when Bowman was running the Sabres, he exasperated another former Peterborough Pete, Craig Ramsay, a gifted defensive forward who won the Selke Trophy in 1985 at the end of his final playing season (during which he also served as assistant coach). Ramsay had been coached by Roger Neilson in Peterborough and greatly admired him as a coach and a person. Ramsay also played under Neilson in Buffalo, when Bowman tried Neilson as his coach in 1980–81, only to fire him after just one season. It turned out to be the longest tenure of any coach in Buffalo under Bowman. Retiring as a player before the start of the 1985–86 season, Ramsay carried on as an assistant coach for Bowman, and one of Bowman's last acts as general manager in Buffalo was to give Ramsay the head coaching job in the fall of 1986.

Ramsay lost his coaching job after twenty-three games, at the same time Bowman was fired, but he remained in the Sabres organization through 1992–93 as the director of professional evaluation and development and then as assistant to the general manager. He went on to serve as an assistant coach with Neilson in Florida, Ottawa and Philadelphia, and was named head coach of Philadelphia in February 2000 when Neilson was diagnosed with cancer. Hired as an associate coach by Tampa Bay in January 2001 by general manager Rick Dudley—a former Buffalo teammate of his—Ramsay was considered so critical to the development of the Lightning's young talent that the Florida Panthers were refused permission to interview him after they fired Mike Keenan as head coach in November 2003. As an assistant coach to John Tortorella, Ramsay was behind the Lightning bench when Tampa Bay won the Stanley Cup in June 2004.

Both as a player and as a coach, Ramsay was frustrated by a lot of what Bowman did in Buffalo, but he nevertheless developed a good feel for the man's merits. "Not everybody is going to be able to deal with what Scotty has to offer," Ramsay has told this writer. "Steve Yzerman was a great player, but a great player on a bad team for a few years, and then a great player on a good team that couldn't win. And now, everybody has to love to watch Steve Yzerman play. He dives to block shots, he backchecks, he wins face-offs. This guy does absolutely everything for his team, while still being a great offensive player.

"Scotty wants a complete player. In Buffalo, he wouldn't put up with a purely checking guy who had no offensive skills. He couldn't understand why guys couldn't make great plays. He wants a guy who can legitimately play in both ends of the rink. He doesn't want a one-dimensional player. He admires talent, and determination, guys that will fight through.

"If you're willing at some point to put up with Scotty and work at it, you'll find out that, hey, I can do a lot of great things, and win. Instead of just trying to score goals, I can do more than that, and be a better player. I don't think anybody in the game today can look at Yzerman and not say, 'This guy is a topnotch, two-way, dedicated and determined hockey player.' He's learned how to be a winner."

Yzerman put up with a lot. For a time, he was shifted from center to play left wing in a Bowman experiment—for that matter, Bowman also tried Sergei Fedorov as a defenseman in the last six weeks of the 1996–97 season, before turning the bewildered superstar back into a forward for the playoffs. Playing left wing made Yzerman the "lock" in the left wing lock, the checking system that the Red Wings ended up using to perfection in the 1997 playoffs, particularly against Colorado and Philadelphia in Detroit's four-game sweep of the finals.

There are many variations on the system, but the Red Wings' associate coach Barry Smith is credited with its successful introduction to the NHL with Detroit in 1996–97 (even though Errey says they were using a version of it in Pittsburgh, when Smith was there). Smith got the idea in Sweden, where he served as assistant coach of Team Sweden in the 1996 World Cup, then coached Malmo of the Swedish elite league during a leave of absence over the 1996–97 season before rejoining Detroit for their commanding playoff run that spring. Under the lock, the attacking team divides the opponent's end of the rink into three lanes of defensive responsibility. The left defenseman takes the center lane, the right defenseman the right lane, and the left winger the left lane. The center and right winger forecheck in an attempt to flush their opponent's breakout around to the left side, where the left winger is hanging back in a defensive role and has "locked up" his opposing winger. The left winger stays with his opposing winger if a breakout occurs, while the center and right winger pursue the puck carrier in a backchecking mode, while the defensemen tie up whomever tries to come down their lanes.

The system requires a lot of coordination among the forwards, and benefits teams with speed, as they can quickly counterattack from neutral-zone turnovers, rather than simply rely on a defensive trap in the neutral zone to thwart rushes. It also rewards teams with highly mobile defensemen, as they can attack the breakout by the opposing center and right winger in their lanes and launch counterattacks of their own through the neutral zone. It helps explain why Bowman would want to try Fedorov, already a defensively gifted forward, as a defenseman, and why the Red Wings defensive corps had such fast, mobile members as Nicklas Lidstrom, Chris Chelios and Paul Coffey (until he was traded in October 1996 to Hartford, along with Keith Primeau and Detroit's 1997 first-round pick, to get Brendan Shanahan and Brian Glynn).

At some point, Yzerman clearly understood what Bowman was trying to do, both with him and with the Red Wings overall. "He's the guy who really turned the organization around," Yzerman said after winning the Stanley Cup in 2002—Bowman's last title before he retired. "He didn't come in impressed with anybody, and he forced players to prove themselves. We wouldn't have won three Cups without him."

In the mind of Jacques Demers, Bowman's greatest contribution to Yzerman's transformation from a great individual player into a champion was in reengineering the team around him—relieving the burden of being the offensive workhorse of the club, giving him teammates who complemented his abilities and allowing him, within a disciplined defensive system, to use the diversity of skills that were obvious back in Peterborough to the ultimate benefit of the entire club.

"When Fedorov came to the team," Yzerman's junior coach Dick Todd reflects, "I don't know whether that was a threat to Steve at the time, or if he recognized that, boy, you know, maybe as time went along he could assume a different role, now that he had someone to help."

"He became better with Lidstrom, with Fedorov, with Larionov," says Demers. "He became better when they put together that checking line, maybe the best in the last fifteen years, with him, Darren McCarty and Kris Draper. The game was always there in what he did, but he became a better hockey player overall with the team he had in front of him. He didn't have to do it all. That was probably Scotty's biggest contribution. Steve didn't have to carry the team anymore."

The trade rumors that had surrounded Yzerman—for LaFontaine, Yashin and others—would baffle Demers after he left Detroit. "I love Scotty Bowman, an unbelievable coach, and just before him there was Bryan Murray, but I don't know why they wanted to trade him. I really believe that under myself and then under Murray, he was a complete hockey player."

Dave Lewis doesn't necessarily agree. The 1990s found Yzerman with room and opportunity to grow, and he still had new levels to reach after the 1995 loss to New Jersey. "I think he still had to go through the process of being as strong defensively as you are offensively, of being a leader in that, regardless of your size, you're going to battle along the boards to get the puck out. You're going to block shots. You're going to drive to the net and get dirty, to score that goal. And you're doing it because you want everybody else to be doing it, because you know that that's the way you have to play to win."

Lewis considers the suggestion made by some that Fedorov's arrival was an apparent threat to Yzerman's stature, but that he was able to recognize it as an opportunity for both himself and the team. "That came with maturity, and with Lidstrom being drafted, and Konstantinov arriving, and the addition of other important players. The supporting cast got stronger. There were people that had won before, like Larry Murphy. The goaltending was solidified in Mike Vernon. No one player can do it all."

No one player can do it all, but when the Philadelphia Flyers were defeated 2–1 at Joe Louis Arena on Saturday, June 7, 1997, to complete Detroit's sweep of the finals, one player became the focal point of the celebrations.

There were others who had particular reason to celebrate. Red Wings goaltender Mike Vernon deservedly received the Conn Smythe Trophy as playoff MVP. And Scotty Bowman, in logging his seventh coaching Stanley Cup, made history of his own by strapping on a pair of skates so he could join his players in the on-ice celebrations. But when it came time to actually celebrate, the attention of Bowman and everyone else in the Red Wings organization turned to the captain.

When the Cup was presented to Yzerman by league commisioner Gary Bettman, Yzerman looked to Bowman for advice on what to do next. Yzerman thought the whole team should go for a skate around the rink, but Bowman urged him to take the first lap himself.

As his teammates applauded and the capacity crowd of nearly 20,000 in The Joe roared in deafening approval, as his parents, his wife, and many friends waved back to him from the stands, Yzerman heard no sound. Success had carved out its own time and space for him. Yzerman was fulfilling a dream he had nourished since he was five years old, and the sensation of winning met every expectation, and then some.

Jim Devellano wept as he watched Yzerman skate around the rink, the Cup raised over his head. "Tears of joy," he explained.

Then the trophy began to feel heavy; Yzerman worried about dropping it. Turning to the Detroit bench, he placed the Cup in the hands of Mike Ilitch, the owner who had slumped at the Red Wings table at the 1983 draft, visibly disappointed with having narrowly missed the chance to land Pat LaFontaine; the owner who, in the end, had stood by Yzerman, and had been—and would continue to be—rewarded for this mutual loyalty, so rare in the recent history of professional sport.

The Red Wings, under Bowman, had learned to win as a

team, led by a captain who had come to understand what success demanded of them, individually and collectively. He had learned how to lead not only on the ice, but with carefully chosen words at opportune times.

The Red Wings had not been the best team in the 1996–97 regular season. They had finished fifth overall, with eleven fewer wins than Colorado, the defending champions and overall season winner. No Red Wings made the All-Star Teams or won any individual hardware. Brendan Shanahan was the club's only top-ten scorer. But the Wings had also endured twenty-seven overtime games in the regular season, more than any other club, and lost only two of them. And this in a season in which they won a total of 38 games. The team had been hardened by the regular season, not exhausted by it.

And when Detroit seemed in danger of another playoff collapse, Yzerman took command. Leading St. Louis two games to one in the opening round, the Wings suffered a 4–0 defeat that put the Blues back in the series. In a team meeting that followed, Yzerman made clear what he expected of his club, in firm, heartfelt words.

"His speech was one of the prime motivators for this team to accomplish what it has," trainer John Wharton would recall for the *Detroit Free Press*. "The line from the speech I remember most is, 'We can be beaten, but we're not going to be outworked.' Since then, we haven't been outworked, except for a period or two in sixteen games." Wharton would also remark: "He never verbalized how much he wanted the Cup, but you could see it in his eyes and in his determination."

The Red Wings rebounded with wins of 5–2 and 3–1 to set the Blues aside, then swept San Jose to advance to the conference finals against Colorado. The teams' last playoff meeting, in the spring of 1996, had been an emotional and sometimes bloody brawl, the low point being Claude Lemieux's vicious hit on Kris Draper. In their last regular-season meeting in 1996–97 (a Red Wings win), the teams had engaged in an old-fashioned bench-clearing brawl which included goalie Mike Vernon tackling his opposite number, Patrick Roy. The playoff reunion promised more of the same, but Yzerman had been striving to insist on a no-nonsense, focused approach to the job of winning.

"He was putting us in a business state of mind that we couldn't get out of," right winger Martin Lapointe told the *Detroit Free Press*. "It was boring. For the first couple of series, it was hard to do. But after that, we started believing, 'Hey, it works.'" Yzerman's message was: "Don't say too much, and when the time comes, you can say whatever you want."

The message paid off against Colorado, as Patrick Roy's boasts about eliminating Detroit backfired, and Avalanche coach Marc Crawford embarrassed himself with a spittle-flecked verbal lashing of Scotty Bowman in the middle of a 6–0 loss in game four that put the Avalanche a game away from elimination. For calling Bowman "Platehead," Crawford was fined $10,000 by the league and moved to extend a public apology. (In his junior play-ing days, Bowman suffered a slash to the head that caused a nasty cut—but not, as legend would have it, a skull fracture that required a metal plate to repair.) Colorado rebounded with a 6–0 win of its own, but Detroit iced the series in game six with a 3–1 victory and proceeded to meet Philadelphia in the finals.

Detroit had improved with every series, and by the time Philadelphia came along there was no question within the organ-ization that it could keep right on winning. A sweep was not nec-essarily in the cards, but the Flyers found themselves as masterfully outplayed as Detroit had been by New Jersey in 1995.

Having been swept in four and outscored 17–6 by the Devils, Detroit swept the Flyers and outscored *them*, 16–6.

The fourth and final game was the hardest. "Coming to the game tonight, I said, 'Just relax, we're going to win,'" Yzerman would relate. "'If it's game four, five or six, we're going to win,' but it was nerve-racking." Of Yzerman's pregame dressing-room speech, Lapointe recalled to the *Free Press*: "He said, 'Let's make sure we come out hard and we do our job. We're professionals. It doesn't matter what we did in the past, it only matters what we do tonight. We've got to play the game of our lives.'" With a few minutes left before they had to hit the ice, Yzerman tried to loosen up with Shanahan by firing movie trivia questions at him. It would leave Shanahan laughing, wondering why his captain was asking him about *Tootsie* just moments before the start of the most important game they'd ever played.

When the game had been played and the burden of fourteen seasons of expectations were removed from his shoulders, Yzerman bubbled over with loquacious joy. The *Detroit Free Press* assembled a "greatest hits" collection of the captain's comments for posterity, among them:

"I don't know how to describe the way I feel. I'm glad the game is over, but I wish it never ended."

"Sometimes you hold your dream way out there and wonder if you can ever be as good as your dream. It was almost like I wanted to sit back and watch it all and not miss a minute of it."

"I'm glad we endured, the organization didn't quit and I didn't quit or move on. I really think I appreciate it more after playing a number of years."

"There were some tough losses and disappointments and injuries—and I don't know if I'm a better skater or scorer—but I think I'm a better player by going through it all."

"It was the one thing in my career I didn't have. I wanted dearly to have my name on the Stanley Cup before I retired."

"There's the Stanley Cup champion and everybody else. When you have a good team for two or three years and don't win, you're not considered a great team but an underachiever."

His teammates were captured in full flight of tribute. "I don't think there can be an individual that I have as much admiration for as Stevie Yzerman," said Vernon to *Detroit Free Press*. "He's been unbelievable with myself when things were down, saying to me, 'You're going to be the guy.' He was a class act. I was so happy for the guy when he grabbed the Cup for the first time."

"Stevie deserves it more than anyone," added Kirk Maltby, expressing a virtually unanimous team sentiment. "Every single guy in this organization loves that he finally got his due."

When the dressing-room celebrations were over, Yzerman headed to the players' parking lot with the Stanley Cup. After forty-two years, Stanley had finally come home to Detroit. And Stanley was going to spend his first night back in town in the Yzerman household. He plopped the Cup into the passenger seat next to him and tore off in his Porsche into the early hours of June 8. It was fourteen years to the day that Jim Devellano had drafted him.

The 1996–97 season had played out much differently for Pat LaFontaine. Sitting alone on October 17, 1996, in the Buffalo

Sabres dressing room in his team's new home rink, Marine Midland Arena, he wondered how he'd gotten there. Thirteen years after the 1983 entry draft had consigned him to the New York Islanders, more than a few admirers were asking essentially the same question.

That same night, the Detroit Red Wings, the team for which he'd seemed destined to play, were in Chicago. The Wings had added Brendan Shanahan to the lineup in a major deal with Hartford nine days earlier, and Steve Yzerman had been welcomed by the fans at the Red Wings' first home game with the chants of *Stevie . . . Stevie . . .* after the negotiations to trade him to Ottawa fell through. But Detroit that night in Chicago did not look like a club that would end the season as Stanley Cup champions. The Wings were losing a chippy game to the Blackhawks, who hadn't beaten them in eight previous meetings. Detroit's power play went 0–4; Steve Yzerman was held off the score sheet in the 2–1 loss and took a double minor for slashing and high-sticking late in the third period.

When LaFontaine wanted out of Long Island in October 1991, Bryan Murray tried, but failed, to execute a deal to swap Yzerman for him. So instead, LaFontaine had gone to Buffalo. It proved to be a professional boon for him. He was given a young Alexander Mogilny as his right-winger, and together they ran amok on opposing goaltenders. While he hadn't been traded to Detroit for Yzerman, Buffalo suited him fine.

And then everything started to go wrong, so quickly, the way it can and does in hockey, the way it had for Gerard Gallant when his back started to give out, the way it threatened to for Steve Yzerman when he seriously injured his knee moments after reaching fifty goals in an NHL season for the first time in March 1988. During the 1992–93 playoffs, problems surfaced with LaFontaine's own right knee. The next fall, it was learned that he had torn the anterior cruciate ligament. After just 16 games in 1993–94, surgery removed him from the lineup. Reconstructive surgery followed in the summer of 1994 and kept him off the ice for all but 22 games of the lockout-shortened 1994–95 season. For the effort it took to return, LaFontaine was awarded the Masterton trophy in 1995, a foreshadowing of Yzerman's comeback from knee surgery in 2002–03.

The 1995–96 season was LaFontaine's unequivocal comeback. He had a very respectable 91 points, the fifth-highest season total of his career, and in September 1996 he was part of the Team USA squad that upset Canada in the World Cup. Yzerman had at last been able to represent Canada in the tournament that Mike Keenan had shut him out of when it was known as the Canada Cup, in 1987 and 1991, and for that personal breakthrough he got to lose to LaFontaine. Having played for his country in an Olympic Games, two previous Canada Cups and a world championship without any hardware to show for it, and after thirteen NHL seasons (in whole and in part), LaFontaine could call himself a champion after Team USA's 5–2 shocker over Canada in the deciding World Cup game.

Then came the game against Pittsburgh on October 17, 1996. The first period was less than two minutes old when LaFontaine, carrying the puck across the Penguins' blueline, met a straight arm from defenseman Francois Leroux. The head of the five-and-double-digit LaFontaine met the mass of the six-foot-six, 235-pound Leroux. Leroux's elbow knocked LaFontaine's helmet off and probably delivered him a concussion on its own. LaFontaine then pitched backwards, smashing the back of his unprotected head on the ice for the second concussive blow. Technically, this single incident qualified as his fifth concussion in just six years.

LaFontaine would recount in his book *Companions in Courage*: "The last thing I remember about that injury was waking up. I had been conscious for a good half hour but nothing registered." And so he found himself sitting in the lounge area of the Sabres' locker room, still in his game gear, with no idea of why he was there. Sabres trainer Rip Simonick heard his voice and came in to find LaFontaine uttering nonsense as he watched the lounge's television.

By his own admission, the remainder of his 1996–97 season was physically and emotionally trying. Supported by coach Ted Nolan, he got the time off to recuperate. As LaFontaine struggled with depression, mood swings, headaches and insomnia, Yzerman and the Red Wings fused as a team and rolled toward the championship that Detroit had been pining for since 1955.

After the summer of 1997, LaFontaine felt he was ready to return to play. But when Buffalo insisted that a doctor of their own choosing assess LaFontaine rather than rely solely on the green-light from LaFontaine's medical experts, LaFontaine demanded to be traded. The Sabres obliged, sending him to the Rangers on September 29.

In New York, LaFontaine produced 62 points in 67 games, and was able to pass the career 1,000-point mark. "I was always a player who was told I was too small and wouldn't make it," LaFontaine said after reaching the milestone. Before he could play his sixty-eighth game as a Ranger, LaFontaine collided with teammate Mike Keane during practice. The resulting concussion, his sixth, was the end of LaFontaine in hockey. He had just played for the United States in one more Olympics. He had both the numbers (468 goals, 545 assists, 1,013 points in 1,056 games) and the reputation to assure him a place in the Hockey Hall of Fame. But he had never made it back to Detroit.

It was oddly appropriate that LaFontaine was inducted into the Hall of Fame at the same time as Mike Ilitch was, in the builder's category. The two Detroit men shared the limelight on November 4, 2003, and Ilitch could not help but remark on the interest he once had at the NHL draft in getting LaFontaine in a Red Wings uniform. It had not worked out. When LaFontaine officially announced his retirement in August 1998, two months had passed since Steve Yzerman, the kid Jim Devellano supposedly was stuck with when the Islanders chose LaFontaine third overall, had led the Wings to their second consecutive Stanley Cup and earned himself the Conn Smythe trophy.

Was there something about LaFontaine's physiology that made him more susceptible to concussions than Yzerman and other players? Even if he had ended up in Detroit—through either some fortuitous change in the way the 1983 draft played out, or a trade that Bryan Murray was actually able to make— would he have been able to survive in the game long enough to earn the Red Wings the Cup wins that Yzerman eventually brought them?

Dick Todd, Yzerman's Junior coach in Peterborough, has wondered about the different paths taken by the lives of these gifted players since the teenage talent pool was divvied up on June 8, 1983. "If he'd not had the concussions and had been on different teams," Todd suggests, "LaFontaine's career and Steve's would have mirrored each other very closely. Steve has the character you wanted, and I think Patty probably did, too."

As Jim Devellano had said of Yzerman and LaFontaine back on draft day in 1983, "They're both still kids. I mean, who the hell knows?" Twenty years later, who still knew how it could have, should have, turned out for both of them?

TEN

RATHER THAN CAPPING AN ALREADY LONG AND DISTIN-
guished career, Steve Yzerman's 1997 Stanley Cup win was the
beginning of a final phase of his career, one in which he would
be seen as an undisputed champion and leader. He had more seasons ahead of him, more victories in store. The Red Wings
repeated as Cup champions in 1998, after a season in which they
finished third overall and had a shaky playoff start against
Phoenix, before setting down St. Louis and Dallas to meet
Washington in the finals.

The run had been bittersweet. The celebrations of the
Detroit Red Wings' victory in the 1997 Stanley Cup finals were
marred by a car crash on, of all days, Friday, June 13. Vladimir
Konstantinov, Viacheslav Fetisov and trainer Sergei Mnatsakanov
had hired a limousine to take them home from a team golf outing, only to have their driver almost kill them all. Fetisov was able
to return to play, but Konstantinov and Mnatsakanov were left
with severe brain injuries.

Yzerman had long admired the dedication of the Russian veterans on the Red Wings team. After skating around with the Cup
in 1997 and letting Mike Ilitch hold it, the first players Yzerman

handed it off to were Fetisov and Igor Larionov. "The last couple of days I thought [about] who I wanted to give the Cup to," Yzerman explained to *Detroit Free Press* at the time. "I thought about Slava. He and Igor, what they stand for, are good examples for younger players. He has been through a lot in his career . . . All five Russian players were significant players and great guys."

Yzerman would not let the injured men be forgotten. The team sported special patches on their jerseys in 1997–98 with the word "believe" written in Russian. The team was determined that Konstantinov and Mnatsakanov remain part of their next Cup drive, and during the finals, Konstantinov could be seen in his wheelchair sporting his Red Wings jersey, sometimes managing a smile and a wave. When the Cup was won, in another four-game sweep, he was wheeled onto the ice for the team photos and had the Cup placed in his lap.

"It was a collaborative effort by Fetisov and Larionov and Steve," says Dave Lewis of the continued involvement of Konstantinov and Mnatsakanov. "It was an ongoing thing that those guys were part of us and with us."

"I knew we weren't going to lose," Lewis adds about the 1998 finals. "I knew going into the playoffs that, regardless of what happened, we were going to win in '98. There was that drive, that depth, even after losing the second- or third-best defenseman in the league in Konstantinov."

Yzerman had also endured the bone-deep ache of Canada's Olympic debacle at Nagano that season. Heavily favored to contest the gold medal, the Canadians were knocked out of contention in a penalty-shot tiebreaker against the Czech Republic. Yzerman's fellow Red Wing, Brendan Shanahan, had drawn the short straw, becoming the last Canadian shooter stopped by Czech goalie Dominik Hasek. After being left off of Canada Cup teams by Mike Keenan in 1987 and 1991, Yzerman had now participated in two of Canada's most disheartening losses in international competition: the loss to Team USA in the 1996 World Cup, and the 1998 Olympic tournament, at which the country did not produce a medal of any color.

It was more than coincidental that Yzerman rebounded from the World Cup loss in September 1996 to win his first Stanley Cup the following spring, and that he responded to the Olympic disappointment of February 1998 with another Cup for Detroit. The high level of play in international tournaments gave Yzerman added inspiration, and he credited the Nagano loss with pushing him toward a second consecutive Cup.

This time, the Conn Smythe went to Yzerman. He had led the Wings with 24 points in 22 playoff games, all the while playing his two-way game. That alone was enough to earn him the trophy. But really, it was his leadership, and the way in which he had made Konstantinov and Mnatsakanov's participation such a priority (and would continue to do so), that had made him more valuable than anyone else on the ice in that postseason run.

To paraphrase Dave Lewis, to be recognized as a leader who can win, you have to be a leader who has won. There's no real way around this. Until you've actually fulfilled the promises made by you or on your behalf, you're just potential energy as far as winning goes. In terms of accolades, payment is strictly on delivery.

Winning in 1997 and '98 raised Steve Yzerman into that special category of player who wins by leading and by producing. And with the pressure of that first championship behind him, he just got better. The Selke Trophy voters in 2000 at last recognized the strong defensive qualities his game had long exhibited. Not even the deep disappointment of the 1998 Olympic tournament could harm this special status. On the contrary, he had become part of an elite for whom having lost in a shootout to the Czechs naturally meant regrouping and trying all over again in 2002. As had been the case at Nagano in 1998, the Games at Salt Lake City affirmed his status as a competitor who could be relied upon to do his utmost to get the job done, and who understood the alchemy of a championship club. As he had told his teammates during the St. Louis series in 1997, he could be beaten, but he could never be outworked. For years, Yzerman had looked to others for the wisdom of what was required to win. Now, that wisdom rested in him.

By the 2001–02 season, Yzerman's desire to keep playing and winning at the highest level was forcing him to subject his body to crippling punishment. His right knee was a mess. In October 2000, Yzerman underwent an arthroscopic procedure called microfracture surgery, in which holes were drilled in an effort to stimulate cartilage growth. After resting for twenty-two games, he returned to play, but the latest surgical intervention clearly was a stopgap measure. Slackness in key ligaments was causing the joint to grind itself to pieces. In the fall of 2001, the team's staff could see that the knee wouldn't get him through the campaign. Yzerman submitted to another round of surgery, almost thirteen years after he slammed into the goalpost at Joe Louis Arena. On January 28, 2002, team doctor David Collon went to work on it at Henry Ford Hospital in Detroit, repairing a tear in the meniscus and cleaning away loose cartilage. Yzerman was expected to be out of action for two weeks, and if all went well, he could be back in the Red Wings lineup for a game or two before joining the Canadian Olympic team in Salt Lake City.

Wayne Gretzky—a teammate of Yzerman's at Nagano who, now retired, was GM of the Olympic squad—was playing it close to the vest on the issue of whether Yzerman should take part. Owen Nolan of the San Jose Sharks had injured his shoulder, and had told the press that he wouldn't show up if he didn't think he was sufficiently healed to make a full contribution. Gretzky had praised Nolan for this selflessness, expecting that other players would behave the same way. The press naturally turned to Yzerman to see what his plans were.

On February 7, with eight days to go before Canada's first game, against Sweden, Yzerman said he hadn't heard Nolan's comments. "I don't foresee a problem, but if I can't play, I won't be going," Yzerman told the media in a conference call from Detroit. "It doesn't make sense to play at 70 percent. There are other guys as good who are healthy and who can go." Gretzky had at least two alternative choices standing by: Yzerman's former teammate, Keith Primeau, now with Philadelphia, and Boston's new young star, Joe Thornton.

Red Wings general manager Ken Holland gave Yzerman's participation his full blessing. Detroit had ten players in the Olympic tournament, more than any other NHL team, and he understood how important it was for them to represent their countries. "Everyone knows your [NHL] team is number one, and you're not going to take any chances from an injury standpoint," Holland said to *The Detroit News* before the tournament. "But if you feel absolutely 100 percent healthy, and you have a chance to represent your country in the Olympics in Salt Lake City, who wouldn't want to play? Why wouldn't you want to participate? It's an incredible honor and opportunity." Holland had also witnessed the boost the Nagano experience had given Yzerman in 1998, and the positive effect it had on his playoff run with the Red Wings. So, yes, Stevie Y should be there if he felt he could be.

Whether or not Yzerman was 100 percent healthy is a matter for debate by physicians. And, in any event, "100 percent healthy" doesn't mean the same thing in professional sports that it does in civilian life. But whether or not Yzerman contributed to the full extent of his capabilities went without question. Like Mario Lemieux, who was nursing a bad hip, like Brendan Shanahan, who had a broken thumb, Yzerman simply played through the pain. The team became stronger with every game, building toward the dream matchup with Team USA in the gold medal game. Lining up opposite them in that match would be, among others, their teammates Chris Chelios and Brett Hull.

Yzerman didn't record a shot on net, yet his was one of the standout efforts of the deciding game, as he played the full sheet of the 100-foot wide Olympic rink with the acumen that had earned him the Selke in 2000. After two periods, Canada had outshot the U.S. 28–24 and was clinging to a precarious 3–2 lead. Mario Lemieux had missed, point blank, a wide-open net that could have salted the game away, and there were a few butterflies being stirred within Canadian stomachs by memories of the deciding game of the 1996 World Cup, when a largely outplayed Team USA had rebounded with a flurry of third-period goals.

At 13:43 of the third period, Yzerman took a tripping penalty, the only infraction of the frame. His occasionally explosive temper had appeared to get the better of him, and threatened to give Team USA the chance to get back in the game. But his teammates killed off the penalty, and Yzerman stepped from the box to gather the puck from Joe Sakic and nail Jarome Iginla with a perfect pass, which the Calgary Flames star buried behind goalie Mike Richter, who had backstopped the 1996 World Cup upset.

Yzerman leapt into Iginla's arms, not once but twice. Canada was up, 4–2, with 3:59 left to play. As the Americans pressed their luck, Iginla fed Sakic, who broke away to beat Richter with one of the prettiest goals ever seen in international hockey. It was 5–2, there was 1:20 left on the clock, and the Americans were finished.

"It's hard to contain your emotions," Yzerman told Bob Wojnowski of *The Detroit News*, after receiving his gold medal. "Guys were trying to be all calm and stoic, but you can't. You let it loose. You become a kid again, and the boyishness just comes out." With a fifty-year Olympic drought vanquished, the enormity of what he had helped to accomplish began to sink in. "You're secluded in the athlete's village, so you don't realize the pressure back home," Yzerman added. "Canadians are like everybody else. They love to win. But if we had lost, it's not like they wouldn't let us back in the country. They let us come home in '98."

Canada had gone even longer without a gold medal in Olympic hockey than Detroit had been without a Stanley Cup winner. Yzerman had now been a key part of both efforts to erase a grating losing streak. His dedication to the Canadian effort had been as deep and as long-standing as his determination to make Detroit a winner. It had taken him to the Junior World Championships, three World Championship tournaments, one Canada Cup, one World Cup, and two Olympic tournaments.

Yet, as thrilled as he was to have been part of Canadian sporting history, he didn't forget that he was the captain of the Red Wings. Once the gold and silver medals were distributed, he gathered Shanahan, Chelios and Hull for an on-ice photo.

The Olympics had, again, renewed Yzerman's inspiration to achieve as a Red Wing. While some fans heaped abuse on his decision to play in the Olympics, he stayed out of the Detroit lineup, preparing his knee for the playoff run. Despite being limited to 52 games that season, Yzerman still managed to finish fifth on the Red Wings scoring list, with a 48-point effort that demonstrated he could still be an offensive threat at age thirty-seven and in his precarious physical condition.

In the months leading up to the 2002 playoffs, Yzerman endured a complex regimen of therapy, whether he was playing or not. Thrice daily, he wore a sequential pressure boot on his knee, to reduce swelling. Lubricant was injected into the joint to replace lost synovial fluid. And the usual physio and muscle-strengthening routines continued.

"You've got to play through it," Yzerman told *The Detroit News* when the playoffs began. "You've got to figure out a way."

The way turned out to involve plenty of ice packs, applied at all hours and in all places; ultrasound examinations; injections of painkillers into his rump before every game; and several interventions by Detroit's training staff to drain fluid from the knee. It also involved the willingness to put up with the pain that the injections couldn't deaden. Warming up for game two of the opening round against Vancouver, Yzerman didn't think he could carry on. But Scotty Bowman encouraged him to try, to do what he could, even if it just meant focusing on winning face-offs.

"The first couple of games in the playoffs," trainer John Wharton would tell *The News*, "we were all kind of holding our breath every shift he went out on the ice, just hoping he could make it back to the bench in one piece, let alone make it through the game or the series or the playoffs."

Bowman talked him into trying because he truly needed him. The Wings, despite winning the regular season, were in danger of making an early exit, as Vancouver won the first two games.

It was up to Yzerman to lead, and he did it with another low-key speech to the club after the second loss that reiterated his confidence in their goaltender, Dominik Hasek, and his conviction that they were through with losing games to the Canucks. But he also did it in leading by example, in making the necessary sacrifices, and in putting up points while playing a complete game.

The Red Wings did win four straight against the Canucks, then moved on to eliminate St. Louis, and, in their toughest test, overcame a three-games-to-two deficit to defeat the Colorado Avalanche in seven. The final series against the Carolina Hurricanes was anticlimactic, as the Red Wings won in five. Yzerman and Shanahan had just joined Ken Morrow—of the New York Islanders and the U.S.'s Miracle on Ice team of 1980—as the only players to have won Olympic gold and a Stanley Cup in the same year.

Yzerman's 23 points in 23 playoff games led his own team and was exceeded only by the superlative effort of Colorado's Peter Forsberg. It took an outstanding blueline effort from Nicklas Lidstrom to deny Yzerman a second Conn Smythe Trophy.

"I don't know why, but this Cup was really rewarding, more special than the other two," Yzerman said to *The Detroit News* when it was over. "Maybe it was because we were a couple years removed from the last one, and I was able to relax and enjoy the whole playoff run instead of being a basket case for two months. It was a collection of players that fit so well together, and that made it really enjoyable. High-profile guys accepted different roles and were willing to get along with everyone. Over the last couple of weeks, I got to thinking, 'Man, I really, really want to win.' I think I wanted to win more than ever."

During the playoffs, Yzerman had denied a rumor broadcast by ABC Sports that he would undergo reconstructive surgery on his knee that summer. Perhaps it was just a matter of semantics.

Instead of reconstruction, he underwent the osteotomy, the realignment that no professional athlete had ever come back from.

And there was, of course, a comeback.

Players rarely get to decide the terms of their retirement. The choice is usually made for them, by injury or by declining skills that teams no longer need or will pay enough money for. Players who do the "right" thing from an aesthetic standpoint, choosing to bow out while they are still capable of playing at a high level, often find themselves driven to return. It happened to Mario Lemieux, to Guy Lafleur, to Dominik Hasek. Many others try to come back but can't make it through training camp.

One of the most misunderstood aspects of retirement is how a player even manages to keep playing to the point when the decision is made, voluntarily or otherwise. The explosion in player salaries, at first through the competition provided by the WHA in the 1970s, then through league expansion and a new collective bargaining agreement in the 1990s, has created the cynical misconception that veteran players stick around, well past their best-before dates, simply to continue drawing their inflated paychecks. It is so easy to forget what a bloody difficult way to make a living professional hockey is. It's physically punishing and emotionally draining, and no matter how big the league is, somebody else is always waiting to take your job. The only players who can afford to float for any length of time (and we're talking about a handful of games at best) are superstars who can justify their meal tickets by putting on the occasional dazzling performance. For the rest, the game has to be loved in order to be tolerated.

"It's an extremely hard game to play professionally," Jim Schoenfeld—who played for Detroit near the end of his career, right before Yzerman showed up—told this writer ten years ago.

"If you don't want to play, it's got to be damned near impossible. There were times when it was hard to go—and I loved the game. You need that passion to get you over the hump. If you didn't have this burning love for the game, I don't know how you would be able to play."

The subject came up in the course of discussing his former defense partner on the Buffalo Sabres, Tim Horton, whose NHL career lasted for twenty-two full seasons (after three years in the American league). In fact, the only thing that took Horton out of the game was a fatal car crash halfway through the 1973–74 season, which occurred after he showed up to play a Wednesday-night match in Toronto with a broken jaw and a body full of painkillers. Horton had just turned forty-four, and unlike most professional players he had a lucrative business, the eponymous chain of donut shops, practically begging him to retire so that he could give it his full attention. But he kept playing.

Horton's tragic end contradicts the notion that players don't retire when they should because they have nowhere else to go. Very often, as was the case with Horton, they don't retire because there's nothing they'd love to be doing more. Few people actually get the chance to have the job they dreamed of when they were in grade school, so they can hardly be condemned for not wanting to stop doing what passion had driven them to do in the first place. Passion is what makes a player want to play, what keeps them playing, and what makes them not want to stop—and sometimes, when they *have* stopped, it is what makes them want to go back to playing again.

Schoenfeld's description of the game's grip on Horton, who tried more than once to retire, only to show up at training camp every September, is a textbook explanation why every player who stays with the game as long as Yzerman has, despite injuries and inevitable career low points, seems eternally reluctant to clean out his locker. "He loved being around the guys," Schoenfeld said of Horton. "He loved everything that goes with the game. The practices, the playing, the camaraderie, the same things that most players like. If you *have to* quit, it's a lot easier. You blow your knee out or nobody wants you—there are a lot of ways where you'll have to say, 'Well, okay, I have to move on.'" But if the passion to still play is still alive, Schoenfeld counseled, not playing isn't an option. "It draws you to the rink. If you're capable, it's very hard for people to stop . . ."

The normally terse Yzerman provided his own perspective on what was keeping him from stopping when he accepted the Masterton trophy in June 2003. He delivered a short, sincere speech to the NHL awards audience, thanking the writers for voting for him and his doctors for crafting a new knee for him, as well as the Red Wings organization and the team's fans, "for their incredible desire to do well and their great expectations, [which] provides me with the motivation to come back and play and chase winning the Stanley Cup one more time, hopefully." But the most affecting words were directed at his wife, Lisa, in the audience. "As all players get older and have families, a lot of players at times are forced to give up the game because the commitment to your family becomes more important than playing the game," he explained. "My wife has understood and unselfishly allowed me to continue to play and chase the dream that I have to play in the NHL. I appreciate her patience and understanding."

When Yzerman returned in the fall of 2003, with a new contract and a realigned knee, to play another season, he immediately went on a scoring tear, leading his team in points when many people at this point were just happy to see him lead in the dressing room. It's no exaggeration to say that Red Wings fans were in awe of his effort. Their chat on one Internet bulletin board captured their gape-mouthed wonder.

> For all those who said Yzerman is washed up with a bum knee . . . TOLD YOU SO!!
> I predicted he will have a fifty point season earlier this year and lookie here . . . three points in three games.

> Stevie does look great, I do hope he can continue it. Hopefully he can. Stamina is an issue. What really matters is how well he can play in April, May, and should things go really well, June.

> Stamina has never been an issue with Yzerman. The question is will the knee hold up through April, May, and should things go really well, June. He's looking good, though. Have faith. The man is just too focused to let a little thing like an osteotomy ruin his contributions to the 'Wings next cup.

> Yzerman is showing exactly [why] he wears the 'C' on his jersey.

> He's persevered before, why should now be any different?

> Focused for sure. Just look at his eyes. He's always been this way. I don't know how he keeps doing it year after year after year . . .

> Because he loves the game. Walter Payton was the same kind of player . . . I have never been there—but you know it when you see it.

As Gerard Gallant has noted, "He enjoys playing the game, and that's what's made him a superstar and such a character player." The fans respond to that joy; they understand it is what makes Yzerman keep coming to the rink, and playing at such a high level, when his body should be resting under the care of a battery of physiotherapists. Unlike Horton, he has never struggled publicly with what he thinks he should be doing—retiring— and what he really wants to be doing—playing.

Nevertheless, the desire to keep playing in 2003–04, to keep living the dream of playing in the NHL and to chase one more Cup win, had traumatic consequences. Less than two seconds were left in regulation time in a game in Denver against the Avalanche on February 5 when Avs defenseman Adam Foote attempted to lift Yzerman's stick. Foote missed, and delivered a brutal upper cut with his composite stick to Yzerman's face. The blow knocked out one tooth and drove several more into the roof of Yzerman's mouth, and stitches were required to repair his upper lip. (Yzerman actually couldn't remember how many teeth his chosen profession had cost him to that point. Maybe two. Maybe six.) A dentist pulled the loosened teeth back into position, and Yzerman joined his family for a ski holiday out west over the weekend, as the league entered its All Star break. Only on Monday did he have braces applied to realign the teeth. On Tuesday, he was back practicing with the team. He never missed a game. Chock up one more case of the Red Wings captain playing through pain.

The next incident was less easy to shake off. Yzerman's quest for a fourth Stanley Cup had delivered the Red Wings into a tough second-round series against a young, swift Calgary Flames club. The series was tied at two games apiece when Yzerman led the Wings into the Saddledome for the pivotal game five on May 1, eight days before his thirty-ninth birthday. Halfway through the second period in a scoreless game, Yzerman was hovering near the right side of Flames goaltender Miikka Kiprusoff, waiting for a rebound, when a shot from Wings defenseman Mathieu Schneider ricocheted up into Yzerman's face. The puck smashed into his left eye, scratching the cornea and fracturing the surrounding orbital bone. Yzerman was rushed off for four-and-a-half hours of surgery. With Yzerman lost for the rest of the post season (after Detroit lost the game, 1–0), his Red Wings went down in six to the Flames, who continued on their march to the finals. Many wondered if they had just seen Steve Yzerman play for the last time.

The Red Wings announced the day after the injury that Yzerman would recover fully. And Yzerman himself soon made it clear that he was not going to allow the latest injury to serve as the epitaph for his career. "I plan on playing next year, but the collective bargaining agreement will determine that," Yzerman had already told the Associated Press before the playoffs began. "I'm just going to wait and see what happens. I'm prepared to wait a year." The eye injury changed nothing . . . except that when he did come back, he promised he would be sporting a visor. "I really believe guys should be wearing them. I wouldn't have said that a week ago," he told *The Detroit News* the day after the incident.

"I don't know what the final point is going to be when I say that's it," Yzerman told AP on May 7, reiterating his intention to keep playing. "But I'm not there."

Two weeks after his traumatic eye injury in Calgary, Yzerman was named to Team Canada for the upcoming World Cup tournament. Canada's stature internationally had never been stronger. The women's national team had followed up their 2002 Olympic gold medal with another world title in 2004. (The 2003 tournament in China had been scrapped because of the SARS epidemic.) The men's team had just won a second consecutive world title on May 9 in Prague. The new World Cup team was built by Wayne Gretzky's brain trust around the nucleus of the 2002 Olympic gold-medal winners. It represented to many observers a changing of the guard in the country's international game. At centre were acknowledged veteran leaders: Yzerman, Sakic, Lemieux, players who had led teams to Stanley Cups and helped craft the recent Olympic victory. Joining them were the next-generation pivots: Jarome Iginla and Joe Thornton, the young stars who were expected to perpetuate the Canadian game's supremacy well into the new millennia. Yzerman was the oldest skater (only goaltender Ed Belfour was older), and some of his teammates—Dan Heatley, Brad Richards, Robyn Regehr, Simon Gagné, to name a few—were still in diapers when Yzerman was in juniors. It went without saying (although naturally it had to be said) that the 2004 World Cup would be the last chance for fans to watch Yzerman on the international stage, and for players like Iginla and Thornton to learn from him. But in July, that last chance appeared to have passed. Team Canada's executive director, Wayne Gretzky, announced through Hockey Canada that Yzerman had informed him that his eye would not have healed sufficiently to allow him to attend Team Canada's training camp. Yzerman's decision opened up a spot for Vincent Lecavalier, who had just won a Stanley Cup with Tampa Bay, and had been a surprise oversight in the original roster selection. Yzerman himself made no public statement on his condition, but the fact that his eye was problematic enough to keep him out of a September tournament he would otherwise not allow himself to miss, raised the question of whether he would even be healthy for another NHL season, should a lockout be avoided. Which then raised the unfortunate possibility that the last sight fans might have had of

Yzerman in action was of him writhing in pain, his own eyesight
in jeopardy.

Were the fans who so admired Yzerman's comeback after the knee
realignment celebrating the continuation of a career that should
have been cause for at least some misgiving? Not because of
Yzerman personally, but because of the kind of game he had come
to play? There would seem to have been a downside to Yzerman's
transformation from a scoring star to an all-around player who
could produce championships, no matter how much it had prof-
ited the Red Wings overall. One might argue that such a change
in a player with Yzerman's offensive gifts should be cause for
regret, not accolades. Why should fans have been satisfied watching Yzerman score only 46 goals in 1996–97 and 1997–98 combined? Were they not more entertained when he was averaging
more than sixty a year in 1989–90 and 1990–91? Perhaps
Yzerman's change was symptomatic of a league that had become
too enamored of a grinding, defensive style. Had Yzerman
changed only to confront the reality of what it now took to win
in a league that had overexpanded and was thin on talent, one
which had largely embraced the neutral-zone trap that the Devils
had used so effectively in shutting down the Red Wings in the
1995 finals?

There may be something to that, and Mike O'Connell for one
won't dismiss it completely. But he still sees Yzerman's transformation as something above and beyond current defensive fads. "Some
great players never understand what they have to develop into," he
says. "And there are other players who have gotten it. Look at
Messier, and what he's accomplished. Gretzky and Lemieux, you
can't put them in that list, because they were so far ahead, skillwise,
of anyone else. It wasn't that they weren't leaders. It was just that they

were so gifted, they could go out and win the game themselves.

"You can see the sacrifices that team players make. You can see it in Yzerman, in Bourque, in Messier, in Ronnie Francis, in Scott Stevens. The sacrifices these players make change the game so that they win more. That's what you're trying to get to in understanding Steve Yzerman. Steve made that choice, and not all players make that choice. The list I gave you is very short. Everyone on it has had to make adjustments to their game for the sake of winning."

The fact that Yzerman made the choice he did is what is most impressive to his teammate from the 1983 World Juniors, Mike Eagles, an NHL grinder turned award-winning university coach.

"Everybody's appreciation of Steve has two phases," he explains. "In his early stage, he was seen as a pure scorer. Maybe he wasn't necessarily so, because he did small things that people didn't notice. But it seemed that when the Red Wings started winning, Stevie took his game from a level where he was a pure point-getter to being a guy who would do anything to win, whether that meant checking or diving in front of pucks. That's what you admire so much about a guy like Steve. Because in order to play in the league, he *doesn't have to do that stuff*. And those type of guys make the best leaders, in my mind. They go outside of what they have to do to survive in the game, in order to win.

"Looking at myself, I dove in front of pucks and blocked shots and hit. But I did that to survive, and to help the team to win at the same time. Other top guys stay within their own game, and do what they feel they need to do, but not necessarily what they need to do *to win*. And I think Steve has done that."

What continues to attract people to Steve Yzerman? He is the player's player, the embodiment of skill, dedication, sacrifice and leadership. He has achieved on every level: as an offensive marvel, a defensive master, a competitor who quietly makes sacrifices without complaint, and a star by the measures of both individual accomplishment and team-based success.

One could also argue that his personality, so locked within the on-ice performance, is not what is needed by a struggling professional sport that is, really, a branch of the entertainment industry. Sport requires a few outsized figures like Babe Ruth, Joe Namath and Dennis Rodman, who raise the business of playing games to some sustainable level of public fascination. Yzerman obviously has never performed that role, and few hockey players ever have. His teammate, Brett Hull, is a rare example of an iconoclast who tends to say whatever he feels while still being gainfully employed by the hand he occasionally bites. Wayne Gretzky became such an icon of greatness and goodness for this, the fourth-ranked professional team sport in America, that he dominated its marketability, and at times has seemed frozen in the headlights of responsibility, both as a spokesman for corporate sponsors and as a standard-bearer of what makes the game great. Though Gretzky is long retired, there has been almost no room for any current player in the game to compete with his fame at the commercial level. And clearly, Yzerman hasn't even tried. "If Yzerman were any less self-promoting, his tongue would atrophy," wrote Austin Murphy in *Sports Illustrated* fifteen years ago. And nothing has changed since then.

When Canada mounted its ill-fated charge for Olympic gold in Nagano in 1998, it was Yzerman's teammate, Brendan Shanahan, who starred in the breakfast cereal commercials, impishly eating HoneyNut Cheerios out of a trophy bowl. Shanahan could drop the gloves on the ice yet still summon a cuddly twinkle in his eye for the TV cameras. Yzerman's public face, meanwhile, has been set perpetually in stony determination, relieved only by the occasional wry smile. It's impossible to envisage Yzerman ever agreeing to have his legs shaved and painted with the black-and-white pattern of a Holstein's hide, as Doug Gilmour did for an Ontario Milk Marketing Board commercial at the peak of his public appeal as captain of the Maple Leafs. Or laughing infectiously as a potato chip addict, the way Mark Messier has been able to in Frito-Lay television spots.

Yzerman has gone into the game and never really come out of it. He has been like Joe DiMaggio in his iconic ability to be no more and no less than someone who gets paid to play a game very well, and have that game be something that its fans see as more than another entertainment product. And if life continues to be kind to him, his fans will never suffer the shock of seeing him flog coffeemakers in his later years, the way DiMaggio had to.

"He *is* a very private person," says Mike O'Connell. "His attitude is, 'Yeah, I play hockey. I don't save the world.'"

To expect Yzerman to be more than what he is—to be a spokesperson for (or an inside critic of) the modern NHL, which is struggling to maintain the attention span of the American sporting audience—is also probably to ask him to be less than what he is. His admirers appreciate him for being a ferociously committed hockey player, whose stardom no longer depends on raw offensive output but on absolute commitment. There has been an unwavering purity to Yzerman all through his career. He has done nothing beyond the ice rink to demand attention. Apart from endorsements of equipment suppliers like Easton, there's not much going on in the way of creating and marketing an Yzerman brand. For one thing, he doesn't lack for money. For another, it's the polar opposite of his nature to put on a salesman's grin and tell people they should choose a particular kind of household appliance. Which is how the fans like him. The Yzerman brand is the anti-brand: the hockey player who sells the idea of being a hockey player. A good one, as Aaron Brown succinctly put it on *News Night* in May 2003.

"I have no intentions to look back at my time as a hockey player," Yzerman asserted to *Inside Hockey* in 1996–97, before winning his first of three Stanley Cups. "When it's over, it's over." Given all that he's accomplished since that breakthrough playoff season, it's hard to imagine him never looking back and taking some satisfaction in a career marked more by plateaus of excellence than by milestones of games played or goals scored. And if the game itself has a lick of sense, it will continue to value this rare commodity, and miss it dearly when he skates his last NHL shift.

SOURCES & BIBLIOGRAPHY

INTERVIEWS

My thanks to the following (in alphabetical order) for agreeing to be interviewed for this project: Jacques Demers, Dale Derkatch, Jim Devellano, Mike Eagles, Bob Errey, Gerard Gallant, Larry Kelly, Dave Lewis, Ken Linseman, Mike O'Connell, John Ollson, Dick Todd.

Portions of an interview I conducted with Craig Ramsay for my 1998 book *Scotty Bowman: A Life in Hockey*, appear in Chapter Nine.

Portions of an interview I conducted with Jim Schoenfeld for my 1994 book *Open Ice: the Tim Horton Story*, appear in Chapter Ten.

PRINT AND WEB SOURCES

In addition to official NHL and NHLPA player and individual team guides, and official team websites from a variety of leagues, I have consulted (and fact-checked with) the following on-line resources:

The Internet Hockey Database: www.hockeyDB.com
Hockey Canada: www.hockeycanada.ca
TSN: www.tsn.ca
Outside the Garden: www.outsidethegarden.com
Hockey Draft Central: www.hockeydraftcentral.com

GAME ACCOUNTS AND GENERAL REPORTAGE

It's impossible to write a sports biography without relying on the daily reportage that records the events in a playing career. I have striven to note specific media sources in the course of the story. In general, the *Detroit Free Press* and *The Detroit News* were key sources of game accounts and post-game quotes, and deserve special mention.

OTHER

Daniel Otten's description of the left-wing lock system on the Hockey Coaching home page (www.geocities.com/Colosseum/1571/lock1.htm) was appreciated, as was Jim Stevens' "The Left-Wing Lock: Cracking the secrets of the Red Wings' Cup-winning defense," posted at www.hockeyplayer.com.

My discussion of the history of Detroit's Olympia Stadium (Chapter 3) was abetted by a Tom Henderson article posted to the website www.ballparks.com which originally appeared in the *Detroit Free Press* in 1980.

Indispensable to my review of Detroit's urban woes (Chapter 3) was the study by John Parr, "Detroit: Struggling Against History," from *Boundary Crossers: Case Studies of How Ten of*

America's Metropolitan Regions Work (Academy of Leadership, University of Maryland, 1998), as well as "Detroit Fights Back," by Julia Vitullo-Martin, *City Journal,* Summer 1995.

SPORTS MEDICINE

Online resources:
- Ligament Injuries of the Knee: sportsmedicine.about.com
- Bone spurs (osteophytes) and back pain: www.spine-health.com
- B.C. Injury Research and Prevention Unit www.injuryresearch.bc.ca
- Medial collateral ligament injury: www.ovphysio.com

Published resources:
"Prospective Analysis of Ice Hockey Injuries at the Junior A Level over the Course of One Season," by M. Pinto, J.E. Kuhn, M. Greenfield et al. *Clinical Journal of Sport Medicine* 9: 70-74, 1999.

"The Posterior Cruciate Ligament: Injury, Treatment & Rehabilitation," by Michael J. Mullin, ATC, PTA, and Kevin R. Stone, MD. *Orthopedic Technology Review,* November 2000, Case 17. (www.orthopedictechreview.com)

BOOKS

Champions: The Illustrated History of Hockey's Greatest Dynasties, Douglas Hunter. Viking, 1997

Companions in Courage, Pat LaFontaine, Ernie Valutis, MD, Chas Griffin and Larry Weisman. Time Warner, 2001

The Memorial Cup: Canada's National Junior Hockey Championship, Richard M. Lapp and Alec Macaulay. Harbour Publishing, 1997

Net Worth: Exploding the Myths of Pro Hockey, David Cruise and Alison Griffiths. Viking, 1991.

Power Plays: An Inside Look at the Big Business of the National Hockey League, Gil Stein. Birch Lane Press, 1997

Scotty Bowman: A Life in Hockey, Douglas Hunter. Viking, 1998

Total Hockey: The Official Encyclopedia of the National Hockey League. Dan Diamond, editor. Total Sports, 1998

ACKNOWLEDGMENTS

My particular thanks go out to Jim Devellano and Larry Kelly, who were generous with their time and also put in a good word for me with other interview subjects.

I was well served on the editing front by Martha Kanya-Forstner and Meg Masters, both of whom believe that a hockey biography is not a compilation of seasons and scores, but should exhibit a logical narrative arc. Their advice and input on shaping that arc were invaluable.

In addition, copyeditor Lloyd Davis did double duty as a fact checker, and saved me from more than a few dumb mistakes and made a number of valuable suggestions on content.

INDEX